Speech and Harm

Speech and Harm

Controversies over Free Speech

EDITED BY
Ishani Maitra and Mary Kate McGowan

OXFORD
UNIVERSITY PRESS

OXFORD

UNIVERSITY PRESS

Great Clarendon Street, Oxford OX2 6DP
United Kingdom

Oxford University Press is a department of the University of Oxford.
It furthers the University's objective of excellence in research, scholarship,
and education by publishing worldwide. Oxford is a registered trade mark of
Oxford University Press in the UK and in certain other countries

First edition published in 2012
Reprinted 2013

British Library Cataloguing in Publication Data
Data available

Library of Congress Cataloging in Publication Data
Data available

ISBN 978-0-19-923627-5

Contents

Foreword[*]

Catharine A. MacKinnon

The reality of pornography, not its abstract or linguistic features, was the ground of the confrontation with the buried harms of "speech" by Andrea Dworkin and me in the late 1970s and early 1980s.[1] Our goal, embodied in the civil rights ordinances against pornography we conceived and drafted,[2] was to stop and remedy the real damage it did to the real people who had come to us for help—mostly women or girls, some men, some boys. There the materials were: active in their violations and indignities, including their sexual abuse as children, rape, and prostitution. These peoples' lives are not a philosophical claim or a causal proof or an interesting example or a debating point. They are what happened to them. Their accounts were not stories or narrative. They are testimony. The materials integral to their abuse do not, relevantly to this setting, make statements or take positions. They are a practice of sex.

Without apology, with the survivors' permission and at their urgent request, we made what they said public. We tried to understand how pornography worked as a sexual practice in the inequality of which we found it is an active vehicle, to clarify the meaning of the insights and experiences those subjected to it told us, and to effectuate what they said they wanted done about it. Their realities and their voices, not Foucault or Austin, framed and drove this work and its insights. Misogyny, racism, and class bias were exposed all at once. The human beings and their abuse, the law and its obstacles and obliviousness, the academy and its posturing and irrelevance, the opposition and its poison and privilege, our speaking and writing and its engagement and punishments were real. In this crucible,

[*] The excellent research assistance of Lisa Cardyn is gratefully acknowledged. The time to write this Foreword was in large part supported by The Diane Middlebrook and Carl Djerassi Visiting Professorship at the Centre for Gender Studies at the University of Cambridge in Lent Term, 2011.
[1] The documents and introductions in *In Harm's Way: The Pornography Civil Rights Hearings* (Catharine A. MacKinnon and Andrea Dworkin eds., 1997) offer an historical perspective on the initial years of this effort.
[2] See *id* at Appendix.

the harm theory of speech—grounded in evidence of inequality done through some of what is called "speech," argued to provide a legal basis for stopping it as a violation of human rights—was born.

Since then, the work we did has provided, among other things, fodder for caricature and pornography and libel, ideas to be appropriated without reference or attributed to others, concepts to be twisted or made superficial as their clear original articulation is elided, intellectual background to be taken for granted, and grist for numerous academic mills, as various schools of thought contend to dismiss it from or subordinate it to pre-existing methodologies. Sometimes the attempts have been tortured, sometimes illuminating, if frankly modestly so. Frequently our work is treated as a trampoline on which others perform showy tricks or described as a distant land seen from an overflying jet or a war zone visited by tourists. The square challenge of the harms uncovered and their omission from prior approaches has yet to be met as what it is, nor have prior frameworks been grasped as determinately inadequate to the degree they did not, even cannot, address its reality in anything close to its widespread prevalence or complete dynamics. Andrea Dworkin's writing in particular has been sublimated and ignored, treated as naïve, rhetorical, and merely activist, rather than the sophisticated, subtle, and indispensible analysis it is.

In general, and increasingly in recent years, scholars have labored to place the facts of abuse uncovered and analysis of dynamics developed on its own ground into one academic straightjacket after another, attempting to prise apart and recategorize and cabin and control and ratiocinate their meanings and implications, abstracting the work into tiny fractionated bits to be confined and domesticated and thus, seemingly, made newly credible and acceptable, even important. The process could be a subject of study in itself. Why are ideas seen as valuable, exciting, worth thinking about, only if cast backwards into already familiar words and pre-existing frameworks, only when reconfigured within the principles of some big man's prior thought? Why are they worth thinking about only when they can be subsumed under someone else's theory? Perhaps Kuhn has partly described this process.[3] Granting that making extrinsic insights into terms of art in each discipline is a very specific process, difficult to evaluate from the outside, such a study would surely want to include the translation of life into law, which flattens reality into the "facts" of complaints and indictments, compressing real ideas into already authoritative "doctrine."

---

[3] Thomas S. Kuhn, *The Structure of Scientific Revolutions* (3d ed. 1996) (1962) (describing subsuming challenging approaches to ordinary science).

In a related but distinct phenomenon, why and how does it become acceptable, even de rigueur in some academic quarters, to elide the origins of a body of thought in which all the basic terms and moves originated and were first mapped out? More deeply, when and why does a whole way of thinking become intellectual wallpaper, so present it is not even seen to be there, so that succeeding academics can presume upon its content, or even propose it as their own, as if no one already put it there? This may be what success looks like, but it can also feel like someone (even a whole crowd of someones) walking over one's grave. In the process, missed in the present instance is the fact that no previous philosopher of language was apparently thinking about pornography in any central way when building their theories, far less did they see what light its elision might shed on the theories they spun in its absence about how language works.[4] Might it just be that this material works in a way that is truly distinct from any other, calling for a new theory, one Andrea Dworkin and I laid the original groundwork for? In this connection, someone might more fully theorize "the example" in philosophy, given its place in the vexed relation between the abstract and the material, a discussion in which the reflexive, even desperate, grab for the least real conceivable example for any point of argument deserves a central place.[5]

An intrepid and insightful group of analytic philosophers has made a real contribution to thinking on the subject of speech and its harms, if without interrogating the methodological assumptions of their discipline, by fitting certain aspects of what we said pornography does into the simpler terms that analytic philosophers of language find less possible to

---

[4] One telling instance involves my reference to J. L. Austin's *How to Do Things with Words* (1962) in *Only Words*, which made clear that we were well aware of his work as close to what we were saying, yet our approach was clearly distinguished from his in some respects. "While he does not confine himself to inequality, which is crucial to my argument here, neither does he generalize the performative to all speech, as have many speech act theorists who came after him. Austin is less an authority for my particular development of 'doing things with words' and more a foundational exploration of the view in language theory that some speech can be action." Catharine A. MacKinnon, *Only Words* 121 n.31 (1993). The intervening years have seen the attachment of "speech act" to our work, see, for example, Judith Butler, *Excitable Speech: A Politics of the Performative* 20–1 (1997), alternating between shoehorning our analysis into such prior terms and multiplying new ones, typically without references, as if our work, now unnamed, is really, although we didn't know it, a subprovince of Austin to be confined and tilled as such, also implying we cannot be doing something he did not do.

[5] The burgeoning literature on thought experiments and intuitions is more an example of what I am criticizing here than the analysis I am calling for. See, e.g., Tamar Szabo Gendler, *Thought Experiment: On the Powers and Limits of Imaginary Cases* (2000); Roy A. Sorenson, *Thought Experiments* (1992).

reject or deny out of hand. Rae Langton brilliantly showed, in speech act theory's terms, that, as we had argued and demonstrated from lived examples, utterances can subordinate.[6] She then went far toward showing that pornography subordinates women, as well as causes subordination, within that approach.[7] She has also, along with Jennifer Hornsby,[8] made the dynamics of silencing more accessible to philosophers of language and linguists, opening potentially productive debates within their discipline. Using a theory of communication, Caroline West further showed that the kind of silencing with which Langton and Hornsby are concerned can plausibly be regarded as a violation of free speech.[9] Extending her own prior work and that of Ishani Maitra, Mary Kate McGowan shows in this volume—again in terms analytic philosophers of language need—how speech can enact facts about what is permissible or acceptable by triggering the norms of certain social practices, thus can oppress or discriminate in sneaky ways.[10] If much can be lost in translation, such analysis, intentionally limited as it is, can anatomize and clarify dynamics and structures of argumentation and, in so doing, speak to varying audiences, open spaces for dialogue, and expand understanding. Many in this group come together in this volume to extend their prior contributions.

Further exceptional to most academic responses to the pornography work has been the legal scholarship of Mari Matsuda, Richard Delgado,

---

[6] See Rae Langton, Speech Acts and Unspeakable Acts, 22 *Phil. & Pub. Aff.* 293 (1993).

[7] See Rae Langton, *Sexual Solipsism: Philosophical Essays on Pornography and Objectification* (2009); Rae Langton, Subordination, Silence, and Pornography's Authority, in *Censorship and Silencing: Practices of Cultural Regulation* 261 (Robert Post ed., 1998).

[8] See Jennifer Hornsby, Disempowered Speech, 23 *Phil. Topics* 127 (1995); Jennifer Hornsby, Speech Acts and Pornography, 10 *Women's Phil. Rev.* 38 (1993); Rae Langton and Jennifer Hornsby, Free Speech and Illocution, 4 *Legal Theory* 21 (1998).

[9] See Caroline West, The Free Speech Argument against Pornography, 33 *Canadian J. Phil.* 391 (2003). For further discussion of the Hornsby and Langton account of silencing, see Ishani Maitra and Mary Kate McGowan, On Silencing, Rape and Responsibility 88 *Australasian J. Phil.* 167 (2010), and Mary Kate McGowan et al., A Partial Defense of Illocutionary Silencing, 26 *Hypatia* 132 (2011).

[10] See Mary Kate McGowan, *infra*; see also Mary Kate McGowan, Conversational Exercitives and the Force of Pornography, 31 *Phil. & Pub. Aff.* 155 (2003); Mary Kate McGowan, Oppressive Speech, 87 *Australasian J. Phil.* 389 (2009). Related contributions have been made by Ishani Maitra, Jennifer Saul, Claudia Bianchi, Nicole Wyatt, and Nellie Wieland, among others. Sally Haslanger's work on objectification, On Being Objective and Being Objectified, in *A Mind of One's Own: Feminist Essays on Reason and Objectivity* 209 (Louise M. Antony and Charlotte Witt eds., 1993), has been helpful in similar ways. Susan Brison's brilliant *Aftermath: Violence and the Remaking of a Self* (2001) goes the step deeper, interrogating philosophy's methodological foundations in light of experience of rape and attempted murder. No one has yet done this for analytic philosophy of language in light of pornography.

Charles Lawrence, and Kimberle Crenshaw on racist hate speech.[11] Their deep, astute, and accurate engagement with the pornography work emerged with new insights and arguments, making a true contribution on its own terms. The legal scholars Cass Sunstein, Owen Fiss, Frank Michelman, and Fred Schauer—realizing that, in the civil rights work against pornography, they were hearing something that they had not heard before—took on some of the doctrinal dimensions of the legal theorizing about pornography with special creativity,[12] rather than recycling First Amendment canards, the more usual response. Other liberal legal theorists responded with arguments ranging from those of Ronald Dworkin on the one end to Jeremy Waldron on the other, with a lot of room in between.

Ronald Dworkin maintained that laws against pornography would undermine prohibitions on other forms of sex discrimination, laws against racist hate speech would undermine prohibitions on race discrimination, because discrimination laws only become legitimate when the debate surrounding them remains unrestricted.[13] Well, the debate over pornography certainly has been unrestricted, even by the law of libel. Yet pornography must be the price "we" pay for equal pay we do not even receive? Nothing is real here except its revealing psychology, the desperate straining for an equality reason for supporting pornography that is bigger than the equality reasons that so decisively indict it. Along with functioning to clarify pornography as a particular kind of bottom line in male supremacy, Ronald Dworkin's analysis has a thuggish undertone: touch that pornography, honey, risk what rights you have.

---

[11] See Mari J. Matsuda et al., *Words That Wound: Critical Race Theory, Assaultive Speech, and the First Amendment* (1993).

[12] See Cass R. Sunstein, Pornography and the First Amendment, 1986 *Duke L.J.* 589; Owen M. Fiss, Freedom and Feminism, 80 *Geo. L.J.* 2041 (1992); Frank I. Michelman, Conceptions of Democracy in American Constitutional Argument: The Case of Pornography Regulation, 56 *Tenn. L. Rev.* 291 (1989), taking our work seriously. Frederick Schauer was a principal author of the *Attorney General's Commission on Pornography: Final Report* (1986), which tracked many features of the harm approach and recommended that the civil rights approach to legislation be considered. *Id.* at 1: 747–54 (setting forth "Recommendation 87: Legislatures Should Conduct Hearings and Consider Legislation Recognizing a Civil Remedy for Harm Attributable to Pornography"). This intrepid cohort of younger legal scholars, defying threats to their careers, include Alexander Tsesis, *Destructive Messages: How Hate Speech Paves the Way for Harmful Social Movements* (2002), Ann Bartow, Pornography Coercion, and Copyright Law 2.0, 10 *Vand. J. Ent. & Tech. L.* 799 (2008), and Mary Anne Franks, Unwilling Avatars: Idealism and Discrimination in Cyberspace, 20 *Colum. J. Gender & L.* 224 2011); Mary Anne Franks, Sexual Harassment 2.0, 71 *Maryland L. Rev.* (forthcoming, 2012), among others.

[13] See Ronald Dworkin, *Freedom's Law: The Moral Reading of the American Constitution* 219 (1996).

No evidence is offered for his causal claim. Indeed, none can exist, because pornography is not effectively restricted by law anywhere. But his proposed dynamic is embarrassed by the facts on racism. Democracies all over the world have both hate speech laws and racial discrimination laws with no apparent loss of efficacy (such as it is anywhere) or legitimacy. His position also defies logic: women must be discriminatorily abused or laws against discriminatorily abusing them will lose their legitimacy? From experimental evidence of pornography's effects, which has only strengthened in the intervening years,[14] more plausible is the view that the absence of laws addressing pornography, an engine of misogyny, may undermine laws against sex inequality from rape to battering to sexual harassment to, arguably, equal pay and political representation. Juries differentially refuse to convict rapists after exposure to pornography.[15] If women mattered, if women had equal social status, if sex equality standards existed to which regimes were held accountable, the lack of laws against this driver of their use as sexual things—not the presence of such laws—would undermine the legitimacy of the regimes that have failed them. In this light, it is the role of pornography in maintaining unequal status based on sex that calls into question the legitimacy of regimes that continue to allow it.

Ronald Dworkin is not alone in failing to grasp that pornography is not a political argument nor is the sex industry a debating society, but arms of prostitution on both production and consumption sides. Pornography, a sexual practice, is not "speech" in the conventional sense that liberals aim to protect, but a form of sex discrimination with some visual and verbal moving parts. To get at its complex reality, pornography's critics in the human rights tradition have not sought to restrict what it says as such, although defending against that is the purported focus of its supporters,

[14] A comprehensive literature review summarized, "experimental research shows that exposure to nonviolent or violent pornography results in increases in both attitudes supporting sexual aggression and in actual sexual aggression." Neil M. Malamuth et al., Pornography and Sexual Aggression: Are There Reliable Effects and Can We Understand Them? 11 *Ann. Rev. Sex Res.* 26, 44 (2000). The same conclusion has been reached in a review of nonexperimental studies. Gert Martin Hald et al., Pornography and Attitudes Supporting Violence against Women: Revisiting the Relationship in Nonexperimental Studies, 36 *Aggressive Behav.* 14 (2010). Recent empirical work and meta-analyses on the nexus between pornography and violence include Mike Allen et al., A Meta-Analysis Summarizing the Effects of Pornography II: Aggression after Exposure, 22 *Hum. Comm. Res.* 258 (1995), Drew A. Kingston et al., The Importance of Individual Differences in Pornography Use: Theoretical Perspectives and Implications for Treating Sexual Offenders, 46 *J. Sex. Res.* 216 (2009), and Vanessa Vega and Neil M. Malamuth, Predicting Sexual Aggression: The Role of Pornography in the Context of General and Specific Factors, 33 *Aggressive Behav.* 104 (2007).

[15] The experiments on this effect are reviewed by Dolf Zillmann, Effects of Prolonged Consumption of Pornography, in *Pornography: Research Advances & Policy Considerations* 127 (Dolf Zillmann and Jennings Bryant eds., 1989).

serving to deflect from its practical harms. Misogynist content and sexually violent advocacy would still flourish in the form of art and political argument if the antipornography civil rights ordinances were law. Rest assured, the debate over women's inferiority to men would continue. What could not continue is this particular practice of that inferiority, this multi-billion-dollar-a-year industry of sex trafficking.[16] This, clearly, is the rub—that it could no longer exist if its harms could no longer be done—the fancy fears being so much eyewash. Child pornography has been criminalized in the United States and the republic still stands. Hate propaganda and pornography are crimes in Canada on the equality theory created,[17] and democracy goes on, and pornography does as well. Nations would survive, one suspects its laws against discrimination even gaining in legitimacy, certainly expanding women's speech, if women's status and treatment could be addressed with this weapon.

Jeremy Waldron's temperate confrontation with the liberal illogic of opposition to restrictions on racist hate speech implicitly builds on the work against pornography in inequality terms, focusing as he does on the effects of "the visible environment" on status—precisely the problematic opened by the pornography work—including, emphasized in his work, the goal of assurance that all groups are regarded as full members of society with dignity.[18] With materials that "becom[e] established as a visible feature of the environment,"[19] "attacks predicated upon the characteristics of some particular social group"[20] become organized and normative "as the wolves call to one another"[21] through "the appearance of symbols and scrawls in places for all to see provid[ing] a focal point for the proliferation and coordination of the attacks the actions express."[22] For him, the effect hate speech laws have of driving this material underground is "the whole point,"[23] unlike for pornography's opponents, for whom there is no true underground where women are not being violated. Of course nothing in racist hate speech is anywhere close to being as visible in creating the social and cultural environment as pornography is, which is

---

[16] For an argument that pornography is a form of sex trafficking, see Catharine A. MacKinnon, Pornography as Trafficking, 26 *Mich. J. Int'l L.* 993 (2005).

[17] See R. v. Keegstra, [1990] 3 S.C.R. 697; Butler v. Regina, [1992] 1 S.C.R. 452; Little Sister's Book and Art Emporium v. Canada (Minister of Justice), [2000] 2 S.C.R. 1120.

[18] Jeremy Waldron, Dignity and Defamation: The Visibility of Hate (2009 Oliver Wendell Holmes Lectures), 123 *Harv. L. Rev.* 1596 (2010).

[19] *Id.* at 1604.

[20] *Id.* at 1605.

[21] *Id.* at 1631.

[22] *Id.*

[23] *Id.*

nothing if not "visible, public, and semi-permanent."[24] Nor are the consequences of hate speech anywhere close to being as well-supported by empirical social science evidence as the effects of pornography are[25]— although there is no lack of cultural presence or material indications, past and present, of the potency of its damage.[26]

If both these scholars hold our work at a distance while standing on it to look in opposite directions—Dworkin pretending to understand it when he does not remotely, Waldron not to when he does profoundly—Judith Butler purports to contend with what she appears largely not to have read. Her assertion that I construe pornography as "a kind of hate speech,"[27] exploiting the reality of one ("the sign of racial violence") to make the other ("the putatively injurious power of pornography") real,[28] is simply wrong, if anything backwards. Noting that both enact abuse, I repeatedly distinguish the way the two work, at one point analyzing hate speech as potentially working like pornography, to the degree it is sexual.[29] The implication that I try to hijack the political legitimacy of opposition to hate speech to bolster my case against pornography[30] is pure invention, likely projection. To the extent Butler's position on the substance of the issues can be discerned, she would have it two ways, supporting laws against hate speech while opposing civil rights laws against pornography. How racist propaganda is subordinating while pornography can unleash liberatory possibilities, how exactly the "visual text of pornography cannot 'threaten' or 'demean' or 'debase' in the same way that the burning cross can[,]"[31] the reader is never told. Her discussion of homosexual speech does not consider gaybashing or even really homophobia or any actual sexual abuse, including in the military as a result of Don't Ask, Don't Tell. Offensiveness is falsely imagined to be the central injury we address[32] when it is no part of our theory at all. Being called a cunt or a nigger opening a freer future[33]

---

[24] *Id.* at 1601.

[25] See *supra* note 14.

[26] Among the clearer instances is the propagation of anti-Semitic pornography in Weimar and Nazi Germany by the popular newspaper, *Der Stürmer* published by Julius Streicher, who was hanged at Nuremberg for crimes against humanity. See generally Randall L. Bytwerk, *Julius Streicher: Nazi Editor of the Notorious Anti-Semitic Newspaper Der Stürmer* (1988).

[27] Butler, *supra* note 4, at 18.

[28] *Id.* at 21.

[29] MacKinnon, *Only Words, supra* note 4, at 20–1.

[30] Butler, *supra* note 4 at 21.

[31] *Id.*

[32] *Id.* at 22.

[33] *Id.* at 38 ("Keeping such terms unsaid and unsayable can also work to lock them in place, preserving their power to injure, and arresting the possibility of a reworking that might shift their content and purpose").

is Orwellian doublethink, as if imposing a status opens the way to changing it even as action to change it is precluded. The fixation on "agency" appeals to the desire to feel free (hence self-respecting) under conditions of abuse, violation, humiliation, and discrimination that, in her hands, remain unchanged. There is nothing about gender at all. The play of opposites and inversions that substitutes for analysis provides a study in denial, evasion, obfuscation, and tortured logic, not to mention opportunism.

It makes one long for the lucidity, humility, and discipline of the analytic philosophers, whose next generation of work, together with scholars of other disciplines, is provided in this volume. Most of its authors realize that harm can be done through speech. In general, they are critical of how hate speech works in society and how it has been addressed, advancing the project of grasping the way hate propaganda works in the world and the implications of that realization for existing paradigms. As a whole, this book takes power and authority, hence social determination, seriously, which liberals often do not seem to know how to do. It challenges some of the orthodoxies that give "speech" hegemony over all other rights and values, such as the inverse arithmetic of free speech (the less you favor its content, the more you must support its existence), balancing of harms (trading off harm to living beings against harms to inanimate objects), and the view that abusive materials represent speech values and restricting them cannot.

This volume's confrontation with the facile "more speech" riposte to subordinating expression is especially usefully developed, as is the analysis of the dynamics of some racist speech. Lynne Tirrell examines the impact of group-based propaganda on genocide in Rwanda, skillfully showing how derogatory terms "regularly enact power, incite crimes, rationalize cruelty,"[34] in which authority is key.[35] Cogent and penetrating is Laura Beth Nielsen's critical anatomization of begging being legally rendered behavior while racism remains protected content, explained as the targets of begging being socially valued while those of racism are not.[36] The American fetishism of "speech" is in some respects overcome by focus on Canada, Australia, and Rwanda. Silencing is further developed,[37] although

---

[34] Lynne Tirrell, in Genocidal Language Games, p. 192 this volume.

[35] *Id.* at p. 211.

[36] Laura Beth Nielsen, in Power in Public: Reactions, Responses, and Resistance to Offensive Public Speech, this volume.

[37] In addition to the work of Langton and Hornsby, see Ishani Maitra, Silence and Responsibility, 18 Phil. Persp. 189 (2004); Ishani Maitra, Silencing Speech, 39 *Can. J. Phil.* 309 (2009) (exploring a communication framework for analyzing silencing, as opposed to an illocutionary one); Mary Kate McGowan, Debate: On Silencing and Sexual Refusal, 17

the complexity, depth, and potency given to it by Andrea Dworkin and others,[38] in a dynamic inseparable from pornography's sexual function, remain to be fully clarified in this philosophical vocabulary.

Their contributions aside, one cannot help wondering why some schools of philosophy have become a place where what something actually does is not considered pertinent to the exploration of what it could or might do. Life is not a game of logic, an argument's plausibility is not unaffected by the social reality to which it refers, and power's denial of abuse is not a function of not having read a philosophical proof that such abuse is possible. Realizing that gathering and evaluating evidence is not the specialty of philosophy, particularly in its analytic mode,[39] information still has something to offer. For one instance, the powerful documentation of "stereotype threat" in psychology shows an unquestionable harm done by racist speech. Stereotype threat, with its measurable and reversible detrimental effects, captures one harm we said pornography

---

J. Pol. Phil. 487 (2009) (arguing that interference with the hearer's recognition of the speaker's authority is a different sort of silencing that pornography may also bring about).

[38] Of course analytic philosophers do not purport to capture how this process works as a whole, only to explicate and spell out the plausibility of claims made for how it may work in certain instances. Noting Andrea Dworkin had said that pornography is not speech for women, but is the silence of women, Speech Delivered in Toronto, Canada (Feb. 1984) (reprinted in *Healthsharing* 25 (Summer 1984), cited in Catharine A. MacKinnon, Francis Biddle's Sister, in *Feminism Unmodified: Discourses on Life and Law* 163, 194, 300 n.159 (1987), I expanded the point: "Remember the mouth taped, the woman gagged, 'Smile, I can get a lot of money for that.' The smile is not her expression, it is her silence. It is not her expression not because it didn't happen, but because it *did* happen. The screams of the women in pornography are silence, like the screams of Kitty Genovese, whose plight was misinterpreted by some onlookers as a lovers' quarrel. The flat expressionless voice of the woman in the New Bedford gang rape, testifying, is silence. She was raped as men cheered and watched, as they do in and with the pornography. When women resist and men say, 'Like this, you stupid bitch, here is how to do it' and shove their faces into the pornography, this 'truth of sex' is the silence of women. When they say, 'If you love me, you'll try,' the enjoyment we fake, the enjoyment we learn is silence. Women who submit because there is more dignity in it than in losing the fight over and over live in silence. Having to sleep with your publisher or director to get access to what men call speech is silence. Being humiliated on the basis of your appearance, whether by approval or disapproval, because you have to look a certain way for a certain job, whether you get the job or not, is silence. The absence of a woman's voice, everywhere that it cannot be heard, is silence. And anyone who thinks that what women say in pornography is women's speech—the 'Fuck me, do it to me, harder,' all of that—has never heard the sound of a woman's voice." *Id.* at 194–5. A stunning articulation of silencing that remains to be captured by the academic exegeses is contained in Malka Marcovich, The Violence of Silence: Survivor Testimony in Political Struggle, in *Making the Harm Visible: Global Sexual Exploitation of Women and Girls* 121 (Donna M. Hughes and Claire Roche eds., 1999), available at http://www.uri.edu/artsci/wms/hughes/mhvtest.htm.

[39] For an accessible discussion of the role of evidence in analytic philosophy, see, for example, Timothy Williamson, *The Philosophy of Philosophy* 208 (2007).

also does: it authoritatively constructs one as a member of a group that is socially inferior, producing behavior consistent with this prognostication in the victim group.[40] Pace Austin and his acolytes, this is not really either illocutionary or perlocutionary, although it is closer to the former, and the difference is not just a matter of timing. Although Butler does not seem to understand it, both illocution and perlocution are causal theories, the former more immediately and with fewer intervening contingencies than the latter. But they do not exhaust the ways speech acts. Stereotype threat is not something specific racist or sexist utterances plausibly could do. It is something they have been empirically proven to have done, although when articulated, the stereotypical statements merely state an opinion in the form of a fact. Now imagine the stereotypes producing orgasms to see what a threat looks like.

Pornography is a sexual practice. This is distinctively key to the way it functions, not a feature that can be abstracted away in order to treat it in simpler linguistic terms. It is because of the way it works sexually that pornography functions to deprive saying "no" to sex of being a speech act at all, so that it can do nothing in the saying and produce no consequences according to the speaker's expressed intent. In the social world created by pornography—pornography participates in creating its own context— saying no to sex simply reports an ignorable subjective internal state that can genuinely be heard as its opposite by the hearer. The no may also stimulate further aggression, making the sex sexier by signaling a lust for redoubled force. Legally, saying no to sex may not even constitute a lack of consent. The point is, *sexuality* is where pornography lives, not in the realm of nonsexual language or (even) discourse.

Perhaps most remarkably in the present setting, "hate," a concept Andrea Dworkin used and analyzed productively,[41] the utility and aptness of which I have questioned,[42] is not theorized in these pages, opening a

---

[40] See, e.g., Claude M. Steele, A Threat in the Air: How Stereotypes Shape Intellectual Identity and Performance, 52 *Am. Psychologist* 613 (1997); Claude M. Steele et al., Contending with Group Image: The Psychology of Stereotype and Social Identity Threat, 34 *Advances Experimental Soc. Psychol.* 379 (2002); Claude M. Steele and Paul G. Davies, Stereotype Threat and Employment Testing: A Commentary, 16 *Hum. Performance* 311 (2003).

[41] See, e.g., Andrea Dworkin, *Woman Hating* (1974); Andrea Dworkin, Jew-Hate/ Woman-Hate, in *Scapegoat: The Jews, Israel, and Women's Liberation* 16 (2000).

[42] One example is Catharine A. MacKinnon, Pornography as Defamation and Discrimination, 71 *B.U. L. Rev.* 793, 808 (1991) ("Hatred rationalizes and impels genocide, certainly, but so do some things far colder, like self-interest, sense of superiority, or fun, and something far more banal, like indifference or system. In the case of women and men, love deals at least as much death, and so does something hotter, like pleasure. The fact that pornography so often presents itself as love, indeed resembles much of what passes for it under male dominance, makes its construction as hate literature a challenging exercise in demystification,

further opportunity for analysis. Related is the fact that, other than by Laura Beth Nielsen and Lynne Tirrell—who contribute significantly in this respect and in part for this reason—the actual voices of the victims and perpetrators tend to be a long way away from this text. Why pretty up what the perpetrators say? It protects them to distance the reader through reducing what they do to descriptive abstractions or generalizations. In such a rarified reductive atmosphere, the fist in the gut that provides the experience of hate speech and pornography is muffled. The result is a failure to call into question what is considered "speech," its broader transnational concept "expression," that is, what is being protected and why. Equality and inequality are not interrogated in any sustained way either, although they are sometimes mentioned,[43] and the substance of inequality frames the insights of Nielsen and Tirrell, although it is largely not mentioned as such. Why all these topics must be considered within the confines of liberalism is not broached even sideways, leaving liberalism assumed rather than interrogated. It is as if liberalism alone makes this discussion possible rather than also creates some of these issues and limits the means of effectively grappling with them. This becomes particularly interesting when the responses of liberals to the human rights critique of pornography have ranged from receptive engagement to vociferous support of pornography while smugly, even aggressively, ignoring its harms.

Meantime, at least from a legal perspective in which words enact as well as clarify, the action is far ahead and taking place elsewhere. Some prosecutors labor to make obscenity law, which has no express element of harm, function against violent pornography.[44] Civil lawyers pursue predators like Joe Francis, architect of Girls Gone Wild, to get him to pay for his violations of girls, recognizing harms that include a lifetime of being trafficked as pornography under your name on the Internet.[45] Congress requires child pornography prosecutions include restitution for its victims.[46] And since September 11, 2001, it suddenly became less forbidden in the United States to consider publicly the relation between what people

to say the least. The concept of discrimination aims not at what is felt by perpetrator or victim or what is said as such, but at what is done, including through words".)

[43] See articles by Altman, West, Gelber, and McGowan this volume.

[44] See, e.g., United States v. Extreme Associates, Inc., 431 F.3d 150 (3d Cir. 2005).

[45] See, e.g., Doe v. Francis, No. 5:03cv260-RS-WSC (N.D. Fla. 2003) (suing Francis for his actions as producer of *Girls Gone Wild*); Plaintiff B v. Francis, 631 F.3d 1310 (11 Cir. 2011) (granting plaintiffs' request to proceed anonymously in subsequent case on similar facts).

[46] 18 U.S.C. § 2259(a) (mandating issuance of restitution order for any offense committed under Chapter 110 ("Sexual Exploitation and Other Abuse of Children"), including acts relating to child pornography).

List of contributors

ANDREW ALTMAN is a Professor of Philosophy and Director of Research for the Jean Beer Blumenfeld Center for Ethics at Georgia State University.

KATHARINE GELBER is an Associate Professor in Politics and an Australian Research Council Fellow at the University of Queensland.

RAE LANGTON is a Professor of Philosophy at the Massachusetts Institute of Technology.

ISHANI MAITRA is an Associate Professor of Philosophy at the University of Michigan.

CATHARINE A. MACKINNON is the Elizabeth A. Long Professor of Law at the University of Michigan Law School and James Barr Ames Visiting Professor of Law (long term) at Harvard Law School.

MARY KATE McGOWAN is a Professor of Philosophy at Wellesley College.

LAURA BETH NIELSEN is a Research Professor at the American Bar Foundation and an Associate Professor of Sociology and Director of the Center for Legal Studies at Northwestern University.

LYNNE TIRRELL is an Associate Professor of Philosophy at the University of Massachusetts, Boston.

CAROLINE WEST is a Senior Lecturer in Philosophy at the University of Sydney.

We thank Jennifer Hazelton for research assistance and Dmitri Gallow for help compiling the index.

Introduction and Overview

Ishani Maitra and Mary Kate McGowan

I. The Theme of the Book

Most liberal societies are deeply committed to a principle of free speech. As a result of this commitment, such societies tolerate some very disagreeable speech. Suppose, for example, that Joe says that all disabled people should be kept out of the public eye, since it is such a bummer to see them out in public. As ignorant and as offensive as Joe's opinion is, most of us would agree that he nevertheless has the free speech right to express it. Tolerating such disagreeable speech is just part and parcel of our deep-seated commitment to free speech.

Some speech, however, is more than just disagreeable. In fact, some speech is downright harmful. There is evidence to suggest, for example, that racist hate speech causes things like racial discrimination. If this is right, then such speech is detrimental to racial equality. Might a genuine commitment to free speech require that we legally permit speech even when it is harmful, and even when doing so is in conflict with our commitment to other important liberal values, such as equality? Even if such speech is to be legally permitted, does our commitment to free speech allow us to provide material and institutional support to those who would contest such harmful speech? And finally, and perhaps most importantly, which kinds of speech are harmful in ways that merit response, either in the form of legal regulation or in some other form?

Given that a principle of free speech is among the most fundamental of liberal political principles, it is crucial that we be as clear as possible about what our commitment to free speech involves. This requires being able to answer the questions listed above. Drawing on expertise in philosophy, sociology, political science, feminist theory, and legal theory, the contributors to this book do just that. By attending to the precise functioning of speech, the essays contained here shed light on these questions by, for example, clarifying the relationship between speech and harm. Understanding how speech functions can help us figure out which kinds of speech are harmful, what those harms are, and how the speech in question brings them about. As we shall see, all of these issues are crucially important when it comes to deciding what ought to be done about allegedly harmful speech.

In this Introduction, we will provide the theoretical background that is necessary to understand the discussions in the articles in this collection. We will also identify some of the principal themes in those articles, and locate them with respect to the literature on these topics. In doing so, we will provide a guide for using this book as the basis for a course. Finally, we will end this Introduction with summaries of the individual articles contained in this collection.

II. The Value of Speech, and a Principle of Free Speech

As we shall see, a commitment to free speech involves extending to speech special protections that we don't extend to other actions. We shall consider, both in this Introduction and throughout this book, what form these protections do, and should, take. But before moving to that, let us briefly consider a prior question, namely, what warrants these special protections in the first place. That is, what makes speech so valuable, and hence, worthy of such protections?

Theorists disagree about the right answer to this question, but many offer one (or a combination) of the following three sorts of answers. The first answer maintains that speech ought to be protected because the free flow of ideas is the best (or only) way for us to access truth (or knowledge). By saying what we think, and by attending to the opinions and reactions of others, we, as a society, are more likely to form true (and better justified) beliefs (Mill 1978). The second answer contends that speech must be protected in order for a democracy to function well. A society will be genuinely democratic only if we are free to criticize the government, tell our representatives what we want them to do, and freely discuss matters of public concern (Meiklejohn 1960). Finally, the third answer maintains that speech must be free in order for persons to be genuinely autonomous (by deciding for themselves what to think and do). If the state limits expression, then we are prevented from *even considering* some possibilities when deciding what to do and think. In this way, then, the free expression of ideas is a requirement of autonomy (Scanlon 1972).

But to say that speech is valuable, and that we are therefore deeply committed to a principle of free speech, is *not* to say that a person is—or should be—free to say whatever she wants. As we shall see, plenty of speech is currently regulated, e.g. criminal solicitation, insider trading, and speech used in contracts, to mention but a few examples. Furthermore, most of us—though we'll discuss some exceptions below—think that many such regulations are perfectly compatible with a commitment to free speech. If this is right, then a commitment to free speech does not *prohibit* the regulation of speech. Rather, it just makes it *more difficult* to regulate speech.

To put this idea slightly differently, we might say that a principle of free speech consists in a presumption of liberty in favor of speech (Greenawalt 1989). This presumption may be strong, since, after all, the principle of free speech is a fundamental political principle, but it is no more than a presumption. As such, it can be overridden. Thus, a principle of free speech implies that justifications for regulating speech must meet (much) higher standards of scrutiny than justifications for regulating non-speech action. We shall have much more to say about these raised standards in a later section.

Of course, not everyone subscribes to the picture sketched above. Free speech absolutists, for instance, would argue that a genuine commitment to free speech is far less compatible with regulation of speech than this picture suggests. A naïve version of free speech absolutism claims that speech cannot ever legitimately be regulated. Such a strong claim is implausible, for it implies, among other things, that there cannot be any regulation of contracts. In fact, one might wonder whether there really are absolutists (in this naïve sense), exactly because everyone agrees that at least *some* speech can legitimately be regulated.

A more plausible version of free speech absolutism claims that it is a mistake to regulate additional categories of speech. So, for example, if a certain category of speech is currently protected (i.e. unregulated), then, according to this view, it would be a mistake to begin to regulate speech in that category. We disagree with this position. We think that it is possible for categories of speech to be protected even though they shouldn't be. We also think that circumstances can change in a way that makes a certain category of speech much more harmful than it used to be, and that such a change might warrant new regulation. Whether a particular category of speech ought to be regulated depends on whether the justifications for regulating it meet the raised standards of scrutiny mentioned above. We think that the question of regulation must be decided separately for every category of speech, and that sometimes, the burden of justification can be met.

Nevertheless, though we disagree with absolutism, it is a useful position to keep in mind. This is because at the heart of absolutism is a reluctance to regulate speech. Even if everyone concedes that *some* speech ought to be regulated, theorists differ with respect to how reluctant they are to regulate additional categories of speech, and thus, with respect to how close they come to an absolutist position. Therefore, absolutism provides a useful way of differentiating between theories, by considering to what degree they approximate an absolutist position. As such, free speech absolutism has theoretical utility.

III. Harmful Speech

There are, as we have already noted, good reasons to value speech, and so, good reasons to be deeply committed to a principle of free speech. Nevertheless, though it is clear that speech is valuable, it is equally clear that some speech is deeply harmful. Suppose, for example, that a newspaper publishes a (false) report that a candidate for public office used to be addicted to drugs. Or that Joe tells his buddy Hank, who is drunk and known to have a violent temper, that Hank's wife has been stepping out on him. Or that Emily, a teacher in an overwhelmingly white school, tells her students that they will have to make allowances for their only African-American classmate, since African-Americans need extra time to learn. If the newspaper article convinces its readers to vote against the candidate, or if Joe's report results in Hank beating up his wife, or if Emily's announcement brings it about that her white students treat their African-American classmate as a moron, then the speech in question is clearly harmful.

It is worth emphasizing that in each of the examples above, we are talking about genuine harm, not mere offense (Feinberg 1985, MacKinnon 1987a). The newspaper article, for instance, might well annoy the candidate and her supporters. Furthermore, they will certainly disagree with its content. But mere (passing) annoyance and disagreement are not genuine harms. Losing an election, by contrast, especially an important election, is a genuine harm.[1]

---

[1] We are here operating with a somewhat broad conception of harm. On a narrow conception, a harm must be due to a single act, and must injure the interests of some identifiable individual. On our broader conception, a harm can be due to a series of acts none of which is individually harmful, and it can injure the interests of a group, rather than any identifiable individual. Consider discrimination, which the law recognizes as a harm. Since discrimination can involve structural elements, it need not be a localized phenomenon, and it need not harm individuals *qua* individuals. Thus, by recognizing discrimination as a harm, the law operates with a broader notion of harm.

Of course, these examples of harmful speech are (relatively) uncontroversial. For other kinds of speech, however, there is a great deal of controversy regarding whether they actually harm anyone. Consider here the long-running and extensive debates over pornography and racist hate speech. Some theorists argue, for example, that pornography does not harm women because its viewers are well aware that it is just a form of fantasy, and so, they do not learn from it. Others argue that speech itself rarely harms, and that any associated harm is really due to those listening to the speech. Similar controversies arise around many other kinds of speech as well, including speech that abuses sexual minorities, speech that denies the Holocaust, and speech that evinces certain kinds of nationalistic fervor.

Even where there is agreement that a given kind of speech is harmful, there is disagreement about other related—and equally important—questions. First, when a kind of speech is harmful, what are the harms in question? Second, *how* does the speech bring about these harms? And third, and perhaps most crucially, *what ought to be done* about these harms? In the remainder of this section, we will briefly take up the first two of these questions. We will return to the third question in §§ IV and V.

In order to fix ideas, let's focus for the moment on racist hate speech. Some allege that racist hate speech directly harms those persons addressed by it. According to Delgado (1993), for example, some of the harms to the addressee are immediate (e.g. anxiety, fear), while others are cumulative and long term (e.g. high blood pressure, low self-esteem, and even mental illness). Racist hate speech is also alleged to cause more widespread social harms, like racial violence, racial discrimination, and the political disempowerment of persons of color (Lawrence 1993, Matsuda 1993). Some allege that racist hate speech subordinates persons of color (Lawrence 1993). In this collection, Maitra argues that (some) ordinary hate speakers can come to have authority, and so, be in a position to subordinate persons of color; McGowan argues that (some) racist hate speech constitutes an otherwise illegal act of racial discrimination, and West argues that (some) racist hate speech silences persons of color in a way that actually violates their free speech right.

Thus, even among those who agree that racist hate speech is harmful, there is still room for difference about which particular harms result from such speech. But getting clear about the harms in question is important, for at least two reasons. First, the kind of empirical evidence that is needed to establish that such speech is harmful will vary greatly according to which kind of harm one has in mind. Second, as we shall see later, what ought to be done about the harms of such speech depends greatly on what the harms in fact are.

Theorists can also disagree with respect to the precise relationship between the speech and the harm, i.e. how precisely the speech in question brings about these harms. For example, some argue that racist hate speech (merely) *causes* harm, while others claim that it also *constitutes* harm. The following examples will help illuminate the difference. Suppose that, in a policy-enacting meeting, the CEO of a company says: "Women shouldn't be promoted to positions of power, because they are just too damn irrational to lead." Suppose further that when the CEO says this, he thereby enacts a new promotion policy for his company. Since the CEO's utterance enacts this policy, and since the policy is discriminatory, the utterance constitutes a harm to women. Contrast that case with the very same words being uttered by a disgruntled low-level employee at the very same company. The low-level employee's utterance may cause other employees to believe that it is permissible to be disrespectful to women in the company, and thus, cause harm to women. But because his words do not enact company policy, his utterance does not constitute harm in the way that the CEO's utterance does.

Even among causal (and constitutive) theorists, however, there are differences with respect to precisely *how* the speech causes (or constitutes) the harm. Consider first causal theories. One way that speech can cause harm is by *persuading* hearers to believe things that, in turn, cause harmful conduct. Such harms are sometimes said to be 'mentally mediated,' and are often alleged to be the responsibility of the hearer/actor. Relatedly, speech can also cause harm by shaping hearers' desires, instead of—or in addition to—affecting their beliefs (MacKinnon 1987b). A third way that speech can cause harm is by *conditioning* its hearers. According to MacKinnon, for example, pornography conditions its consumers to be sexually aroused by degrading images of women (MacKinnon 1993, Scoccia 1996). Moreover, such conditioning is taken to be unconscious, and thus, not 'mentally mediated.' A final way that speech can cause harm is by causing its hearers to *imitate* what is represented. Empirical studies establish that humans have an extremely strong tendency to, and capacity for, imitation (Hurley 2004). If this is right, then we may imitate what we see in pornography and violent movies, without being aware that and why we are doing so.

Some of the contributors here explore potential causal connections between speech and harm. Altman, for example, weighs the harms caused by Holocaust denial literature against those that would be caused by its regulation. He argues that, although such speech is harmful, it nevertheless ought to remain protected. Gelber considers how one might prevent the harms caused by various categories of speech by supporting, and thus increasing the causal effectiveness of, counter-speech.[2] There are also causal components to several of the other accounts offered.

Let's turn next to constitutive theories. Catharine MacKinnon has famously argued that pornography *constitutes* the subordination of women (MacKinnon 1987b). In their much discussed anti-pornography civil rights ordinance, she and Andrea Dworkin treat pornography as an act of gender discrimination that subordinates women both sexually and socially (MacKinnon and Dworkin 1997). Developing this line of thought, Langton argues that speech can subordinate in virtue of unfairly ranking women as inferior, depriving them of important powers and capacities, and legitimating discriminatory behavior towards them (Langton 1993). Additionally, MacKinnon also claims that pornography violates the free speech rights of women by silencing them (MacKinnon 1987b, 1993). Several theorists have since offered accounts of such silencing, and its relation to women's free speech right (Hornsby 1993, 1995, Langton 1993, Maitra 2009, McGowan 2009, West 2003). Parallel claims to the effect that racist hate speech constitutes the subordination of racial minorities were (independently) made by critical race theorists (Lawrence 1993, Matsuda 1993).

A theme that runs through the work of these constitutive theorists is that speech can harm not just directly, such as by causing fear and anxiety in its targets, but also somewhat indirectly, by affecting the positions of groups to which those targets belong within the social hierarchy. That is to say, speech can fix facts about the distribution of social power, including facts about who has this power, and who lacks it. For example, when a celebrant pronounces a couple to be husband and wife, he grants them powers and abilities they didn't have previously. (Moreover, these are powers and abilities that are not available to all other couples, in many jurisdictions.) Similarly, when a legislator declares that members of a certain minority group no longer have the right to vote, he deprives them of powers and abilities that they previously had, and that members of other groups continue to have. In doing so, he (the legislator) makes it the case that members of this group occupy a subordinate position within the social hierarchy.

Several theorists in this collection also explore potential constitutive connections between speech and harm. For example, Langton considers the hypothesis that pornography subordinates women, by enacting changes to desires (in addition to altering beliefs). Maitra explores different notions of speaker authority that might enable even ordinary speakers to

---

[2] Gelber is also interested in speech that constitutes discrimination.

constitute subordinating norms for others. McGowan argues there are two quite different mechanisms by which speech enacts norms, and thus by which speech can constitute harm. Tirrell maintains, among other things, that speech generates "action engendering permissions," which can themselves be harms. Finally, West explores the possibility that racist hate speech both causes and constitutes silencing. Thus, although this constitutive approach is somewhat neglected in the overall free speech literature, this volume does much to address this gap.

As one can see, even among those who agree that speech harms, there is much debate about the precise relationship between the speech and the harm. Again, getting clear on this question is important for the same reasons that identifying the harms is important. First, the kind of empirical evidence that is needed to establish that speech of a given kind is harmful will vary greatly according to how the speech brings about the harm. Evidence that speech of that kind constitutes harm by, for example, enacting a harmful policy will be quite different from evidence that the speech causes harm by, for example, altering the hearer's beliefs via persuasion. Second, what ought to be done about the harms depends greatly on how they are created. The correct remedy for the harm constituted by the enacting of a harmful policy, for example, may be to dismantle that policy, while the correct remedy for the harm caused via persuasion may well be counter-speech. We will consider some of the different possible remedies for harmful speech in the next two sections.

IV. Remedies

In the previous sections, we've focused on theorizing about the relationship between speech and harm, especially on theories that attempt to answer questions about what harms are associated with a given kind of speech, and what the precise relationship between the speech and the harm is. Even once these questions have been answered, there is still a further question about what ought to be done. One option is to regulate the harmful speech. But, given our commitment to free speech, regulation is not, and should not be, the first option to consider. If there are other remedies that can be effective while not restricting speech, then those options should be preferred.

Many believe that the best remedy for harmful speech is more speech.[3] Rather than regulate speech, what we ought to do, according to this line

---

[3] Justice Brandeis took this stance particularly memorably when he wrote, "If there be time to expose through discussion the falsehood and fallacies, to avert the evil by the process

of thinking, is to counteract its harmful effects with counter-speech. For example, if confronted with racist hate speech, one might explicitly disagree with what the speaker has said. Or else, since it may be daunting for a target of such speech to take on the speaker directly, the target (and others) can take later opportunities to speak out against racist hate speech, and racism more generally. Similarly, many suggest that the proper response to the harms associated with (some) pornography is to speak out in opposition to the pernicious view of women so often portrayed and even endorsed in pornography (Carse 1995, Kipnis 1996).

This 'more speech' response is certainly not without its critics. One important concern about this response is that not everyone is equally able to engage effectively in counter-speech because of differences in social position and power, some of which are due to the very speech that needs to be countered (Crenshaw 1995, Nielsen 2004). Relatedly, insofar as the burden of challenging, say, racist hate speech will fall disproportionately on persons of color who are already disadvantaged socially, the 'more speech' response seems unfair (Schauer 1992).[4]

A further criticism of the 'more speech' response is based on the idea that some speech *silences* others' speech (MacKinnon 1987b, Hornsby 1993, 1995, Langton 1993, West 2003). It is well known that some speakers can do more with their words than others. Only someone having the right kind of authority, for example, can command others. Until the passage of the Nineteenth Amendment to the U.S. Constitution, women lacked the power to use their speech to vote in U.S. federal elections. Further, speech can set the conditions for what speakers are able to do with their words. When the Nineteenth Amendment was enacted, it made it possible for women to vote. In this case, U.S. legislators' speech empowered U.S. women's speech. On the flip side, speech can also disable speech. If a legislator enacts a law that says that green-eyed persons can no longer vote, then the legislator's speech disables the speech of green-eyed persons. Appealing to such possibilities, some have argued that the speech of some disables the speech of others. If this is correct, then the disabled speakers may thereby be prevented from using speech to fight back against others' harmful speech. This further undermines the 'more speech' response.

---

of education, the remedy to be proposed is more speech, not enforced silence" (*Whitney v. California*).

[4] A further problem for the 'more speech' response may be that in many cases, it is not clear what the content of the counter-speech should be. For example, when a racial epithet is thrown at a person of color, it is hard to imagine what she can say in response to contradict the hateful message conveyed, or to counteract the harmful effects of the speech. As a result, it is unclear what would even count as counter-speech in such cases.

Finally, the empirical evidence suggests that targets of harmful speech do not in fact speak back in the way required by the 'more speech' response (Nielsen 2004). In her essay for this volume, for example, Laura Beth Nielsen presents her own original sociological research supporting this last point. As a matter of fact, she argues, targets of offensive race- and gender-related speech in public rarely ever speak back. Nielsen also argues that the law perpetuates social inequality by protecting those (relatively privileged persons) made uncomfortable by street begging, even at the cost of curtailing the speech of beggars, while refusing to protect those individuals (women and persons of color) targeted by offensive race- and gender-related speech in our public spaces.

One possible response to the criticisms outlined above is to offer institutional support for counter-speech, instead of depending on the courage and perseverance of isolated individuals to effectively challenge harmful speech. According to this more sophisticated version of the 'more speech' strategy, the state would not itself regulate harmful speech. Rather, the state would provide material and symbolic support for those who would engage in counter-speech. This strategy might alleviate some of the concerns mentioned above, such as the concern that the burden of speaking back falls disproportionately on those who are least able to do so. But it also raises a different question, namely, whether, and to what extent, such state support for counter-speech is compatible with a commitment to a principle of free speech. In fact, this is the question pursued by Katherine Gelber. She argues here that a version of this policy is defensible in a broad range of free speech contexts.

Although the 'more speech' response is perhaps the most discussed potential remedy to harmful speech, there are other possibilities as well. We might, for example, seek to prevent or remedy the harms of a certain category of speech through education, by making us less receptive audiences to certain sorts of messages. Or else, we could tighten enforcement for those crimes allegedly caused by speech, and thereby send a message about the state's attitude toward such crimes. So, for instance, if pornography causes rape, or if racist hate speech causes racial violence, we could step up efforts to make sure that rapists and violent racists are caught and held accountable for their egregious crimes.

Although our discussion thus far (in §§ III–IV especially) has focused on pornography and racist hate speech, the very same questions arise about other categories of allegedly harmful speech. In fact, it is a peculiarity of the current state of the literature that so much attention is focused on pornography and racist hate speech, and so little on other categories of speech, or for that matter, on connections *between* categories of speech. This book attempts to remedy this state of affairs by including essays on Holocaust denial (Altman), the use of radio broadcasts in setting the social conditions for genocide (Tirrell), and 'Whites Only' signs (McGowan). Moreover, some of the essays also consider connections between categories of speech. Both Langton and West, for instance, consider some of the cross-categorial connections between pornography and racist hate speech. By considering previously overlooked categories, and by considering connections between categories, these essays open up fertile ground for further exploration.

V. Regulating Speech

Where other remedies prove inadequate, because they are either ineffective or impractical, regulation of harmful speech may be necessary. But as has already been mentioned, to say that a principle of free speech involves a presumption of liberty in favor of speech is to say that justifications for regulating speech must meet a higher standard of scrutiny than justifications for regulating non-speech action. Thus, a proposed regulation of speech is legitimate, then, only if its justification is able to meet this raised standard.

Theorists differ about what this raised standard of scrutiny is, and what it ought to be (Volokh 1997). Despite this, it is generally agreed that the state should not interfere with speech unless it does so to prevent harm (Mill 1978).[5] But the mere fact that a particular category of speech is harmful is not generally thought to be sufficient to warrant its regulation. It must also be shown, at the very least, that the harms associated with that category of speech outweigh the considerations in favor of permitting it.[6]

Typically, this involves what might be called the 'balancing of harms' approach. On this approach, to determine whether a proposed regulation of speech is permissible, we need to balance the costs of the regulation against the costs of not regulating. Such a regulation is justified only when failing to regulate the speech in question would actually be worse than regulating it. To see how this approach might be applied, consider defamation.[7] Let's imagine what the world would be like if (false) defamation

---

[5] There are some who would disagree. For example, Joel Feinberg has argued that some speech can be regulated even though it is merely offensive, rather than harmful, if the offenses in question are such that they wrong someone (Feinberg 1985). We will not consider such views in any detail here.

[6] For these purposes, the harms associated with a category of speech should include both the harms caused by speech in that category, as well as the harms constituted by such speech.

[7] As we are using the term, not all defamation is false. If the argument outlined below is correct, then there may be reason to regulate false defamation. But the argument says nothing about true defamation.

were not regulated. In such a world, one could say false and damaging things about other people without facing any legal sanctions. One could falsely malign enemies and competitors in an attempt to get ahead. One could unjustly damage reputations, out of pure spite. Even worse than this, though, if false defamatory speech were widespread, then we might well cease to believe negative reports about other people. But if we cease to believe much of what others say, then it becomes unclear whether a system of free speech can realize the values that it is intended to realize, such as leading to the discovery of truth, or contributing to a well-functioning democracy. These are all significant costs of failing to regulate (false) defamation.

By comparison, the costs of regulating such speech seem minor. Any regulation of speech, it should be allowed, will have some 'chilling effect' on other speech. But beyond this, it seems that singling out (false) defamatory utterances for regulation would not significantly undermine the values underwriting our system of free speech (more on this below). If this is right, then on such a balancing approach, regulations of (at least some) defamation can be justified.

It is generally supposed that the balancing of harms works out differently with other categories of speech. Consider next an example of political speech. While discussing the school budget in her town, Cindy says: "The government ought to spend more money on education, because only a society with an educated workforce can compete in today's global market economy!" Suppose further that several people attending the meeting are very upset by this, because they prefer that the money be spent on new roads. Nevertheless, despite the offense caused by Cindy's words, it seems unlikely that anyone is actually harmed. By contrast, it is argued, regulating such speech would certainly be harmful. For one thing, the 'chilling effect' of such regulation on other speech is potentially substantial. Moreover, we have reason to distrust state decisions about what can and cannot be said regarding issues of public concern, since it may be in the state's interest to regulate speech that is critical of it. Thus, it seems that the costs of permitting political speech like Cindy's are minor, whereas the costs of regulating such speech would be substantial. If that's right, then the balancing approach thus tells us that regulations of such speech cannot be justified.[8]

---

[8] We have some reservations about this sort of argument. Because the category of 'political speech' is such a broad and ill-defined category, it seems to us that the balancing of harms might turn out rather differently for some speech in this category than for other speech. Nevertheless, we do think that this argument is sound for some *kinds* of political speech.

With still other categories of speech—e.g. pornography, racist hate speech—it is (even) more controversial how such balancing of harms works out. Let's focus here on pornography. As mentioned already, theorists disagree with respect to how harmful pornography is. Some contend that pornography is so harmful that regulation is warranted. More specifically, some theorists have argued that pornography harms women during its production, and that the production, distribution, and consumption of pornography causes things like rape and gender discrimination, and constitutes the subordination of women (MacKinnon 1987b, Russell 2000). As mentioned above, some also claim that pornography 'silences' women in a way that violates their right to free speech. Others maintain that pornography has liberatory and culture-enhancing aspects which outweigh its harms. In fact, some see pornography as a deeply subversive form of cultural expression that helpfully, but jarringly, exposes our socially shared prejudices and hypocrisies (Kipnis 1996). On such views, pornography does more good than harm, and thus, there is certainly not sufficient reason to regulate it.

In addition to disagreement about how harmful pornography is, there is also considerable disagreement about how harmful it would be to regulate. There are slippery slope concerns to the effect that the regulation of pornography would open the door to the regulation of speech that clearly ought to remain protected (Carse 1995, Kipnis 1996). This concern is perhaps exacerbated by the difficulty of finding an adequate definition of pornography, that distinguishes it from other sexually explicit material such as documentaries about survivors of rape (Longino 1980). There are also concerns that regulating pornography might open the door to inappropriate governmental interference with sexuality, which might in turn ultimately and disproportionately harm homosexuals and those with non-standard sexual identities (Butler 1997, Green 2000). Finally, as with any regulation of speech, there is also the potential 'chilling effect' of any regulation of pornography.

These questions about the costs of regulating (and not regulating) pornography are difficult to settle because they each depend on complex and notoriously difficult to establish empirical claims. Moreover, even once we know the harms of regulating versus the harms of failing to regulate, there is still the further question of how to weigh these harms against one another. Thus, although the balancing of harms approach affords a reasonable necessary condition for legitimate regulation, the correct application of this approach can be a source of deep and widespread disagreement.

Some of the contributors to this volume use this balancing of harms approach. Altman, for example, argues that holocaust denial laws are unwarranted exactly because regulating such speech would be significantly more harmful than permitting it. On his view, this is so because regulating such speech would undermine and thus harm our commitment to free speech itself. In addition, Gelber implicitly relies on the same approach when she explores ways to counterbalance the harms of harmful speech while, at the same time, avoiding the harms of regulation.

As mentioned at the beginning of the section, establishing that some category of speech is harmful is generally not thought to be enough to justify its regulation. Some further conditions must be met, though there is disagreement about what those conditions should be. For one thing, it might be required that alternate remedies, such as the ones considered in § IV, be shown to be inadequate (Volokh 1997). Moreover, even once it is established that regulation is warranted, the regulations themselves must meet certain constraints. In what follows, we will return once again to the example of defamation to illustrate some constraints on regulations of speech that have been imposed by U.S. courts in recent years. (Similar constraints have been imposed in other legal contexts as well, though we won't say much about such contexts here.)

As we suggested above, (false) defamatory speech can reasonably be supposed to be more harmful than its regulation would be. In light of this, and assuming that alternate remedies have been demonstrated to be inadequate, suppose that the government decides to discourage such speech by prohibiting all accusations that citizens make about one another. Even if this law manages to regulate the speech that the government has good reason to target (i.e. false defamatory speech), it would also target much else besides. Furthermore, much of the speech that it would regulate (e.g. *true* accusations about fellow citizens) clearly ought to remain protected. After all, our entire criminal justice system would break down if the government interfered thusly with the accusing of wrongdoers! Therefore, legitimate regulations of (regulable) speech must be crafted so as to not restrict speech any more than is absolutely necessary to prevent the harms in question (Schauer 1982). That is to say, legitimate regulations must be carefully crafted to target as closely as possible the speech that is to be regulated, and not other speech besides.

Next, the example in the previous paragraph brings to light an additional constraint on regulations. A regulation that targets all accusations, besides being overbroad, can also be criticized for being overly vague. After all, what counts as an accusation is not so easy to characterize. Most accusations do not involve any distinctive locutions. They certainly aren't generally prefaced with the words "I hereby accuse . . .", or any other such characteristic phrase. Accordingly, we might worry that it would be unclear, for quite a lot of speech, whether it counts as an accusation, and so, whether it is prohibited by this regulation. The potential 'chilling effect' of such a regulation, then, is enormous. To avoid this result, legitimate regulations must eschew overly vague terms.

Finally, legitimate regulations must also be content (or viewpoint) neutral. That is, the grounds for regulation must not be based on the content (or viewpoint) expressed by the speech in question. This is generally agreed to be illegitimate, since it seems dangerous to trust the government to decide which messages should and should not be communicated. Regulating speech in order to prevent considerable harm, by contrast, is generally agreed to be a legitimate reason for state intervention.

It is worth mentioning that differences between civil and criminal law have repercussions for the treatment of speech in each sphere. In civil law, the regulation of speech typically involves providing injunctive relief and/or awarding damages. If a defendant loses a (civil) defamation case, for instance, he is liable for damages, but he is not likely to be sent to jail. In criminal law, by contrast, the regulation of speech can involve imprisonment. The punishment for both perjury and contempt, for example, can include incarceration. Civil and criminal law also differ with respect to the required standards of proof. Proving a charge of perjury, for example, requires establishing guilt beyond a reasonable doubt, whereas proving a civil suit of defamation requires meeting a lower standard, such as showing either that a preponderance of the evidence favors the plaintiff, or that there is clear and convincing evidence in the plaintiff's favor. Thus, the characteristic differences between the civil and criminal systems have repercussions for what it takes to regulate speech within each system.

Finally, although we have been talking thus far as if all regulation of speech must meet the conditions discussed above, there is reason to believe that the truth is considerably more complex. As we shall see in the following section, when it comes to free speech, it seems that the word 'speech' is being used in a special technical sense. To this important issue, we now turn.

VI. Speech and 'Speech'

Thus far, we have been avoiding a question that should be central to all discussions of a free speech principle, namely, what counts as speech for the purposes of such a principle. One might think that the answer to this question is straightforward: everything that counts as speech in the ordinary sense of the word should fall within the scope of a principle of free speech, and nothing else besides. Thus, such a principle should make it more difficult to regulate anything that is speech (in the ordinary sense) than anything that isn't speech (in the ordinary sense).

Though this answer is simple and intuitive, it is not correct. For one thing, there is much that *isn't* speech in the ordinary sense that is generally taken to fall within the scope of a free speech principle. Neither burning a flag nor wearing a swastika is speech in the ordinary sense. Nevertheless, both actions are protected by current First Amendment law (*Village of Skokie v. Nationalist Socialist Party of America, Texas v. Johnson*). Moreover, this is as it should be. Such actions *should* fall within the scope of a free speech principle, even though they aren't speech (in the ordinary sense of that word).

More controversially, some theorists have argued that much that is speech in the ordinary sense does (and should) fall beyond the scope of a free speech principle (Greenawalt 1989, Schauer 1982, 2004, Maitra and McGowan 2007, 2010). To see why this is plausible, consider speech that is used to create or modify contracts. Such speech is heavily regulated, yet the regulations are rarely, if ever, challenged on free speech grounds. In other words, regulations of contracts, though they are generally regulations on speech, rarely seem to raise free speech concerns. In a similar vein, consider speech that is used in the commission of verbal crimes, such as criminal solicitation, or criminal conspiracy. Regulations of such speech (e.g. "I'll pay you five thousand dollars if you'll kill my boss") also seem to raise no free speech concerns.

If this is right, then the correct answer to the question with which we began this section—namely, what counts as speech for the purposes of a principle of free speech—is far more complicated than initially supposed. 'Speech' for these purposes must be given a special, technical sense, different from its ordinary sense, that both includes some things (e.g. wearing a swastika) that don't count as speech in the ordinary sense, and excludes others things (e.g. "I'll pay you five thousand dollars if you'll kill my boss") that do clearly count as speech in the ordinary sense. On this interpretation, the free speech principle extends special protections to all and only speech in this special, technical sense. Such a principle then entails that the justification for any proposed regulation of speech in this special, technical sense must be subject to the raised standards of scrutiny discussed in § V.

The approach sketched above raises two important questions. The first of these is a descriptive question, regarding what actually counts as speech in this technical sense. The answer to this question will, of course, be different for different free speech systems. But for any such system, the answer to this descriptive question matters enormously, since it determines how difficult a given action is to regulate. If the action counts as speech (in this technical sense), then it falls within the scope of a free speech principle. Then, the justification for any proposed regulation is subject to a raised standard of scrutiny, of the sort discussed in § V. If, however, the action in question does not count as speech (in this technical sense), then it does not have the special protections of a free speech principle extended to it. Consequently, as far as such a principle is concerned, the action would be quite easy to regulate.

Besides the descriptive question, there is also a normative question, regarding what ought to count as speech in this technical sense. It seems plausible that the answer to this question should depend on the answer given to a question we discussed earlier (§ II), about what makes speech valuable in the first place. That is to say, it seems that what ought to count as speech (in the technical sense relevant to a principle of free speech) should be whatever has the property (or properties) that make speech valuable in the first place. For example, if speech is valuable because it is conducive to the discovery of truth, then a principle of free speech should cover all those actions that are most conducive to truth-discovery (and perhaps also those actions that don't actively and substantially impede truth discovery). By contrast, on this line of thought, actions that actively and substantially impede truth discovery, even if they count as speech in the ordinary sense, ought to fall beyond the scope of a free speech principle.

In this volume, both Langton and McGowan touch on such issues. Langton raises the question of whether pornography ought to count as speech for the purposes of a free speech principle. McGowan argues that some racist hate speech should not so count, because it constitutes an otherwise illegal act of racial discrimination.

VII. This Collection

It should be clear by this point that the issues here are complex, and that they require expertise in various disciplines. Moreover, although there has already been important work done by legal scholars, philosophers of language, political philosophers, sociologists, philosophers of law, and political scientists, this collection brings them into fruitful contact with one another. By focusing on the precise functioning of the speech in question, these essays also clarify the all-important relationship between speech and harm. As argued above, by identifying which speech is harmful, what the harms are, and how the speech in question brings about those harms, these essays clarify the various issues surrounding the appropriate remedy for harmful speech. In doing so, they both heighten our awareness of the relationship between speech and harm, and educate us about the possibilities for response.

Although the contributions to this volume represent a wide variety of views on these issues, there is nevertheless sufficient common ground to facilitate a productive interaction. All contributors recognize, for example, that a clear and detailed understanding of the precise functioning of the speech in question is mandatory for successful work on such complex problems. All recognize that free speech absolutism is both a gross over-simplification of actual practice, and an unworkable stance in the face of the complexities embodied. All are keenly aware of the importance of social justice, and all acknowledge that speech can be powerful, harmful, and connected to social power in ways that are politically important. These essays offer a fruitful and inter-disciplinary exploration of this common ground.

This collection also brings together theorists who are working on free speech issues from the perspective of quite different theoretical frameworks. Here we have the speech act approach (McGowan), the pragmatic approach (Langton, Maitra), inferential role semantics (Tirrell), and Habermas' theory of communication (Gelber), all applied to free speech issues. In this way, many different theoretical tools from the philosophy of language are used to illuminate and clarify the relevant issues. As mentioned earlier, this volume also theorizes less discussed categories of speech, and some of the essays even cross-theorize, thus applying the insights from studying one category of speech to that of another. Finally, the collection is genuinely international in scope. Although several of the essays are primarily concerned with U.S. free speech law, others are explicitly international in focus. Altman, for example, considers the laws governing Holocaust denial speech in Europe, Gelber considers hate speech codes in Australia, and Tirrell discusses pre-genocidal speech in Rwanda.

Finally, this volume is also accessible to a wider audience. Rather than essays pitched to academics with rarified expertise, this volume consists of articles that are informative and comprehensible for interested readers outside the academy. We therefore hope that this collection will inform free speech discussions in the public arena. Furthermore, because it is so accessible, the collection is suitable for use as the basis for a course. We have found that, given the immediacy of the social, political, and legal issues at play, otherwise dry and technical matters in language and law really come alive for undergraduates. This introduction is also intended to foster the development of such a course. By presenting the core issues involved, and by flagging relevant complexities and controversies, it introduces the theoretical landscape to be explored there.

VIII. Overview of Articles

The articles in this collection are listed alphabetically, by author.

Andrew Altman, "Freedom of Expression and Human Rights Law: The Case of Holocaust Denial": Altman critically examines the jurisprudence of free expression under human rights law and American constitutional doctrine, focusing on the issue of Holocaust denial. He argues that legal prohibitions aimed at Holocaust denial are unjustifiable in any existing liberal state. The argument hinges on a revised form of a doctrine at the heart of a key American free speech case, *Brandenburg v. Ohio*. The revised *Brandenburg* doctrine holds that speech ought not to be prohibited, regardless of the viewpoint it advocates, unless the speech is a) intended and likely to bring about immediate lawless conduct, or b) reasonably expected to contribute substantially to widespread violence. Altman defends this doctrine, and shows that it tells against prohibitions on Holocaust denial in existing liberal states.

Katharine Gelber, "'Speaking Back': The Likely Fate of Hate Speech Policy in the United States and Australia": A central idea within free speech arguments is that the most appropriate response to speech with which one disagrees, or which one finds intolerable, is to speak back. Some scholars have argued there may even be a basis for governmental or state support to assist some in speaking. Gelber develops this argument in relation to hate speech, arguing that because and to the extent to which hate speech may prevent its targets from speaking back, institutional, educational, and material support ought to be provided to enable the targets of hate speech to 'speak back'. This would enable them both to contradict the messages contained within the hate speech and to counteract the effects of that speech on their ability to respond. The policy thus aims to ameliorate the potential effects of hate speech, and also to preserve and enhance speech opportunities. Gelber discusses the likely fortunes of a 'speaking back' policy in the United States and Australia; two jurisdictions with widely variant institutional mechanisms for the protection of free speech. She concludes that the speaking back policy is conceptually and practically useful in combating hate speech, and also potentially robust in differing constitutional environments.

Rae Langton, "Beyond Belief: Pragmatics in Hate Speech and Pornography": Pragmatics can shed light on racial hate speech and pornography, but only if we bring it down to earth. Langton distinguishes five models for hate speech and pornography: a conditioning model, an imitation model, an argument model, a speech act model, and its descendant, the pragmatic model. A speech act model distinguishes illocutionary and perlocutionary dimensions of speech: e.g. hate speech can incite, and cause, hatred and violence. The pragmatic model tries to capture these dimensions via an account of accommodation. It can indeed illuminate racial hate speech and pornography, but only with amendments that go 'beyond belief'. Lewis and Stalnaker showed how 'score' or 'common ground' of conversation accommodates to moves speakers make, and how the hearer's belief adjusts accordingly. Langton argues that this picture needs extending to make sense of hate speech and pornography: we need to allow for the accommodation of other attitudes, such as desire and hate.

Ishani Maitra, "Subordinating Speech": Maitra considers whether ordinary instances of racist hate speech can be authoritative, thereby constituting the subordination of people of color. It is often said that ordinary speakers cannot subordinate because they lack authority. Maitra argues that there are more ways in which speakers can come to have authority than have been generally recognized. In part, this is because authority has been taken to be too closely tied to social position. Maitra presents a series of examples which show that speaker authority needn't derive from social position at all. In fact, these examples show that a speaker can come to have authority even when they *lack* it prior to speaking. After distinguishing different ways in which speakers can come to have authority, Maitra concludes that there is ample reason to think that even producers of ordinary instances of racist hate speech can *sometimes* have authority in these ways.

Mary Kate McGowan, "On 'Whites Only' Signs and Racist Hate Speech: Verbal Acts of Racial Discrimination": McGowan argues that some instances of racist hate speech are speech acts that constitute illegal acts of racial discrimination. By identifying a previously overlooked mechanism by which utterances enact norms (the covert exercitive), one comes to see that some racist hate speech enacts discriminatory norms in public places. Such speech thus acts very similarly to 'Whites Only' signs. This result has two important consequences. First, it affords at least a prima facie case for the regulation of this subset of racist hate speech. Second, it disproves a certain naïve conception of so-called political speech. Although both racist hate speech and 'Whites Only' signs express political messages, they do not and should not count as political speech for the purposes of a free speech principle. Thus, McGowan concludes, expressing a political opinion is insufficient for being political speech (in the relevant sense).

Laura Beth Nielsen, "Power in Public: Reactions, Responses, and Resistance to Offensive Public Speech": Many maintain that the proper remedy for harmful speech is 'more speech.' Nielsen argues that this prescription relies on faulty empirical assumptions. As the empirical evidence shows, targets of problematic race- and gender-related public speech do not in fact 'talk back,' for many reasons. The legal treatment of such speech contrasts with that of begging. Because there are already a variety of formal mechanisms in place that discourage begging, it is easier for targets to respond to begging. In this way, the law protects the powerful from harassment in public places, while placing on its less privileged members a burdensome choice between responding or accepting their own subordination.

Lynne Tirrell, "Genocidal Language Games": Tirrell examines the role played by derogatory terms (e.g. *'inyenzi'* or cockroach, *'inzoka'* or snake) in laying the social groundwork for the genocide of the Tutsi in Rwanda in 1994. The genocide was preceded by an increase in the use of anti-Tutsi derogatory terms among the Hutu. As these linguistic practices evolved, the terms became more openly and directly aimed at Tutsi. Then, during the 100 days of the genocide, derogatory terms and coded euphemisms were used to direct killers to their victims. Understanding these speech acts helps to illuminate the important ways that power is enacted through discourse, how speech acts can prepare the way for physical and material acts, and how speech generates permissions for actions hitherto uncountenanced. Studying the role of speech acts and linguistic practices in laying the groundwork of the genocide illuminates how patterns of speech acts become linguistic practices that constitute permissibility conditions for non-linguistic behaviors. Further, Tirrell's analysis helps to make sense of the view that a steady, deep, and widespread derogation of a group can be part and parcel of genocide, not only an antecedent to it.

Caroline West, "Words that Silence? Freedom of Expression and Racist Hate Speech": West examines the prevailing assumption that the value of freedom of speech itself is necessarily only or best served by permitting racist hate speech. She argues that anything worthy of the label 'freedom of speech' must satisfy three relatively minimal conditions, namely, minimal distribution, minimal comprehension, and minimal consideration. If racist hate speech silences other speech by interfering with its production/distribution, comprehension, or consideration, then racist hate speech may function to undermine, rather than exemplify or enhance, freedom of speech. If so, there might be a free speech argument against permitting racist hate speech. West provides a novel framework within which such claims can be evaluated.

References

Butler, J. 1997. *Excitable Speech: A Politics of the Performative*. New York and London: Routledge.

Carse, A. 1995. Pornography: An Uncivil Liberty. *Hypatia* 10 (1): 155–82.

Crenshaw, K. 1995. Comments of an Outsider on the First Amendment. In L. Lederer and R. Delgado (eds.), *The Price We Pay: The Case Against Racist Speech, Hate Propaganda, and Pornography*. New York: Hill and Wang: 167–75.

Delgado, R. 1993. Words that Wound: A Tort Action for Racial Insults, Epithets, and Name Calling. In M. Matsuda, C. Lawrence, R. Delgado, and K. Crenshaw (eds.), *Words that Wound: Critical Race Theory, Assaultive Speech, and the First Amendment*. Boulder, CO: Westview Press: 89–110.

Feinberg, J. 1985. *Offense to Others: The Moral Limits of the Criminal Law*, Volume 2. Oxford: Oxford University Press.

Green, L. 2000. Pornographies. *The Journal of Political Philosophy* 8 (1): 27–52.

Greenawalt, K. 1989. *Speech, Crime and the Uses of Language*. Oxford: Oxford University Press.

Hornsby, J. 1993. Speech Acts and Pornography. *Women's Philosophy Review* 10: 38–45.

Hornsby, J. 1995. Disempowered Speech. In S. Haslanger (ed.), *Philosophical Topics* 23 (2): 127–47.

Hurley, S. 2004. Imitation, Media Violence, and Freedom of Speech. *Philosophical Studies* 117 (1–2): 165–218.

Kipnis, L. 1996. *Bound and Gagged: Pornography and the Politics of Fantasy in America*. New York: Grove Press.

Langton, R. 1993. Speech Acts and Unspeakable Acts. *Philosophy & Public Affairs* 22 (4): 293–330.

Lawrence, C. 1993. If He Hollers Let Him Go: Regulating Racist Speech on Campus. In M. Matsuda, C. Lawrence, R. Delgado, and K. Crenshaw (eds.), *Words that Wound: Critical Race Theory, Assaultive Speech and the First Amendment*. Boulder, CO: Westview Press: 53–88.

Longino, H. 1980. Pornography, Oppression, and Freedom: A Closer Look. In L. Lederer (ed.), *Take Back the Night: Women on Pornography*. New York: Morrow.

MacKinnon, C. 1987a. Not a Moral Issue. In her *Feminism Unmodified: Discourses on Life and Law*. Cambridge, MA: Harvard University Press: 146–62.

MacKinnon, C. 1987b. Francis Biddle's Sister: Pornography, Civil Rights, and Speech. In her *Feminism Unmodified: Discourses on Life and Law*. Cambridge, MA: Harvard University Press: 163–97.

MacKinnon, C. 1993. *Only Words*. Cambridge, MA: Harvard University Press.

MacKinnon, C. and A. Dworkin (eds.). 1997. *In Harm's Way: The Pornography Civil Rights Hearings*. Cambridge, MA: Harvard University Press.

Maitra, I. 2009. Silencing Speech. *Canadian Journal of Philosophy* 39 (2): 309–38.

Maitra, I. and M. K. McGowan. 2007. The Limits of Free Speech: Pornography and the Question of Coverage. *Legal Theory* 13 (1): 41–68.

Maitra, I. and M. K. McGowan. 2010. On Racist Hate Speech and the Scope of a Free Speech Principle. *Canadian Journal of Law & Jurisprudence* 23 (2): 343–72.

Matsuda, M. 1993. Public Response to Racist Speech: Considering the Victim's Story. In M. Matsuda, C. Lawrence, R. Delgado, and K. Crenshaw (eds.), *Words that Wound: Critical Race Theory, Assaultive Speech, and the First Amendment*. Boulder, CO: Westview Press: 17–51.

Meiklejohn, A. 1960. Free Speech and its Relation to Government. In his *Political Freedom: The Constitutional Powers of the People*. New York: Harper: 3–89.

McGowan, M. K. 2009. On Silencing and Sexual Refusal. *Journal of Political Philosophy* 17 (4): 487–94.

Mill, J. S. 1978. *On Liberty*. E. Rapaport (ed.). Indianapolis, IN: Hackett.

Nielsen, L. B. 2004. *License to Harass: Law, Hierarchy, and Offensive Public Speech*. Princeton, NJ: Princeton University Press.

Russell, D. 2000. Pornography and Rape: A Causal Model. In D. Cornell (ed.), *Feminism & Pornography*. Oxford: Oxford University Press: 48–93.

Scanlon, T. 1972. A Theory of Freedom of Expression. *Philosophy & Public Affairs* 1 (2): 204–26.

Schauer, F. 1982. *Free Speech: A Philosophical Enquiry*. Cambridge: Cambridge University Press.

Schauer, F. 1992. Uncoupling Free Speech. *Columbia Law Review* 92 (6): 1321–57.

Schauer, F. 2004. The Boundaries of the First Amendment: A Preliminary Exploration of Constitutional Salience. *Harvard Law Review* 117 (6): 1765–809.

Scoccia, D. 1996. Can Liberals Support a Ban on Violent Pornography? *Ethics* 106 (4): 776–99.

Texas v. Johnson. 491 U.S. 397 (1989).

Village of Skokie v. Nationalist Socialist Party of America. 373 N.E. 2d 21 (Ill. Sup. Ct. 1978).

Volokh, E. 1997. Freedom of Speech, Permissible Tailoring, and Transcending Strict Scrutiny. *University of Pennsylvania Law Review* 144 (6): 2417–61.

West, C. 2003. The Free Speech Argument Against Pornography. *Canadian Journal of Philosophy* 33 (3): 391–422.

Whitney v. California. 274 U.S. 357 (1957).

Freedom of Expression and Human Rights Law: The Case of Holocaust Denial

Andrew Altman

Relying on an array of sources, historians have assembled a detailed picture of Nazi Germany's efforts to exterminate European Jewry and annihilate Jewish culture. Holocaust denial is a set of theses radically at odds with that picture, and its theses cannot be taken seriously as historical claims. Yet, the persistent allure of denial for some, and its apparent connection to a potentially lethal form of antisemitism, suggest that denial should be taken seriously as a social and political phenomenon. In fact, there are many liberal states—including much of the European Union, Canada, Australia, Germany, and Israel—that have made the public expression of Holocaust denial a criminal offense.

At the same time, freedom of expression is a right protected by several international human rights agreements, and the question inescapably arises as to whether laws prohibiting denial are consistent with this right. The question has been addressed by courts and jurists at the domestic and regional levels in Europe and in other parts of the world, and at the global level by the United Nations' Human Rights Committee. And the consensus among those tribunals and jurists is that prohibiting denial does not violate the right of free expression. A human rights jurisprudence has thus been developed under which states are permitted to outlaw the public expression of Holocaust denial.

This human rights jurisprudence stands in contrast to the understanding of free expression embedded in current American constitutional doctrine. Under American First Amendment jurisprudence, legal prohibitions directed at the viewpoint expressed by a certain instance of communication are almost never constitutional. It would be difficult to find a clearer case of such disfavored "viewpoint-based regulation" than laws prohibiting Holocaust denial, nor an easier case for an American court to decide than one challenging the constitutionality of such a law. Contemporary American jurisprudence rejects as a violation of freedom of speech any legal punishment for public expressions of denial.[1]

In this article, I critically examine the jurisprudence of free expression under human rights law and American constitutional doctrine, focusing on the issue of Holocaust denial. I argue that legal prohibitions aimed at Holocaust denial are unjustifiable in any existing liberal state. The argument hinges on a revised form of a doctrine at the heart of a key American free speech case. The revised doctrine holds that speech ought not to be prohibited, regardless of the viewpoint it advocates, unless the speech is a) intended and likely to bring about immediate lawless conduct, *or* b) reasonably expected to contribute substantially to widespread violence.

The article unfolds as follows. Section I provides an account of the main theses of Holocaust denial. Section II explains the provisions of the major international human rights agreements concerning freedom of expression and shows how those provisions have been understood and applied in cases of Holocaust denial. Section III presents the doctrine enunciated in the U.S. Supreme Court case, *Brandenburg v. Ohio*, and contrasts that doctrine with human rights jurisprudence. Section IV then defends the Brandenburg Doctrine and its implications for Holocaust denial, and criticizes human rights jurisprudence. Section V shows that a revision is needed in the Brandenburg Doctrine to allow viewpoint-based restrictions on speech, but argues that, even in its revised form, the Doctrine still protects Holocaust denial from legal prohibition in any existing liberal state. Finally, section VI rejects the suggestion that their special relation to the Holocaust entitles Germany and Israel to ban denial.

I. An Anatomy of Denial

The chief prosecutor for the United States at the Nuremberg Trial of the Major War Criminals was Associate Justice of the Supreme Court, Robert Jackson. He gave the opening address at the trial, telling the tribunal that the prosecution would "give you undeniable proofs of incredible events" (IMT 1947: 99). Among those incredible events was the Nazi campaign of genocide that had murdered approximately six million Jews. The evidence

---

[1] American free speech doctrine did not embrace Viewpoint Neutrality until the 1960s, and even as late as the 1950s the Supreme Court endorsed the idea of group libel (*Beauharnais v. Illinois* 1952), an idea that is at odds with Viewpoint Neutrality and sometimes invoked to justify the prohibition of Holocaust denial.

adduced at the trial provided the first public view of what later became known as the Holocaust.

Although the trial evidence seems to have been accepted as conclusive by most people in Allied nations, it did not convince the majority of Germans of the scale of the murders. A 1954 poll asking West Germans about the statement that there were five million Jewish victims of the Nazis found that more than one-third of respondents regarded the statement as "very exaggerated," and an additional one-quarter thought it "somewhat exaggerated" (Bergmann and Erb 1997: 252). These figures are not surprising, given natural suspicions that the Germans of the time had about the fairness of the trial combined with the almost incomprehensible scale of the genocide.

It is surprising, though, that two decades after the verdicts were handed down at Nuremberg, a literature began to flower in the United States and Western Europe that challenged the main historical claims about the Nazi genocide that the trial and subsequent research had amply confirmed. Key works included *The Hoax of the Twentieth Century*, authored by Arthur Butz (1992/1976), professor of engineering at Northwestern; *Mémoire en Défense* by Robert Faurisson (1980),[2] former professor of literature at Lyons-2; and a pseudo-technical report written by a self-proclaimed engineering expert, American Fred Leuchter (1989), on gas chambers at Auschwitz and Majdanek.

The essential theses of Holocaust denial fall into three major areas:

A) The treatment of Jews by the Nazi regime during the Second World War;
B) The evidence on which is based the conventional account of the treatment of Jews; and
C) The reasons explaining why the conventional account has been so widely and firmly accepted.

Although there is some variation in the claims of deniers, the following theses constitute the common core of most versions of Holocaust denial.

Under area (A), there are four key theses:

A-1) There was no plan or systematic effort of the Nazi regime to exterminate the Jews of Europe;
A-2) Jews were brought to concentration camps as part of a program of resettlement, not one of extermination;

---

[2] Noam Chomsky became embroiled in a public debate in France over Faurisson's book for defending Faurisson's right to publish it. (Chomsky 1981)

A-3) The deaths of Jews were due mainly to the difficult conditions that the war had created for everyone in Europe (e.g. poor sanitary conditions); and

A-4) The number of Jewish deaths was a fraction of the conventional figure of six million.

As far as the number of Jewish victims is concerned, the claims of deniers vary widely and wildly, from thousands (Harwood n.d.: 38) to hundreds of thousands (Butz 1992: 239), and even as high as one million (*Faurisson v. France* 1996, para. 2.4). This extreme variation is what one might expect from a collection of persons who are only loosely coordinated with one another and who are radically disconnected from the stubborn facts of history. While historians have arrived at varying estimates of the number of Jewish victims, the differences are fully explainable by the ineliminable uncertainties involved in determining how many died during the chaotic and turbulent years of the war. In a recent estimate, Evans writes that "it is certain that at least 5.5 million Jews were deliberately killed in one way or another by the Nazis and their allies" (2009: 318).

Area (B) involves the deniers' "refutation" of the conventional story of World War II. It contains what is possibly the most extensive part of the denial literature, amounting to a shadow reflection of the vast evidence that has been accumulated about the various aspects of the Holocaust. In the denial literature, five theses are most prominent in the effort to undermine that evidence.

B-1) Eyewitness claims that gas chambers were used for mass killings are not reliable, as evidenced by the fact that such claims made about the camps at Dachau, Bergen-Belsen, and Buchenwald were later conclusively proved false;

B-2) Confessions by Germans in which they admitted to participating in the mass murder of Jews are not reliable because they were the product of coercion or else the result of a desire to please the victorious Allies;

B-3) It was physically impossible for the facilities at Auschwitz-Birkenau to be used for the mass killing of humans;

B-4) References to the "extermination" of Jews in various Nazi documents and speeches are mistranslations of German terms that actually refer to resettlement; and

B-5) No written order to exterminate European Jewry has ever been found among the store of German documents from the war.

Although hundreds of thousands of Jews and other prisoners died in the camps at Dachau, Bergen-Belsen, and Buchenwald, historians agree that mass extermination by gassing did not take place in those camps. Yet, there were some eyewitness reports from Dachau, claiming that there was mass, homicidal gassing there. Deniers rely on these incorrect reports to discredit eyewitness reports from all camps. But deniers also need to address the fact that many Germans who worked in the extermination camps confessed to the mass killings. The commandant of Auschwitz, Rudolph Hoess, made a detailed confession to Allied authorities after the war and published an autobiography revealing the operations of the mass killing in the Birkenau section of the camp. Deniers contend that the confessions were the result of torture by the Allies, or, alternatively, the result of the desire of the Germans to curry favor by saying what they knew the Allies wanted to hear. Suffice it to say that these contentions are unsupported by any evidence and that Hoess's confessions are supported by a wide range of physical evidence and eyewitness testimony.

Perhaps the most discussed of the deniers' claims is that there were no homicidal gas chambers at Auschwitz. Leuchter examined remains of the crematoria and performed chemical tests to determine the amount of Zyklon-B residue. He found insufficient residue to support the idea that the buildings were used to gas people to death. Leuchter also asserted that certain design elements made it impossible for the purported extermination facilities to be used for killing persons. His conclusion, heralded by deniers, asserted: "It is the best engineering opinion of this author that the alleged gas chambers . . . could not then have been, or now, be utilized or seriously considered to function as execution chambers" (Leuchter 1989: 19). Leuchter's tests, however, were seriously flawed; for example, they were conducted on materials that had been exposed for decades to the weather. More importantly, Leuchter assumed that it would take more Zyklon-B to kill a person than to kill lice, when in fact the opposite was true. Additionally, when testifying at a Canadian trial of another denier, Ernst Zundel, Leuchter was forced to admit in court that he did not have a degree in engineering (Lipstadt 1993: 164).

The Nazis made a systematic effort to destroy physical and documentary evidence of their genocide, when their regime began to crumble under the assault of the Allied forces. Yet, in addition to the physical remains of the extermination centers, considerable documentary evidence survived, including records of speeches by Hitler and reports of discussions among the Nazi officials in which they referred to the extermination of Jews. The terms used to refer to that extermination were "Ausrottung" and "Vernichtung." Deniers contend that, although these terms might *now* unequivocally mean extermination, Nazi-era Germans used them in a more innocent and metaphorical way to refer to removal and resettlement outside of the Reich. This contention has no basis in reality and is easily refuted by reference to German dictionaries and native German speakers (Shermer and Grobman 2000: 204–8).

The final set of theses addresses the question of why the conventional account of the Holocaust has received such widespread and enduring acceptance. Three theses are central:

C-1) The conventional account of the Nazi treatment of Jews has received widespread acceptance because it has been strongly promoted by Israel and the Zionist-controlled media, even while the Zionists who are involved know full well that the account is false;

C-2) The conventional account is used to legitimize Israel's existence, its oppression of the Palestinians, and its receipt of reparations from Germany; and

C-3) The dearth of dissent from that account is largely the result of the fear of suffering retaliation at the hands of the powerful cadre of Zionists.

The common theme among these three theses is that Israel, Zionism, and a Zionist-controlled media lie behind the conventional account of the Holocaust. Deniers typically claim that the story of the Nazi genocide was originally fabricated by British intelligence during the war. After the war, Zionists deliberately embellished and disingenuously promoted the story in order to build international support for the state of Israel, and, after the founding of the state, Israel and its supporters used the story to bilk Germany of vast sums in reparation payments and to defend Israeli oppression of the Palestinians. And so great is the international power of Zionists that few persons are willing to incur their wrath by openly questioning the conventional account. The received account of the Holocaust is, accordingly, a "Zionist swindle" (*X v. Federal Republic of Germany* 1982: 195). That is the deniers' story, at any rate.[3]

---

[3] Polls in the U.S. suggest that about 1% or 2% of the population regards the conventional account of the Holocaust as a myth. (Smith 1995) A poll in the U.K. found that 15% agreed or strongly agreed that the Holocaust had been exaggerated (Bates 2004), and an Italian poll found that 11% said that Jews are lying when they say that millions were exterminated by the Nazis in gas chambers. (Mannheimer 2003) A 2008 poll of Israeli-Arabs found that 40% of them say that the Holocaust never happened, although there is reason to think that their support for Holocaust denial was in fact not a reflection of what Israeli-Arabs actually believed, but rather was a way of expressing their anger at Israeli policy toward the Palestinians. (Heller 2009)

II. Human Rights Law

International and regional human rights instruments contain explicit and broad protections for freedom of expression. Article 19 of the *Universal Declaration of Human Rights* (*Universal Declaration*) provides, "Everyone has the right to freedom of opinion and expression; this right includes freedom to hold opinions without interference and to seek, receive and impart information and ideas through any media and regardless of frontiers." A virtually identical provision is found in Article 19 of the *International Covenant of Civil and Political Rights* (*International Covenant*). And Article 10 of the Council of Europe's *Convention for the Protection of Human Rights and Fundamental Freedoms* (*European Convention*) contains very similar wording: "Everyone has the right to freedom of expression. This right shall include freedom to hold opinions and to receive and impart information and ideas without interference by public authority and regardless of frontiers."

In construing the *European Convention*, the European Court of Human Rights has given broad scope to freedom of expression. In a key case, the court wrote,

Freedom of expression constitutes one of the essential foundations of... [democratic] society.... [I]t is applicable not only to "information" or "ideas" that are favourably received or regarded as inoffensive or as a matter of indifference, but also to those that offend, shock or disturb the State or any sector of the population. Such are the demands of that pluralism, tolerance and broadmindedness without which there is no "democratic society". (*Handyside* 1976: para. 49)

This statement of the court is best understood as an affirmation of what is called in the American context the "Principle of Viewpoint Neutrality." According to the principle, speech must not be prohibited by government on the basis of the viewpoint it expresses. The term "viewpoint" here refers paradigmatically to beliefs or opinions about general matters of political, ethical, social, and historical significance. In the European Court's understanding, speech is protected from being restricted on the ground that the viewpoint it expresses is offensive, shocking, or otherwise disturbing.

Yet, the same human rights treaties and cases that protect freedom of expression also contain explicit limitations on the right. Some of these limitations are presented as optional: states are permitted but not obligated to impose them. Others are presented as obligatory. Thus, Article 19 of the *International Covenant* permits certain restrictions, declaring that, because the right of free expression "carries with it certain duties and responsibilities," the right may be subject to legal restriction when such restriction is "necessary (a) for respect of the rights or reputations of others; (b) for the protection of national security or of public order (*ordre public*), or of public health or morals." Article 20 requires that "[a]ny advocacy of national, racial or religious hatred that constitutes incitement to discrimination, hostility or violence shall be prohibited by law," and that article is based, in part, on the provision of the *Universal Declaration*, which holds that everyone is "entitled to equal protection against any discrimination in violation of this Declaration and *against any incitement to such discrimination*" (Article 7, emphasis added).

The *European Convention* explicitly permits restrictions on expression when they "are necessary in a democratic society, in the interests of national security, territorial integrity or public safety, for the prevention of disorder or crime, for the protection of health or morals, [or] for the protection of the reputation or the rights of others..." (Article 10). And Article 4 of the *International Convention for the Elimination of All Forms of Racial Discrimination* (*Convention on Racial Discrimination*) contains the requirement that state parties "[s]hall declare an offence punishable by law all dissemination of ideas based on racial superiority or hatred, incitement to racial discrimination, as well as all acts of violence or incitement to such acts against any race or group of persons of another colour or ethnic origin."

All of the foregoing provisions of international human rights law have played a role in the reasoning of courts and other bodies that have considered Holocaust denial cases. In those cases that are of immediate interest, a defendant was found liable under a provision of the domestic legal code of his country of citizenship or residence and filed a complaint on the basis of the provisions of human rights law that protect freedom of expression. Some cases are civil and involve laws against defaming the reputation of others. The criminal cases typically involve laws that fall under one or both of two rough categories. First are general laws that prohibit public incitement of racial or religious hatred, hostility, or discrimination. Second are laws that pick out the Holocaust or, somewhat more broadly, certain genocides or crimes against humanity that include the Holocaust, and criminalize public expression that denies or diminishes such atrocities.

When I speak of the "human rights jurisprudence" regarding freedom of expression and Holocaust denial, I am referring to the view embodied in the jurisprudence that has emerged from the interpretation of the foregoing human rights instruments by the European Commission on Human Rights, the European Court of Human Rights, and the U.N.'s Human Rights Committee. According to that jurisprudence, laws used to prosecute deniers do not violate freedom of expression, because the laws fall within the scope of those provisions of human rights agreements that permit or require certain kinds of restrictions on that freedom. Two main lines of argument appear in the Holocaust denial cases, one revolving around the idea that denial is defamatory and the other that it incites discrimination.

The defamation argument was made initially in a civil case and then extended to criminal prosecutions of deniers. In the case *X. v. Federal Republic of Germany*, the European Commission on Human Rights received an application from someone who had lost a civil suit concerning a pamphlet that he posted publicly in which he characterized the claim that six million Jews were murdered by the Nazis as "a mere invention, an unacceptable lie, and a zionist swindle" (1982: 195). The plaintiff was the grandson of a victim of the Holocaust. The applicant asked the commission for relief on, among other grounds, the claim of an infringement on his human right under international law to freedom of expression. The Commission agreed that there was such infringement, but it asserted that the infringement was justifiable because the pamphlet constituted "a defamatory attack against the Jewish community and against each individual member of this community" (1982: 198).

In *Remer v. Germany*, the European Commission heard a case of a man convicted and punished for inciting racial hatred for having distributed a publication suggesting that Nazi camps did not contain gas chambers and that Jews had invented the story in order to extort money from Germany. The Commission held Remer's application inadmissible on the ground that the racial incitement provisions of the German penal code were within the permissible exceptions to the free expression guarantees of the European Convention. The commission explained, "The public interest in the prevention of crime and disorder ... due to incitement to hatred against Jews, and the requirements of protecting their reputation and rights, outweigh, in a democratic society, the applicant's freedom to impart [sic] publications denying the existence of the gassing of Jews ..." (1995: 122).

In *Garaudy v. France*, the European Court of Human Rights found inadmissible an application by a French author who had been convicted and sentenced in his national courts for denying the Holocaust. France's Gayssot law, adopted in 1990, prohibited persons from publicly contesting the reality of certain crimes against humanity, including the Holocaust. Garaudy had published a book, *The Founding Myths of Israeli Politics*, containing chapters with such titles as, "The Myth of the Nuremberg Trials" and "The Myth of the Holocaust." Although Garaudy sought to downplay the elements of denial contained in the book, portraying it mainly as a criticism of the state of Israel and its policies, the Court of

Human Rights found that the book "systematically denies the crimes against humanity perpetrated by the Nazis against the Jewish community." The court went on to claim that "[d]enying crimes against humanity is...one of the most serious forms of racial defamation of Jews and of incitement to hatred of them" (2003).

Turning from the European human rights system to the U.N.'s Human Rights Committee, the key case concerns Robert Faurisson, a French academic and author who had been prosecuted under the Gayssot law and who filed a communication with the committee contending that his right to freedom of expression under the *International Covenant* had been violated. Faurisson had denied the reality of the Holocaust during an interview that was subsequently published in a French magazine. In the interview, Faurisson stated, "I have excellent reasons not to believe in this policy of the extermination of Jews or in the magic gas chamber" (1996: para. 2.6). The Human Rights Committee rejected Faurisson's complaint and adopted the view that his statements had "violated the rights and reputation of others" (1996: para. 2.6) and "were of a nature as to raise or strengthen antisemitic feelings" (1996: paras. 9.5 and 9.6).

In each of the foregoing cases, the human rights body having jurisdiction found that Holocaust denial fell within the scope of exceptions to freedom of expression enumerated in human rights law. Specifically, denial was regarded as unprotected expression, because states may prohibit speech with laws that are "necessary...for the protection of the reputation or the rights of others" (*European Convention*: Article 10) and because the *Universal Declaration* holds that everyone is "entitled to equal protection against any discrimination in violation of this Declaration *and against any incitement to such discrimination*" (Article 7, emphasis added). The bodies also found that, properly interpreted, the *Convention on Racial Discrimination* covers antisemitic speech and ideas under its provision requiring that State parties "[s]hall declare an offence punishable by law all dissemination of ideas based on racial superiority or hatred, or incitement to racial discrimination," (Article 4), further supporting the legality of Holocaust denial prosecutions.

Human rights bodies have also suggested a potential rationale for the foregoing exceptions to freedom of expression. They have held that such exceptions are justified because the exceptions are "necessary in a democratic society." Unfortunately, there is no elaboration of the criteria for determining what is necessary in a democracy or how such criteria are pertinent to the case of Holocaust denial. Presumably, the core ideas are that democracy requires equal citizenship and that a ban on denial makes an important, or even essential, contribution to maintaining the equal citizenship of Jews. Without the ban, the argument goes, Jews would be denied equal citizenship because they would be subjected to the discrimination incited by denial and to the defamation inherent in denial. In sections IV and V we will examine these arguments. First, let us look at the American alternative.

III. The Brandenburg Doctrine

If the Holocaust denial cases discussed in the previous section had been brought in the judicial system of the United States in recent years, they would have presented especially easy cases for the courts to decide: the deniers would have won hands down (Schauer 2005: 61, n. 28). Indeed, it is, in part, because the cases would have been so easy that there have been no prosecutions in the U.S. for Holocaust denial or any laws purporting to prohibit denial. The pivotal difference between U.S. law and international human rights law hinges on how the Principle of Viewpoint Neutrality is interpreted and, more specifically, what the permissible exceptions to the principle are thought to be. The principle has been very broadly applied by U.S. courts to strike down laws directed at, among other forms of expression, flag burning, pornography, racist speech, and the infamous Nazi march that had been planned to take place in Skokie, Illinois, a town where many Holocaust survivors lived.

One of the central cases in the development of the American understanding of Viewpoint Neutrality is *Brandenburg v. Ohio*. The case involved a prosecution under the state's Criminal Syndicalism Statute, which outlawed "advocat[ing] . . . the duty, necessity, or propriety of crime, sabotage, violence, or unlawful methods of terrorism as a means of accomplishing industrial or political reform" and banned "voluntarily assembl [ing] with any society, group, or assemblage of persons formed to teach or advocate the doctrines of criminal syndicalism" (1969: 444–5). The court invalidated the conviction of a member of the Ku Klux Klan and declared the statute to be unconstitutional. "[C]onstitutional guarantees of free speech and free press," wrote the court, "do not permit a State to forbid or proscribe advocacy of the use of force or of law violation except where such advocacy is directed to inciting or producing imminent lawless action and is likely to incite or produce such action" (1969: 447).

Brandenburg should be construed as affirming the Principle of Viewpoint Neutrality, while adding that there is one, and only one, class of exceptions in which viewpoint-based prohibitions are permitted, namely, cases in which the advocacy of a certain viewpoint is intended and likely to bring about imminent lawless conduct.[4] Let us call this elaboration of the Principle of Viewpoint Neutrality, the Brandenburg Doctrine. If we judge the cases of Holocaust denial examined in the previous section on the basis of this doctrine, the decisions would almost certainly be in favor of the denier. In no case was there any explicit advocacy of force or lawless conduct or any reason to think that the speaker's words were likely to cause imminent lawless conduct. The Brandenburg Doctrine protects Holocaust denial, because denial as such does not fall within the class of exceptions to Viewpoint Neutrality that the doctrine specifies. More generally, under the doctrine, there is no viewpoint that is so egregious that explicitly advocating it is beyond the protection of the Viewpoint Neutrality, unless the advocacy is accompanied by the intention and likelihood of bringing about immediate lawless conduct.

In contrast to the Brandenburg Doctrine, human rights jurisprudence permits a wider range of exceptions to the Principle of Viewpoint Neutrality. In particular, human rights jurisprudence places beyond the protection of Viewpoint Neutrality instances of racist, antisemitic, or similar forms of derogatory speech that do not involve an explicit advocacy of force or other lawlessness and that are not characterized by an intention or likelihood of bringing about imminent lawless conduct. Stephanie Farrior describes this dimension of human rights law: "the bedrock of international law on hate speech is the belief that there is indeed a wholly unacceptable ideology, one that is not deserving of legal protection: that of discrimination on the basis of race, sex, and other prohibited grounds" (1996: 98). Forms of speech that advocate discrimination (or persecution or genocide) against persons based on their race, sex, and so forth express viewpoints that are so egregious that those forms of speech are not protected by Viewpoint Neutrality. Accordingly, under human rights jurisprudence, government is licensed to prohibit speech for advocating viewpoints that are racist, sexist, and so forth. But under *Brandenburg*, such viewpoint-based restrictions are not permitted, and the government is

---

[4] The term "abstract advocacy" is used in American law to refer to speech that advocates a certain viewpoint when there is no intention or likelihood of bringing about imminent lawless action. Although the Court does not distinguish between different categories of lawless action, it is best to construe the doctrine in *Brandenburg* as concerned with lawbreaking that involves serious harm or risk of such harm to persons or their property. The case, after all, is one about the advocacy of political revolution, and it is doubtful that a person should be liable to legal punishment for advocating, in a non-abstract way, that private citizens protest the perks of government officials by parking their cars in spots reserved for those officials. There will undoubtedly be hard cases between advocacy of political revolution and advocacy of parking protest, but that fact reflects the absence of sharp moral lines in important areas relating to freedom of expression.

required to show that any racist or sexist speech that it aims to prohibit is, in each instance, intended and likely to produce imminent lawless conduct.

IV. The Brandenburg Doctrine Defended

In this section, I formulate and defend a revised version of the *Brandenburg Principle*. The revisions move the principle in the direction of human rights jurisprudence, but not so far as to entail that existing liberal democracies are morally permitted to prohibit Holocaust denial. The section starts by examining an argument by Jeremy Waldron against American doctrine.

Referring explicitly to *Brandenburg*, Jeremy Waldron writes, "It is not clear to me that the Europeans are mistaken when they say that a liberal democracy must take affirmative responsibility for protecting the atmosphere of mutual respect against certain forms of vicious [verbal or other symbolic] attack" (2009: 44). He cites the criminalization of Holocaust denial as one step that European states have taken in carrying out that responsibility, and he appears to approve of such a step along with other laws that "protect ethnic and racial groups from threatening, insulting, or abusive publications likely to excite hostility against them or bring them into public contempt" (2009: 42). This line of thinking converges nicely with the human rights decisions examined in section II. His reference to speech that is insulting and "likely to excite hostility" seems to be Waldron's way of talking about incitement to discrimination, while the reference to expression that brings the members of a group into "public contempt" captures the idea of speech that defames a group.

Waldron is concerned to argue that one can endorse the criminalization of denial and still consistently defend the speech rights of Communists, anarchists, fascists, and other revolutionaries who call for the forcible overthrow of government. *Brandenburg* seems to provide firm support for the speech of Communists, for example, as long as their revolutionary rhetoric is not intended and likely to bring about the overthrow of the government (or other such lawless activity). But if the Brandenburg Doctrine is abandoned in order to accommodate the legal prohibition of Holocaust denial, the question arises as to whether Communist and other revolutionary speech are then open to suppression. Waldron does not think so. He writes,

The state and its officials may be strong enough, thick-skinned enough, well-enough-armed, or sufficiently insinuated already into every aspect of public life to be able to shrug off public denunciations. . . . But the position of minority groups as equal members of a multiracial, multiethnic, or religiously pluralistic society is not something that anyone can take for granted. It is a recent and fragile achievement in the United States... (2009: 44)

Waldron's argument rests on the presumption that, in existing liberal states, the revolutionary rhetoric of Communists and other political radicals ought to be protected. The presumption is, I think, correct. Any adequate account of the expressive rights of a Holocaust denier must avoid entailing that revolutionary political speech is legitimately subject to prohibition. If denial is subject to prohibition, then it must be adequately distinguished from revolutionary speech. However, Waldron's effort to draw the line is problematic, because revolutionary denunciations of government are frequently based on the belief that the government has too cozy a relation with some racial or religious group or is even secretly controlled by the group. American neo-Nazis who call for revolution will say that Jews control the U.S. government. The denunciation of the government and the denunciation of Jews go hand-in-hand, and there seems to be no way of protecting neo-Nazi speech insofar as it denounces the government, but prohibiting it insofar as the speech denounces Jews.

Nonetheless, one might argue that certain kinds of restriction on racially charged expression are defensible and seek to show that the Brandenburg doctrine stands in need of revision. Thus, consider the prohibition on cross-burning in various jurisdictions in the U.S. It would seem that the prohibition can be justified on the ground that, given U.S. racial history, cross-burning is reasonably understood as a credible threat of violence against blacks.[5] Such threats need not—in fact, should not—be tolerated by government, the argument goes, even if the cross-burner did not actually intend to issue a threat. It is sufficient that cross-burning (in the U.S.) is reasonably understood as a credible threat of imminent violence.[6] Accordingly, one might suggest the following revised Brandenburg Doctrine: speech should be protected, regardless of the viewpoint it advocates, unless the speech is a) intended and likely to bring about imminent lawless conduct *or* b) reasonably understood as a credible threat of imminent violence.

I agree that cross-burning in the U.S. is reasonably understood as a threat of imminent violence (at least in almost all real cases) and that it is legitimately prohibited as such. However, I am dubious that a revision in Brandenburg is called for on that basis. The prohibition of cross-burning

---

[5] See *Virginia v. Black* 538 U.S. 343 (2003).

[6] I do not wish to get hung up on exactly what counts as "imminent." I doubt that there is anything exact on that matter. But I would not limit the imminent to a few minutes or even a few hours. A few days or, perhaps, weeks would be more like it, but a year would no longer be imminent.

does not target cross-burning for advocating a certain viewpoint; rather, it targets the act for being a threat. Although a communicative action can be both a threat and the advocacy of a viewpoint, it is only *qua* threat that cross-burning is prohibited. Accordingly, there is no need to revise the Brandenburg Doctrine in order to accommodate the prohibition of cross-burning.

But suppose that one thought that bans on cross-burning were (legitimate) viewpoint-based restrictions and that Brandenburg must be revised accordingly. Holocaust denial would still count as protected speech under the revised doctrine. The key reason is that it is not reasonable to construe the advocacy of denial as a threat of imminent violence. Perhaps the subtext of many instances of denial is: "Watch out Jews; some day we admirers of the Fuehrer will again form a powerful political movement, and then you will be in trouble." Even so, denial would be protected, because the imminence requirement would not be met.

But those who defend prohibitions on Holocaust denial are not satisfied with the suggestion that denial does not *now* pose a threat of imminent attack on Jews. Thus, Alexander Tsesis argues that "it is too dangerous to wait until there is an emergent threat" (2002: 145). In his view, Holocaust denial is antisemitic speech, and the historical record shows that bigoted speech is "instrumental" in paving the way for massive crimes against groups such as Jews and Native Americans. Tsesis reasons that "[i]t is better to nip [such crimes] in the bud" than to permit the bigoted speech (2002: 144 and 145). In a similar vein, William Schabas suggests that Holocaust denial might well pave the way for another genocide against Jews. He laments the fact that in many countries, deniers remain free "to spew… hateful propaganda to followers, with their nostalgia for Auschwitz and Treblinka." To those thinkers who are doubtful of the importance of bigoted speech to the origins of a genocide, Schabas writes, "A well-read and well-informed genocidaire will know that at the early stages of planning of the 'crime of crimes', his or her money is best spent not in purchasing machetes, or Kalatchnikovs, or Zyklon B gas, but rather investing in radio transmitters and photocopy machines" (2000: 171).

However, this "better safe than sorry" line of argument sweeps much too broadly. Even conceding the reasonable proposition that Holocaust denial is antisemitic, there is a whole range of antisemitic speech whose prohibition would noncontroversially count as an illegitimate incursion on free expression but which cannot be distinguished in any nonarbitrary way from denial. Thus, consider that the Western cultural tradition contains a great deal of antisemitic writing, penned by some of the tradition's greatest figures, including Luther, Calvin, Voltaire, Kant, and Wagner. It would be implausible to suggest that the antisemitic passages of these authors should be legally suppressed or that the public recitation of the passages be prohibited, even though those passages might well exert as much or more rhetorical force in promoting antisemitic feelings than the works of Holocaust deniers. The following passage from Kant's *Anthropology*, discussing Jews, is illustrative of the problem:

The Palestinians [i.e., Jews] living among us since their exile, or at least the great majority of them, have earned the not unfounded reputation of being cheaters, on account of the spirit of usury. Admittedly, it seems strange to think of a *nation* of cheaters, but it is just as strange to think of a nation of nothing but merchants, the far greater majority of whom are bound by an ancient superstition recognized by the state they live in, seek no civil honor, but rather wish to make up for their loss through the advantage of outwitting the people under whom they find protection, and even one another. (Kant 2006: 100)

Proponents of laws prohibiting denial are placed in a difficult situation by passages such as this: either the proponents must find some way of distinguishing Kant's (or Luther's or Voltaire's, etc.) antisemitic words from Holocaust denial, showing why the former but not the latter are protected speech, or they must argue that Kant's words are not, after all, protected speech. Neither argument has been made, and it is doubtful that any such argument could be successful, consistent with the endorsement of any reasonable understanding of freedom of expression. In contrast, the Brandenburg Doctrine protects Kant's words from viewpoint-based restrictions and treats Kant's text and Holocaust denial as indistinguishable from the perspective of the right of free expression.

It might be said that the Kant example takes unfair advantage of the stature of a thinker who stands out as one of the greatest in history. Who would think of censoring the works of a philosophical titan like Kant? But the point made by the Kant example can just as well be made by considering the antisemitic writings of undistinguished authors. Moreover, the stature of Kant and the other notable thinkers mentioned above arguably lends their antisemitic words greater authority in perceptions of a potential audience than what Holocaust deniers would say. A "well-read and well-informed genocidaire" might, as Schabas says, find it advisable to invest in radio transmitters and photocopy machines. But if the genocidaire's target is European Jews, he or she might well be better off broadcasting quotes from Voltaire and Kant than citing the words of deniers. Indeed, one should not discount the possibility that, at least in existing liberal states, the public expression of Holocaust denial is more likely to give a bad name to antisemitism than it is likely to lead to antisemitic persecution. The reason is that denial is associated in the public mind with antisemitism, and the large majority of people in existing liberal states regard denial as preposterous. Thus, the speech of Holocaust deniers may well inadvertently discredit antisemitism more than it discredits Jews.

One might still be concerned that denial incites antisemitic discrimination. After all, it could be the case that denial discredits antisemitism among the general public but, nonetheless, incites discrimination among some small but significant sector of the population. Moreover, it might seem persuasive to maintain, following human rights jurisprudence, that incitement to discrimination does not require speech to cause (or intend to cause) *imminent* discriminatory conduct[7] (Evatt and Kretzmer 1996: paras. 4 and 9). Rather, it is enough, under that jurisprudence, for words to count as incitement that it is reasonably foreseeable that the words will, at some point, cause discriminatory conduct. Accordingly, one might suggest that the Brandenburg Doctrine is in need of the following revision: speech should be protected, regardless of the viewpoint it advocates, unless the speech is a) intended and likely to bring about imminent lawless conduct, *or* b★) reasonably expected to cause discriminatory conduct, whether the conduct is imminent or not.

Although I will argue in the next section that a second disjunct should be added to Brandenburg, the above suggestion, b★, is overbroad. For example, the public dissemination of Kant's offending passages could be reasonably expected to cause discriminatory conduct. Indeed, it would not be difficult to find antisemitic passages in the writings of many major Christian thinkers across the ages, passages that could be reasonably expected to bring about discriminatory conduct against Jews if publicly disseminated in a way that conveyed the endorsement of those passages. And the potential to cause discriminatory conduct is not limited to Christian or other religiously motivated thinkers. In Nietzsche's work, for example, one can find passages that could foreseeably bring about anti-Christian and antisemitic discrimination.[8] Yet, it is implausible to regard the offending writings of Kant or Nietzsche as legitimate objects of legal suppression.

---

[7] The classic example of incitement from the philosophical literature, Mill's corn dealer hypothetical, involves a high probability of imminent violence, though it is unclear what role intent plays in his analysis (Mill 1978: 53).

[8] "The Jews are the most remarkable nation in world history because, faced with the question of being or not being, they preferred, with a perfectly uncanny conviction, being *at any price*: the price they had to pay was the radical *falsification* of all nature, all naturalness, all reality." (Nietzsche 2003/1895: 146; italics in original) "[W]hat a *monster of falsity* modern man must be that he is none the less *not ashamed* of being called a Christian!" (Nietzsche 2003/1895: 162; italics in original) It should be noted that Nietzsche condemns antisemitism (Nietzsche 1989/1887/1908: 73, 124, 158, and 342), seeing it as a symptom of weakness, but that condemnation in fact does not undermine the claim that there are passages in Nietzsche's work which antisemites could readily misconstrue as affirming their prejudice.

Similar considerations also undercut the argument that Holocaust denial is legitimately prohibited because it is a case of group defamation. Many passages from Kant and other prominent thinkers of the past are at least as defamatory of Jews as Holocaust denial is. For example, Luther's infamous "On the Jews and their Lies" contains a wealth of passages on which a twenty-first-century antisemite might effectively draw to promote discrimination against Jews (1971/1543). Yet, it is difficult to see that the essay is legitimately subject to legal suppression on that account. An individual who publicly recited in an approving way defamatory passages from Luther's essay, which characterizes Jews as mendacious, bloodthirsty, vengeful, boastful, arrogant, and so on, would be engaged in speech that is more explicitly antisemitic than are the recitations of Holocaust deniers. And it would not seem reasonable to assert that the Holocaust denier is subject to legal sanction but the Luther-speaker is protected by freedom of expression.[9]

One might counter that the Holocaust denier's words are given more credibility in society at large than the person who recites from Luther or Kant, but such a claim is of questionable accuracy. The antisemitic stereotypes voiced in Luther's or Kant's writings are arguably more widespread and considered more credible than is Holocaust denial.

Nonetheless, I think that human rights jurisprudence is not entirely off-the-mark in its concern with the potentially discriminatory effects of antisemitic and similar types of derogatory speech. In the next section, I suggest that the examination of one of the cases from Nuremberg helps to show that the reasonable foreseeability of certain kinds of discriminatory consequences can provide sufficient reason to deem speech unprotected, even if the consequences are not imminent. Accordingly, a revision of the Brandenburg Doctrine is in order. Yet, even with this revision, Brandenburg still entails that existing liberal democracies are not permitted to prohibit Holocaust denial. Before turning to that section, though, I would like to consider a certain objection to any use of the Brandenburg doctrine aimed at showing that Holocaust denial is protected speech.

In human rights jurisprudence, a distinction is drawn between statements that purport to represent facts, on the one side, and expressions of opinion or value judgments, on the other. The latter two categories—

---

[9] One might argue that the public recitation of Luther's antisemitic words is protected by freedom of religion rather than by freedom of expression. However, it is more reasonable to hold that the two forms of freedom overlap in such a case and that the recitation is protected under either one. In addition, the example of Nietzsche shows that words denigrating a certain religious or racial group need not be religiously motivated in order to be protected by freedom of expression.

expressions of opinion and value judgments—are said to be protected by the right of free expression, but demonstrably false statements purporting to represent facts are claimed not to be under the protection of that right (Lehideux 1998). In other words, even though government restrictions on speech cannot legitimately be viewpoint-based, "viewpoint" here refers to opinions and value judgments, not to demonstrably false statements of purported fact. Accordingly, it could be objected to my argument that I have misapplied the Principle of Viewpoint Neutrality by assuming that it covers demonstrably false statements of "fact."

I leave aside the difficulty of drawing the distinction on which this objection hinges. Nonetheless, the line of thinking presented by the objection has some anomalous implications that render it dubious. For example, imagine two persons, one of whom says, "The Holocaust never happened" and the other of whom says, "The Holocaust happened, and the world would have been a better place had Hitler only finished the job." The former sentence is a demonstrably false statement of "fact," while the latter is a conjunction of a demonstrably true statement of fact and a value judgment. On the current objection, the utterance of the latter sentence is protected speech, but the utterance of the former is not. But it is difficult to see why the two utterances should be treated differently under free speech principles. It is typically bad for people to make demonstrably false statements of "fact," but it is also typically bad for people to endorse genocide as good.

Some demonstrably false statements should be legally prohibited, namely, defamatory speech, but we have seen that Holocaust denial cannot be legitimately prohibited on the ground that it defames Jews. Moreover, the history section of any library or bookstore is stocked with works that contain some, and often many, false statements of historical "fact." Even books by scholars of history contain demonstrably false statements. There is no reason to pick out the falsehoods of deniers for special, disfavored treatment unless one takes into account the moral horror of what the falsehood covers up. And that horror cannot be taken into account without making a value judgment. In other words, prohibitions of Holocaust denial *are* viewpoint-based, even if we were to agree that only opinions and value judgments legitimately count as "viewpoints."

V. The Brandenburg Doctrine Revised

Most discussions of the principles of freedom of speech proceed on the implicit premise that the issue is arising in the context of a relatively stable and secure liberal state. However, such a premise involves a certain tunnel-vision, because questions of expressive freedom can be quite salient in quite different social-political contexts, for example, ones in which there is widespread violence or the threat of such violence targeted at the members of certain racial or religious groups.[10] In such contexts, speech that demeans or degrades the groups in question can make a substantial contribution to the violence, even when the speech itself is not reasonably understood as a threat of imminent violence and not intended, or likely, to bring about such violence. These situations call for a revision in the Brandenburg Doctrine. To see why this is so, let us examine a key case from international criminal law.

Julius Streicher was tried for crimes against humanity by the International Military Tribunal (IMT) at Nuremberg for publishing the vicious and crudely antisemitic newspaper *Der Stuermer*. At its height in the mid 1930s, the paper often sold over 200,000 copies per issue and, for some issues, reached a circulation of well over 400,000. Additionally, "[t]he readership...was even larger than the circulation figures suggest, for thousands of elaborate [public] display cases were built by loyal readers throughout Germany that displayed each week's issue" (Bytwerk 1983: 61). The paper regularly characterized Jews as "germs and pests," "parasites," and "disseminator[s] of disease who must be destroyed in the interest of mankind" (IMT 1947: 548). The paper was also widely known for its antisemitic cartoons in which Jews were consistently represented as "short, fat, ugly, unshaven, drooling, sexually perverted, bent-nosed [and] with pig-like eyes" (Bytwerk 1983: 56). The IMT found Streicher guilty.

I think that the tribunal was right to find Streicher guilty, but my key point is that he could not have made any valid free-speech claim in his defense: his speech was beyond the protection of any reasonable principle of freedom of speech. It might be said that the articles and cartoons in *Der Stuermer* could not have been reasonably expected to spur readers to immediate violent action. And I agree that it is possible that the harmful effects of the paper were more indirect and long term, serving to shape sensibilities and attitudes. Yet, the society in which the paper circulated was one in which Jews were being victimized by mass persecution. Given that context, it was reasonably foreseeable that *Der Stuermer* would, on account of the viewpoint it advocated and because of the very large number of persons who read it, substantially contribute, even if only

---

[10] Cf. Lynne Tirrell, "Genocidal Language Games," this volume. See also the "Media Cases," *Nahimana et al. v Prosecutor* 2007. These cases were tried before the International Criminal Tribunal for Rwanda. The defendants, who controlled a radio station and newspaper, were found guilty for direct and public incitement to genocide.

indirectly, to the violent victimization of Jews. And that kind of connection to the widespread violence against Jews was sufficient, in my view, to remove Streicher's antisemitic speech from the protection of free-speech principles.

If the foregoing account of the *Streicher* case is sound, then we need a genuine revision of the Brandenburg Doctrine: speech should be protected, regardless of the viewpoint it advocates, unless the speech is a) intended and likely to bring about imminent lawless conduct, *or* b★★) reasonably expected to contribute substantially to widespread violence. To be sure, there are complications to be worked out in interpreting and applying b★★. For example, one might wonder whether what counts as widespread should depend on the absolute number of violent acts, or numbers relative to the size of the group attacked, or numbers relative to the size of the society, and so on. Nonetheless, in whatever way one works out the details of the answers to such questions, speech that affirms the theses of Holocaust denial and that is uttered in the context of any existing liberal state will be protected under the revised Brandenburg Doctrine. Such speech cannot be reasonably expected to contribute substantially to widespread violence against Jews: there is now nothing approximating widespread violence against Jews in any liberal state, and there is no reason to think that Holocaust denial can make a substantial contribution to bringing about that kind of violence. These points are not made in order to deny the existence of antisemitic violence in existing liberal states. Unquestionably, such violence exists, but it is marginal. In today's liberal states, Jews in general are extremely safe from antisemitic attack against their persons and property. Indeed, most of the humans on earth today and almost all of the humans who have ever lived—whether Jewish or not—would consider themselves quite fortunate if they could swap their level of personal safety for that enjoyed by Jews in today's liberal states.

One might ask whether, in a society where antisemitic speech could foreseeably make a substantial contribution to widespread violence against Jews, the antisemitic passages in Kant's *Anthropology* would be unprotected. The answer is that, depending on the precise context and use of Kant's words, they might be unprotected. For example, if the passages were used in the mass media as part of an anti-Jewish campaign, then those responsible for that use might well have no valid free-speech claim. On the other hand, a public university whose library puts on its shelves a copy of Kant's book might still have strong claim that freedom of expression protected the act of making the book available, even if the society were one in which antisemitic speech could foreseeably contribute to widespread violence against Jews. Admittedly, the line between a mass media case and a university library case could become fuzzy, if only because the ideas of reasonable foreseeability and substantial contribution do not provide a bright-line criterion. Moreover, it is possible to imagine cases in which b★★ would arguably be met by a library that made available a copy of Kant's *Anthropology*. Yet, such cases only show that under conditions radically different from any that can be found in existing liberal states, antisemitic speech should be treated in a very different way from how it should be treated in existing liberal states. Under those radically different conditions, Holocaust denial might lose its protection, but in existing liberal states its protection under a suitably revised Brandenburg Doctrine remains secure.

To recap: I have argued that the understanding of Viewpoint Neutrality embodied in the original Brandenburg Doctrine stands in need of some modification, but that the necessary revision still makes it impermissible for existing liberal states to prohibit Holocaust denial. Arguments that purport to show that denial is permissibly prohibited sweep too broadly, implausibly licensing the prohibition of the antisemitic words of many notable thinkers who contributed to the Western intellectual tradition. If the words of Kant and Nietzsche are to be protected, then those of the Holocaust denier must be protected as well.

VI. Germany and Israel

Two countries have a special connection to the Holocaust, which raises the possibility that good arguments can be given in favor of *their* bans on denial, even conceding that freedom of expression rules out bans for all other liberal states. Germany perpetrated the crimes of the Holocaust, and Israel was founded in order to help ensure that Jews would have a safe haven from any future efforts to repeat such crimes. Let us examine Germany first.

In the decade following World War II, in order to quell doubts about its legitimacy, the new democracy in West Germany saw the need to signal to the rest of the world that there had been a radical break with the Nazi past. Part of this break involved a refashioning of the public political culture and of the attitudes of West German citizens toward Jews. The Allied Occupation powers had paved the way for this refashioning of German cultural attitudes by banning the public expression of pro-Nazi attitudes. And the new West German legal system criminalized the Nazi party and the display of various Nazi symbols. There is little doubt that, in light of the historical context and need for a reconstructed and liberal German state, such criminalization was not only legitimate; it was the right thing to do.

Criminalizing Holocaust denial seems to be of a piece with the criminalization of the Swastika. Or at least that is the way many Germans have seen it: denial is understood as "a symbolic affirmation of Nazism" (Kahn 2004: 15). Accordingly, Klaus Guenther defends Germany's criminal laws against denial, arguing that, "[b]ecause one cannot deal with the problem of antisemitism in Germany without regard to the horrific legacy of Nazi atrocities, restrictions on freedom of expression in this context are essentially not comparable to similar restrictions in other countries" (Guenther 2000: 65). The key points, for Guenther, are that "denial of the Holocaust is, first and foremost, a question of German identity" (66) and that such denial amounts to denying "the dishonor of Germans" (66, quoting Guenther Jakobs).

Guenther's argument can be understood as claiming that, because Germany stands in a special moral relation to the Holocaust, the country has a good reason that other nations do not have for banning denial and that this reason applies today, long after Germany has established a stable and secure liberal state. The idea seems to be that Germany should not permit persons within its jurisdiction to proclaim that Germans did not plan and perpetrate the Holocaust. Any such permission would implicate the German state in an effort to deny the dishonor of its own citizens.

However, it is unclear that Guenther's argument can be limited, as he intends, to Germany: other countries and their citizens, e.g. France, aided and abetted the crimes of the Holocaust. It is true that these other countries were either virtual puppet states or had actually been conquered by Germany, but the fact remains that those states and more than a handful of their citizens share some of the dishonor. Additionally, Guenther leaves it unexplained why Germany is permitted to ban today's German citizens from denying "the dishonor" of those Germans who were complicit in the persecution and genocide of Jews during the Nazi era. I do not mean to deny that the German state had, and continues to have, special obligations arising from the Holocaust, including the payment of reparations and the tracking down and punishment of those responsible for the crimes of the Holocaust. Germany also rightly commemorates various dates and sites important to the history of the Holocaust. Moreover, I agree that Germany has a special obligation to do something about Holocaust denial, though not to criminalize it. For example, the schools and media have broadly educated the citizenry about the Holocaust, at least since the late 1970s, and it is sensible to think that the country is obligated to do as much. But Guenther's argument does not explain why Germany's special obligations arising from the Holocaust license it to go beyond reparation, commemoration, the criminal punishment of Nazi perpetrators, and the education of the citizenry, and to suppress the public expression of denial, now that Germany has become a stable liberal state.

What about the German law prohibiting the display of the Swastika? If that law is acceptable, then why not the law against Holocaust denial? The answer is that there is a sensible way of distinguishing the two kinds of laws. Displaying the Swastika and (much) Holocaust denial might both be, as Guenther says, an "affirmation of Nazism." But displaying the Swastika in Germany is also reasonably construed as a threat of imminent violence and so should not be protected. Thus, the display of the Swastika in Germany is akin to cross-burning in the U.S., and each is permissibly subject to criminalization where it is reasonably construed as a threat of imminent violence.

Turning to Israel, we have a state that was founded to ensure that there would be no repetition of the Holocaust. But that fact does not justify the criminalization of denial in Israel. A state cannot, by invoking its founding purposes, circumvent or override the Principle of Viewpoint Neutrality. No state is entitled to suppress speech on the ground that the speech questions or rejects its founding purposes, however legitimate those purposes are, as long as the speech is not intended or likely to bring about lawless conduct and not reasonably expected to contribute substantially to widespread violence.

It might seem unreasonable to demand of the Jewish citizens of Israel that they give up their laws prohibiting Holocaust denial. It certainly seems implausible to think that they will in fact give up those laws anytime soon. But the principles of free expression have moral force, and such force sometimes makes a demand reasonable when otherwise it would be unreasonable. And sometimes such force helps to sway humans to do what is demanded.

References

Bates, Stephen. "One in Seven Britons says Holocaust is Exaggerated," *The Guardian* (January 22, 2004). Available at http://www.guardian.co.uk/uk/2004/jan/23/religion.immigrationpolicy.

Beauharnais v. Illinois. 343 U.S. 250 (1952).

Bergmann, Werner and Rainer Erb 1997. *Antisemitism in Germany: The Post-Nazi Epoch Since 1945.* New Brunswick, NJ: Transaction Publishers.

Brandenburg v. Ohio 396 U.S. 444 (1969).

Butz, Arthur 1992/1976. *The Hoax of the Twentieth Century.* Newport Beach, CA: Institute for Historical Review.

Bytwerk, Randall 1983. *Julius Streicher.* NY: Stein and Day.

Chomsky, Noam "His Right to Say It," *The Nation* (February 28, 1981) 231.

Convention on the Elimination of All Forms of Racial Discrimination. Available at: http://www.hrcr.org/docs/CERD/cerd2.html.

European Convention for the Protection of Human Rights. Available at: http://www.hri.org/docs/ECHR50.html.

Evans, Richard 2009. *The Third Reich at War*. NY: Penguin.

Evatt, Elizabeth and David Kretzmer 1996. "Individual Opinion," in *Faurisson v. France*, Communication No. 550/1993, U.N. Doc. CCPR/C/58/D/550/1993.

Farrior, Stephanie 1996. "Molding the Matrix: The Historical and Theoretical Foundations of International Law Concerning Hate Speech," *Berkeley Journal of International Law* 14 (1996), 1–98.

Faurisson, Robert 1980. *Mémoir en defense*. Paris: Le Vieille Taupe.

Faurisson v. France 1996. Communication No. 550/1993, U.N. Doc. CCPR/C/58/D/550/1993.

Garaudy v. France. European Court of Human Rights. Case no. 65831/01 (2003), http://www.humanrights.is/the-human-rights-project/humanrightscases andmaterials/cases/regionalcases/europeancourtofhumanrights/nr/498.

Guenther, Klaus 2000. "The Denial of the Holocaust: Employing Criminal Law to Combat Antisemitism in Germany," *Tel Aviv University Studies in Law* 15, 51–66.

Handyside v. U.K. 1976. Available at http://www.robin.no/~dadwatch/echr/handy.html.

Heller, Aron "Holocaust Denial Widespread among Israeli Arabs," *Associated Press*, May 18, 2009. Available on Lexis-Nexis at: http://www.lexisnexis.com/us/lnacademic/results/docview/docview.do?docLinkInd=true&risb=21_T70877 27361&format=GNBFI&sort=RELEVANCE&startDocNo=1&resultsUrlKey =29_T7087727365&cisb=22_T7087727364&treeMax=true&treeWidth =0&csi=304478&docNo=1.

International Covenant on Civil and Political Rights. Available at: http://www1.umn.edu/humanrts/instree/b3ccpr.htm.

International Military Tribunal. *Trial of the Major War Criminals, Vol II*. Nuremberg, Germany: 1947.

Kahn, Robert 2004. *Holocaust Denial and the Law*. NY: Palgrave MacMillan.

Kant, Immanuel 2006. *Anthropology from a Pragmatic Point of View*, Robert Louden, ed. Cambridge: Cambridge University Press.

Lehideux and Isorni v. France. European Court of Human Rights. Case no. 55/1997/839/1045, 23 September 1998. Available at http://www.iidh.ed.cr/comunidades/libertadexpresion/docs/le_europeo/lehideux%20and%20isorni%20v.%20france.htm.

Leuchter, Fred 1989. *The End of the Line: The Leuchter Report*. London: Focal Point Publishers.

Lipstadt, Deborah E. 1993. *Denying the Holocaust.* New York: Free Press.

Luther, Martin 1971/1543. "On the Jews and their Lies," trans. by Martin H. Bertram. Available at: http://www.humanitas-international.org/showcase/chronography/documents/luther-jews.htm.

Mannheimer, Renato "E antisemita quasi un italiano su cinque," *Corriere della Sera,* 10 November 2003. See Table 1 at: http://www.corriere.it/Primo_Piano/Cronache/2003/11_Novembre/10/israele.shtml.

Mill, John Stuart 1978. *On Liberty.* Indianapolis, IN: Hackett.

Nahimana et al. v. Prosecutor. Case no. ICTR-99-52-A. November 2007.

Nietzsche, Friedrich 1989/1887/1908. *On the Genealogy of Morals* and *Ecce Homo.* New York: Penguin.

Nietzsche, Friedrich 2003/1895. *Twilight of the Idols* and *The Anti-Christ.* New York: Penguin.

Remer v. Germany. European Commission of Human Rights. Case no. 25096/94, *Decisions and Reports* 82-A, 117–24 (1995).

Schabas, William 2000. "Hate Speech in Rwanda: The Road to Genocide," *McGill Law Journal* 46: 141–71.

Schauer, Frederick 2005. "Freedom of Expression Adjudication in Europe and the United States," in Georg Nolte, ed. *European and US Constitutionalism.* Cambridge: Cambridge University Press, pp. 49–69.

Shermer, Michael and Alex Grobman 2000. *Denying History.* Berkeley, CA: University of California Press.

Smith, Tom W. 1995. "A Review: The Holocaust Denial Controversy," *Public Opinion Quarterly* 59: 269–95.

X v. Federal Republic of Germany. European Commission of Human Rights 29, *Decisions and Reports,* 194–9 (1982).

Tsesis, Alexander 2002. *Destructive Messages.* NY: NYU Press.

Universal Declaration of Human Rights. Available at: http://www.un.org/en/documents/udhr/index.shtml

Virginia v. Black 538 U.S. 343 (2003).

'Speaking Back': The Likely Fate of Hate Speech Policy in the United States and Australia[1]

Katharine Gelber

I. Introduction

A central idea within free speech arguments is that the most appropriate response to speech with which one disagrees, or which one finds intolerable, is to respond with one's own opinions. This is because free speech is so vital that its restriction ought to be minimised as far as possible. Thus, even speech which is abhorrent, pernicious, or abusive ought to be permitted and those who disagree with such speech have the option of saying so, and why they oppose it.

This relatively straightforward idea has been taken further by some scholars who have argued that there may be a basis for governmental or state support to assist some in speaking, because expecting or hoping they will spontaneously do so underestimates and denies the real social conditions which operate to prevent them from speaking. Thus, for example, Cass Sunstein has argued that a civic republican approach to the First Amendment would countenance, indeed require, a greater commitment to political equality and thus permit policies which sought to remove distortions in the political process brought about by disparities in wealth (1988: 1577–8). More recently, Owen Fiss has argued that the state could be utilized to 'further the robustness of public debate' where and when

[1] Many thanks to Adrienne Stone and Dan Meagher for helpful discussions on earlier drafts of this chapter, and to the anonymous reviewers.

some people's voices would not otherwise be heard (1996a: 4), and to 'preserve the fullness and openness of public debate' (1996b: 5). These arguments foster the underlying presumption that broader participation in deliberation is a public good which can bolster democratic legitimacy.

This idea has also been applied to the arena of hate[2] speech. If some people are unable to speak because they have been targets of particularly virulent or powerfully repressive types of speech, they suffer social conditions which prevent them from responding to speech which they find marginalizing or disempowering, and with which they disagree. An excellent elaboration of this proposition appears in the chapter by Laura Beth Nielsen in this volume. In response to this problem, I have developed the idea of a policy of speaking back, in which individuals who are the targets of hate speech are provided with the institutional, educational, and material support to enable them to speak back, both to contradict the messages contained within the hate speech and to counteract the effects of that speech on their ability to respond (Gelber 2002).

My argument differs from Fiss' and Sunstein's in at least two respects that are relevant here. First, it is limited to the arena of hate speech. As such, it does not cover other areas in which a person's ability to speak might be hindered by inequality-producing phenomena such as economic inequality. Second, it is not based only upon a conception of what speech is required in order that democracy might function well or better. It is also based upon a view about what speech is required in order to foster the individual capabilities which underpin a meaningful life, one in which individuals are able to choose to live and function well. Thus the argument has a clear basis in capabilities theory, especially as elucidated by Martha Nussbaum (e.g. 1990, 1999, 2000, 2006).[3]

The outcome of my policy proposal is that it shifts the terrain upon which hate speech policy is debated. Hate speech policy has typically been thought of in binary terms—as necessarily detrimental to the speech opportunities of the hate speaker in order to protect the interests of the target/s. I see this binary conceptualization as ultimately not entirely

---

[2] 'Hate' in the term 'hate speech' is a shorthand for prejudice which exists against identifiable groups on the basis of certain characteristics including but not limited to race. Hate does not denote simply a personal dislike for another individual.

[3] Capabilities theory has been developed by Amartya Sen (1992) and Nussbaum. For clarification of the differences between them, see Nussbaum (2003). Since Nussbaum is more specific about the list of central human functional capabilities, it is from her work that this analysis is derived. For a fuller account of the contribution of capabilities theory to the regulation of hate speech, see Gelber (2010). For regular critical engagement with the ideas of capabilities theory see the *Journal of Human Development* (http://www.tandf.co.uk/journals/carfax/14649888.html).

helpful. Instead, I reconceptualize the dilemma to develop a hate speech policy with the aim of ameliorating the effects of hate speech in such a way that the targets themselves are better able to engage in speech. This does not directly punish, or limit the speech of, hate speakers. But it might do more to assist the targets of hate speech than traditional binary approaches.

One of the most interesting questions to arise from the speaking back policy idea is how well it is suited to the constitutional free speech environments within which free speech debates are taking place. Would such a policy be consistent with the importance placed on free speech in liberal democracies? More specifically, would it be consistent with the spirit of First Amendment jurisprudence in the United States? First Amendment jurisprudence, although exceptional in comparative terms internationally (Stone and Evans 2006, citing Schauer 2005), is neverthe-less also heavily influential in international legal culture (Barendt 1994: 149). Therefore, a full explication of a speaking back policy requires consideration of its viability and potential within this environment. By way of contrast, I will also consider whether such a policy would be consistent with jurisprudential developments around freedom of expression in Australia, which constitute a very different constitutional environment.

In order to answer these questions I will first summarize the key aspects of the speaking back policy. I will then consider whether, how, and to what extent such a policy can be implemented within the context of First Amendment doctrine. Asking whether a policy of speaking back would be compatible with the spirit of decision-making in the Supreme Court in First Amendment matters prompts a highly qualified answer. I will outline this answer and its reasons. This analysis will then be contrasted with a comparative analysis of the likelihood of a speaking back policy finding purchase in Australia. The free speech context and environment in Aus-tralia are unusual, and this comparison may be illuminating in illustrating how different jurisdictions can approach the fundamental liberty of free speech in disparate ways.

II. Speaking Back

A speaking back policy would require the state to provide institutional, educational, and material support to targets of hate speech. The point of providing this support would be to enable targets both to contradict the messages contained in the hate speech and to counteract certain effects of that speech. Specifically, the relevant effects can include marginalization, disempowerment, and the limiting of a response. This may be for several reasons. Targets of hate speech may believe the broader community believes (in part or in whole) the messages conveyed in the hate speech. They may feel that their speech will be disregarded, or they may feel unable to speak and be heard. It may also be that their concrete circumstances make it difficult for them to speak and be heard.[4] The kinds of support that could be provided include providing resources to targets of hate speech to generate a community awareness campaign to combat racist stereotypes, or to write an article or produce an advertisement in the press, or to create a video to be broadcast at a community event.

My argument takes as valid the presumption that the hate-speech acts of hate speakers are acts which are capable of inhibiting the ability of their targets to speak back. They need not always do so, as clearly some people are capable of responding in often very articulate ways to the expressions of hate speakers that are directed at them. Yet hate speech possesses the capacity to inhibit the speech of its targets in often subtle ways. To some this is a controversial claim. Since speech is simply an expression of ideas, a critic might argue I am overplaying the role of hate speech, and thus that my entire argument is based on an unsustainable premise.

To this criticism I respond in several ways. Prejudice and discrimination are not pretty; they produce negative outcomes in concrete ways that impact on people's lives. This has been recognized in many ways in policy responses to other forms of discrimination, such as discrimination in job opportunities or in the provision of housing. That the discrimination in this instance is enacted discursively ought not automatically to discount the possibility that it can occur. It may well be more difficult to identify which speech-acts enact discrimination and which simply hurt someone's feelings, but in my other work (Gelber 2002: 60–82) I have attempted to overcome this problem by establishing an evaluative framework for speech-acts.

I claim that the discrimination enacted by hate-speech acts entails the carrying out of injury or harm[5] to the human persona. This is a claim that has been better made by scholars before me including critical race theorists Delgado,[6] Matsuda,[7] and Lawrence,[8] as well as by other scholars including

---

[4] On this, see the chapter by Laura Beth Nielsen in this volume.

[5] This part of the argument is derived from an Austinian idea about a 'perlocutionary' speech-act (Austin 1975: 94–101, 109) combined with Habermas' insight that perlocutions result where speech-acts are used in contexts of strategic interaction (Habermas 1984: 292–3). See also Gelber (2002: 56–64).

[6] Delgado argues *inter alia* that listeners unconsciously learn and internalize the messages conveyed in racist speech (1993: 90–4).

[7] Matsuda argues *inter alia* that racist speech denies its victims personal security and personal liberty and freedom of association (1993: 17, 22, 24–5).

[8] Lawrence argues that racist speech causes psychological injury, and assaults self-respect and dignity (1987: 351).

Sunstein,[9] Williams,[10] and MacKinnon.[11] My argument differs from these, however, because I argue there is a particular harm carried out in the saying of an act of hate speech that requires consideration in the context of speech policy, namely the harm done to the target's ability to develop central human functional capabilities.

I have developed this idea by utilizing the work of Martha Nussbaum. Her list of central human functional capabilities includes a number to which freedom of speech, and freedom of political speech, are central (Nussbaum 1990: 21–234; 1999: 39–54; 2000: 231–3; 2003: 41–2).[12] These include being able to form a conception of the good, to engage in critical reasoning, to live with and show concern for others. Being able to engage in speech is clearly crucial to the realization of these things. I have applied this idea to the arena of speech policy, arguing that an individual's ability to develop their capabilities can be harmed by the hate-speech acts of others. This means the harms of hate speech risk the very core of what is required for an individual to be able to live a fully human life.

If this is the case, the harms of hate speech are significant indeed. Recognizing this implies that a policy response is needed. What form ought that policy response to take? If hate-speech acts harm their targets' capacity to develop human capabilities, this is what needs to be remedied. Thus, a response which enables the targets of hate-speech acts to engage in speech in a way which will assist in the development of their central human functional capabilities would seem an appropriate way for a society to choose to deal with the harms of hate speech.

Thus, I argue that individual targets of hate-speech acts ought to be provided with the appropriate institutional, educational, and material support to empower them to respond to, and to seek to contradict, the discrimination enacted in hate-speech utterances. This would involve them raising an alternative set of claims which contest the claims made by the hate speaker. By engaging in the processes of speech required to do

---

[9] Sunstein argues that racist hate speech can have 'corrosive consequences on the self respect' of people of colour, and that it can contribute to the maintenance of a 'caste system' in which targeted group members experience 'fears of violence and subordination' and are made aware of the denial of their political equality (1994: 102).

[10] Williams has called the process of injury to self-esteem and self-worth enacted via racist discrimination 'spirit-murder' (1987: 151).

[11] MacKinnon argues that hate speech damages the ability of its actual and potential victims to engage in speech by silencing them (1993: 72).

[12] Nussbaum's 2000 version of her list, as compared with earlier versions (e.g. Nussbaum 1990: 219–34; Nussbaum 1993: 263–5), gives a more central place to 'political liberties' which, she argues, were always incorporated but had previously been granted less prominence (2000: 237).

that, the targets would at one and the same time be given assistance to overcome the silencing and marginalizing effects of hate speech (Gelber 2002: 119–22).[13] This policy is not speech-limiting or speech-restricting, it is speech-enhancing. It is differentially and selectively so, providing not for the enhancement of speech opportunities for everyone but for the enhancement of speech opportunities for those whose speech opportunities are impaired by the hate speech of others.

The policy is focussed on the individual target who experiences an incident of hate speech, and would be triggered by the reporting and verification of a hate speech incident. Of course, the corrosive impact of hate speech is felt not only by its individual targets, but also by the community to which they are perceived to belong and, by extension, to the community as a whole. This might lead one to propose that the policy be written more broadly—to provide institutional, educational, and material support that would empower a group generally and not just in relation to specific acts of hate speech.

However, such a proposal would overlook crucial aspects of the analysis here. The first of these is that the justification for my policy idea is based in the harm enacted to an individual's capabilities. Even if groups are also harmed (and I certainly agree that they are), a policy response is needed that recognizes and responds to the harm suffered by the individual who has been targeted. This is an explicitly individually based policy idea, because a wholesale group response might not be able to respond in a sufficiently nuanced way to remedy the harms of hate speech.

Second, these are harms enacted by speech, one of which is that it may be difficult for a target to respond with more speech. *Speech* is central both to the problem and the proposed solution. A generalized policy that supported communities to respond to persistent prejudice and discrimination, while a good idea for other reasons, would overlook this crucial aspect of the problem. Indeed it would not change the status quo. Numerous policy ideas already exist to combat ingrained and persistent prejudice and discrimination. The difference between those policies and my proposal is that mine is explicitly and deliberately speech-based, in order to capture conceptually, and respond to, discursively enacted harms. Therefore, although a more generalized policy would not raise First Amendment concerns, I have nevertheless chosen to focus on a

[13] There are of course many objections which could be made to this part of the argument. I have canvassed some of them elsewhere, including the problem of identifying those who could benefit from such a policy, and how to avoid the unintended consequence that Nazis (for example) could claim support for their right to answer their critics (Gelber 2002: 125–8).

speech- and individually-based policy proposal. I will move now to analyse whether a policy of this kind might survive a First Amendment context.

III. The First Amendment and 'Speaking Back'

At first glance the First Amendment environment would appear to provide little succour for a policy such as this. Speech-affecting policies have significant hurdles to overcome to be considered constitutionally valid. Generally speaking, the First Amendment is seen to provide protection to speech, especially speech considered part of 'public discourse' (Weinstein 1999: 44–5), to the extent that is necessary to permit individuals to choose what to believe from a marketplace of ideas, and to participate in democratically fashioning their own society. Many incidences of hate speech would very likely constitute public discourse, and thus fall within a category of speech that is highly protected. A very small number of types of speech are considered unprotected, including true threats, fighting words, libel, and obscenity, but the interpretation of when such speech is unprotected is narrow (Weinstein 1999: 30).

Any regulation with a speech-limiting effect is subject to strict scrutiny—an examination of whether it serves a compelling interest is necessary to achieve the goal sought, and is narrowly drawn to achieve that goal. If the same purpose could be achieved with a non-speech-limiting effect, the regulation is invalid (Weinstein 1999: 55). A speech-limiting regulation may be held valid if it is a time, manner, or circumstance regulation which impinges on speech as a coincidental corollary to another legitimate goal and thus is not primarily directed at the regulation of the speech in question (Sumner 2004: 71), and if it does not offend other elements of free speech doctrine.

In this environment there are at least two specific reasons for suggesting a speaking back policy would find little favour in the First Amendment environment. First, it is a well-established principle of First Amendment jurisprudence that content discrimination may not be permitted. I will explain below why the speaking back policy, even though it is not speech-limiting, must still conform to the prohibition against content discrimination. For the moment, I will outline the content distinction prohibition itself to clarify the context for the later discussion. Laws which seek to limit some expressions on the basis of their content, defined as the message they convey, violate the protection afforded by the First Amendment. Viewpoint discrimination, a more specific form of content discrimination, is regarded as particularly egregious (Weinstein 1999: 36). Content-neutrality means the government must take a neutral position in the realm of ideas; it may not endorse one idea and punish another. All ideas are given equal treatment in the marketplace of ideas, including the unorthodox and the hateful (Baker 1992: 8–9), the insulting and the outrageous (Post 1995: 119). This principle operates in the realms of protected, and also to a large extent unprotected, speech.

Hate speech provisions that seek to restrict speech have typically been declared invalid by the Supreme Court on the ground that they are content-based. These include the *R.A.V.* case in which a hate speech ordinance prohibiting words 'producing anger or resentment on the basis of race' and used to prosecute a man for burning a cross on the lawn of a black family was invalidated.[14] It also includes the events in Skokie, when an ordinance prohibiting the dissemination of materials that would promote hatred towards people on the basis of their heritage was declared unconstitutional.[15] Additionally, and as demonstrated in *R.A.V.*, even where a whole class of speech may be proscribed, a type of content within that class may not be proscribed (Weinstein 1999: 75).

There is a caveat to the prohibition on content distinctions. It has been established that content-based distinctions are permissible in unprotected areas of speech, as long as 'the content distinction reflect[s] the distinction and rationale for the initial non-protection' (Schauer 2003: 203). Is it possible this may provide an opening for a speaking back policy to be considered constitutionally permissible? This principle, established in *R.A.V.*, was revisited and reaffirmed in *Virginia v Black*, in which the Supreme Court concluded that a state may, consistently with the First Amendment, ban cross-burning carried out with the intent to intimidate.[16] In making this decision, the Supreme Court upheld the longstanding premise that 'true' threats do not constitute protected speech (Schauer 2003: 201, 210). However, as noted above, incidences of hate speech and their responses are extremely unlikely to be presumed unprotected speech. This would mean that the speaking back policy could not be held constitutionally valid on this ground, and leaves the content distinction problem intact. This raises the related question of the speaking back policy's effect on speech opportunities, a question to which I will now turn before returning to the content-distinction problem.

---

[14] *R.A.V. v City of St Paul*, 505 U.S. 377 (1992).

[15] *Smith v Collin*, 439 U.S. 916 (1978).

[16] *Virginia v Black*, 538 U.S. 343 (2003). It was held in this case that the Virginia statute was nevertheless still invalid due to its treatment of cross-burning as prima facie evidence of intent to intimidate. Since cross-burning could conceivably be carried out for other purposes than intimidation that constitutes a threat, the presumption was invalid (Schauer 2003: 204).

The second reason a speaking back policy looks like it would find little favour is the principle established in *Buckley v Valeo*[17] that the voices of some cannot be restricted in order to enhance the speech of others. The Supreme Court stated that 'the concept that the government may restrict the speech of some elements of our society in order to enhance the relative voice of others is wholly foreign to the First Amendment'. Thus, the idea that an imbalance of speech opportunities might be corrected by governmental intrusion to limit the speech of those who are able to be heard in order to give voice to those who are not, has been rejected.

A key aspect of the speaking back policy is that it is a speech-*enabling*, rather than a speech-restricting, policy. A speaking back policy does not require that the speech of some be silenced *in order that* the speech of others can be made possible. No one is directly silenced by the policy. Hate speakers are not targeted for punishment or restrictions on their speech. It is true that the policy is selectively applied in the sense that it ought only be applied to those whose speech is limited by the hate speech of others. On the one hand, this is a standard aspect of public policy—policies are usually only made available to those who need them. Hospital care is provided to the sick and not to the well, roads are provided to those who drive cars and not to those who ride in trains. On the other hand, the determination of who is entitled to utilize a speaking back policy is of course a great deal more complicated than questions such as who is sick, and who drives a car.

Further, in the realm of speech protection there is a particularly powerful concern when government is the institution that would be charged with the responsibility for deciding who might benefit from a policy such as this. The possibility that government might overlook views with which it disagrees, or might not be competent to decide who could benefit from a speaking back policy, are grounds on which such a policy could be inconsistent with a First Amendment culture which is generally suspicious of government and its motives (Barendt 2005: 53–4). Nevertheless, at the level of principle, to the extent that it is possible to identify people whose ability to speak is limited by the hate speech of others, simply enabling those people to speak back (other concerns aside for the moment) ought not to raise the charge that the speech of the hate speakers is being limited.

The speech of hate speakers may become changed over the longer term by the provision of assistance to the targets of hate speech to speak back. One of the aims of the speaking back policy is enabling a process of argumentation that could lead to changed attitudes and thus behaviour.

---

[17] 424 U.S. 1 (1976). The decision invalidated a law that sought to limit expenditures which could be made by individuals or corporations on behalf of candidates or in relation to political issues.

This could promote and assist respectful interaction between human beings and allow more individuals to participate meaningfully in determining how they want to live their lives. However, this could not properly be conceived of as limiting or restricting the right to speak of hate speakers.

Understanding the speaking back policy as not speech-limiting, however, does not render it immune from constitutional hurdles. This is because it is not only speech-limiting policies which must overcome First Amendment strictures. The idea that the speech of those who are disproportionately unable to speak might be supported to do so (even if it is in a way that does not restrict other speakers) has also been rejected by the Supreme Court on First Amendment grounds. For example, a 'right of reply' of political candidates when attacked in the press has been rejected,[18] thus rejecting a claim that enforced provision of the right of reply was consistent with First Amendment principles. The Supreme Court has also rejected a claim that the First Amendment entailed a right to access the broadcasting media.[19]

As I noted above, a specific question remains unanswered. Does the speech-enabling characteristic of the speaking back policy render it immune from the content-distinction prohibition? Since the very idea of hate speech policy is based around an assessment of the content (although I prefer the 'meaning' or 'force') of an expression, it by definition discriminates on the ground of content. It is speech that does a particular thing that is implicated by this policy—speech that harms on a specified ground.

The answer to this question is that the content-distinction prohibition is still applicable. This is because the prohibition on content discrimination can be extended to laws that enable or promote speech. The speaking back policy does impose a differential burden on speech because of its content. Even worse from a First Amendment point of view, its emphasis on enabling a response by victims of hate speech in such a way as to contradict the messages contained in those utterances could be seen as viewpoint discrimination, and thus entirely and conclusively invalid. As the Supreme Court declared in *Turner Broadcasting System v Federation Communications Commission*,[20] 'government action that . . . requires the utterance of a particular message favoured by the government' contravenes the First Amendment. The speaking back policy does not require that targets speak back, rather it provides support should they wish to do so. But the

---

[18] *Miami Herald Publishing Co. v Tornillo*, 418 U.S. 241 (1974).
[19] *CBS v Democratic National Committee*, 412 U.S. 94 (1973).
[20] 114 St. Ct. 2445 (1994), cited in Chemerinsky 1997, 758.

purpose of that support is to support a particular viewpoint, one contrary to the meaning of the hate speaker.

As such, the speaking back policy would likely be subject to a strict scrutiny test. Since this test, the 'most intensive type of judicial review' (Chemerinsky 1997: 416), requires proof that the law is necessary to achieve a compelling government purpose, it most often results in a law being struck down as invalid. Although it might be possible to argue that a speaking back policy would fulfil a compelling government objective (the elimination of discrimination achieved discursively which impacts negatively and disproportionately on the lives of those targeted by hate speech), it is by no means secure that the courts would agree with this argument. Moreover it is unlikely that the necessity component could be met, since means other than a policy mandating government support in this way could be developed to achieve the same end.

There are areas in relation to the promotion of speech opportunities in which the usual First Amendment hurdles appear less insurmountable. In the arena of speech-enablement the fortunes of specific laws can be surprising. Weinstein argues that the government 'routinely engages in content discrimination when it subsidises expression' (Weinstein 1999: 42). The kind of content discrimination permissible in such instances is that based on standards of merit or excellence (for example, in relation to funding of the arts), so it is not based on the expression of particular ideas. In its current form the speaking back policy is targeted at the promotion of anti-racist and anti-discriminatory views. Thus, the policy cannot take advantage of this particular area of permissibility.

But a more fruitful area of exploration may lie in the Supreme Court's differentiation between instances where the government itself is speaking or conveying its own message, and instances where it subsidizes the speech of private speakers. It has been held that the government can promote its own views, and say what it wishes to say, even if in doing so it discriminates on the basis of content (Weinstein 1999: 42; Chemerinsky 1997: 797).[21] What it cannot do is encourage private speech by funding or subsidizing speech in a way that encourages speech and is simultaneously content-discriminatory (Chemerinsky 1997: 798).[22] The speaking back policy appears to violate the prohibition against government subsidizing private speakers to engage in speech in a content-discriminatory way. Additionally, the government is under no obligation to subsidize the exercise of First Amendment rights (*Ibid*). It cannot be forced to provide

---

[21] Citing *Rust v Sullivan* 500 U.S. 173 (1991).
[22] Citing *Rosenberger v Rector of the University of Virginia* 115 S. Ct. 2510 (1995).

the resources required for any individual or institution to engage in speech.[23]

However, this discussion opens up a new possibility for the development of a different type of hate speech policy which might survive First Amendment constraints. That would be the devising of a policy that is an expression or furtherance of a government's broader anti-discrimination policies by allocating support to anti-discrimination campaigns in response to hate speech. The difference between this proposal and the generalized group-based response rejected above is that this proposal is still speech-centred. An incidence of hate speech, reported and verified, could be used to trigger a subsidized and supported speech-based response by authorities working closely with the target/s. Since it would be the government itself that was speaking, viewpoint discrimination would be permissible. The government could speak, through its own existing institutions or a newly created institution charged with carrying out anti-discrimination policies, in a manner which sought to contradict the messages within, and counteract the effects of, hate speech.

This would shift the onus of responding away from individual targets to government institutions. Such a policy could still be philosophically justified in the same manner as the original speaking back policy, in terms of the need for a response to contradict the messages expressed within hate speech. It does, however, raise some new challenges. The 'government' is not a person, nor is an anti-discrimination institution. If someone were to 'speak back' to hate speech from within a government institution, in a manner which would not be seen as impermissibly (i.e. in a content-distinctive fashion) subsidizing private speakers, then it would be the institution that would need to be seen to be speaking back. Yet an institution is only made up of its individual employees or contracted staff, so inevitably it would be some of these individuals who would do the speaking back.

In order for the aims of the amended policy to be achieved, those employees or contract personnel within an institution charged with carrying out the policy as an anti-discrimination measure would need to be members of the identities targeted by hate speakers. These individuals could be provided with resources within a stated policy objective of countering discrimination, and given policy support as a stated government objective. But would the selection of individual staff to carry out

---

[23] Indeed, this position is not restricted to freedom of speech. The Constitutional framework does not mandate government support to enable the realization of rights (Holmes and Sunstein 1999: 35).

speaking back to hate speech mean the policy would impermissibly be subsidizing private speakers?

The element which would overcome the concern about whether directing the policy through an anti-discrimination institution would be indirectly subsidizing private speakers is that these employees or contracted personnel would not themselves need to have been the target of hate speech in order to engage in the counter-speech response. As members of the targeted identities, their response ought to be capable of having the same potential effect, over time, as the counter-speech of targets (and this is why members of targeted groups would be engaged in such a campaign rather than any staff within the institution).

There is a discrepancy here between the injury caused to the target of the hate speech (who would be potentially individually disempowered and marginalized by the hate speech) and the persons who would be engaged in counter-speech. This kind of approach would less directly fulfil the objective of providing support to enable targets of hate speech to counteract the marginalizing and silencing effects of hate speech. In order to retain compatibility with the First Amendment environment, this amended speaking back policy trades off proximity between the injured targets and the empowering counter-speech for a policy capable of withstanding contextual constitutional strictures. Thus the ability of the counter-speech to achieve the contradiction and counteraction of hate speech required is further removed from the deleterious effects of the hate speech than in the originally envisaged policy.

Additionally, the revised (or original) policy would require an allocation of public funds to the furtherance of specific anti-discriminatory messages in a manner which reaches beyond the historical or current commitments of many governments. Thus, there are political-pragmatic reasons to doubt the viability of such a programme in the concrete circumstances of governing, but the obstacles in this version of the policy may no longer be constitutional. This amended policy might pass constitutional muster, allowing a response to hate speech to be generated that would be logistically located within a broader anti-discrimination framework but nevertheless targeted at ameliorating the messages contained within, and effects of, hate speech. It thus opens up a space for reconsidering the relationship between the First Amendment and hate speech policy.

A final problem raised by this version of the policy would be in relation to the original justification for the speaking back policy. This was that a policy of supporting the marginalized to speak was warranted because it served the broader goal of supporting and making possible that speech which is required to foster the individual capabilities which underpin a meaningful life, one in which individuals are able to choose to live and function well. If the counter-speakers are not the original targets of the hate speech, then to what extent can the policy still be considered to achieve this goal? This is a significant criticism of the revised proposal, one that is only weakly answerable by considering the hope that the counter-speech might achieve changes in attitudes and behaviour over the longer term.

The revised version of the policy therefore might survive constitutional scrutiny, but is less directly of assistance to those harmed by the hate speech of others. The fortunes of a speaking back policy, as originally conceived, in the United States look relatively bleak. It may be that other jurisdictions, especially ones in which the free speech tradition is more qualified against other considerations, might react differently to a speaking back policy. To consider this, I turn now to consider the constitutional viability of a speaking back policy in Australia.

IV. Free Speech and Hate Speech in Australia

In Australia, free speech protection has been achieved through less direct mechanisms than in the United States. The protection of freedom of speech has historically relied on a common law tradition (Chesterman 2000a: 7–13) and not, as in many other jurisdictions internationally, a broad and entrenched constitutional protection or statutory protection in the form of a bill of rights.[24] This tradition has led scholars to describe free speech protection in Australia as 'delicate' (Chesterman 2000a) and 'partial and unsatisfactory' (Gelber 2003: 44). Nevertheless, this is not a uniformly held view. The free speech tradition in Australia has also been argued to have been strong enough to have had a significant influence on the form and reach of hate speech policy (McNamara 2002: 5).

In addition to the common law tradition, a doctrine of an implied constitutional freedom of political communication has been developed in the High Court since 1992 (Chesterman 2000a). This doctrine is significantly limited in its application and scope. It is viewed as an implication from the form of representative and responsible government

---

[24] More recently emerging State/Territory charters of rights have appeared to endorse the idea that anti-hate speech laws ought not to be overridden with free speech protections. In the Australian Capital Territory's *Human Rights Act* 2004, the right to freedom of expression expressed in s16 is qualified by s28, which allows for any right enunciated to be subject to reasonable and lawful limits such as are demonstrably justified in a free and democratic society. In the Victorian *Charter of Human Rights and Responsibilities Act* 2006, the right to freedom of expression is qualified in s15 by the acknowledgement of 'special duties and responsibilities' which apply to that right, and to allow for the lawful restriction of some speech to, among other things, protect the rights of others.

established by the Constitution and operates as a freedom from government restraint, rather than a right conferred on individuals (Patapan 2000: 51–9; Williams 2002: 165–97; Stone 2001; Gelber 2003: 23–32). It is limited to 'political communication', usually understood as discussions relating to matters which might have a bearing on federal politics, although the exact parameters of the term 'political communication' remain contested. It also includes non-verbal expression.[25] However, an expression which constitutes political communication is not automatically protected speech. If a restriction on speech, even political speech, occurs as a result of a law which is appropriately adapted to achieving another legitimate government end, it may be upheld.[26]

In this climate, hate speech laws have become an accepted and normal part of the Australian legal framework. In every State,[27] the Australian Capital Territory,[28] and federally,[29] anti-vilification laws exist. These laws establish that in Australia, governments and communities view hate speech as an unacceptable form of expression, which warrants government intervention to minimize its harms and/or its occurrence. The grounds on which a complaint of vilification may be lodged are specified in the relevant legislation and can include the categories of race, religion, HIV/AIDS status, transgender or gender identity, sexuality, homosexuality, and disability.

The forms that these laws take and the penalties they impose differ markedly. Federally and in Tasmania, only civil provisions have been enacted which provide for complainants to lodge a complaint under anti-discrimination mechanisms.[30] In Western Australia, only criminal

---

[25] *Levy v Victoria* (1997) 189 CLR 579.

[26] The full expression of the 'Lange' test, derived from *Lange v Australian Broadcasting Corporation* (1997) 189 CLR 520 at 567, was that a law must be reasonably appropriate and adapted to serve a legitimate end, the fulfilment of which is compatible with the maintenance of the constitutionally prescribed system of representative and responsible government. The test was slightly altered in *Coleman v Power* (2004) 220 CLR 1 at 66 to be that a law must be reasonably appropriate and adapted to serve a legitimate end in a manner which is compatible with the maintenance of the constitutionally prescribed system of representative and responsible government.

[27] *Anti-Discrimination Act* 1977 (NSW) ss 20B-20D, 38R-38T, 49ZS-49ZTA, 49ZXA-49ZXC; *Anti-Discrimination Act* 1991 (Qld) ss 124A, 131A; *Racial Vilification Act* 1996 (SA); *Civil Liability Act* 1936 (SA) s 73; *Anti-Discrimination Act* 1998 (Tas) ss 17(1), 19; *Racial and Religious Tolerance Act* 2001 (Vic); *Criminal Code* (WA) ss 76-80H.

[28] *Discrimination Act* 1991 (ACT) ss 65-67.

[29] *Racial Discrimination Act* 1975 (Cth) ss 18B-18F.

[30] This tends to result in assessment of the claim by an anti-discrimination authority. If the claim is substantiated, a remedy (which might include an apology, education in a workplace, publication of a retraction, or a commitment not to reoffend) is mediated. Recalcitrant cases are referred to a Tribunal, or in the case of complaints under federal law to the Federal Court,

provisions are in force. In all other States and the Australian Capital Territory, both civil and criminal provisions apply, although the criminal provisions have only been successfully invoked once[31] in nearly two decades of their existence.

This raft of anti-hate speech laws has experienced little—if any— constitutional or statutory impairment on free speech grounds. Unlike the United States, in Australia, anti-vilification laws have survived resistance from quarters emphasizing free speech concerns (McNamara 2002: 1–5). They are generally considered compatible with the common law protection of freedom of expression that exists in Australia, and with the doctrine of an implied constitutional freedom of political communication as developed by the High Court (Gelber 2007: 3–4). Although it has been argued that incidents of hate speech may constitute political communication as conceptualized under the implied constitutional freedom (Chesterman 2000b: 16–18; Meagher 2004: 251–3), this would not render hate speech laws constitutionally invalid. All that is required for them to be constitutionally permissible is that the laws are regarded as reasonably and appropriately adapted to a legitimate government end. Such an end could very likely include minimizing the attendant harms of hate speech or discouraging its practice. Although the High Court has yet to decide upon the constitutionality of hate speech laws, respondents' attempts to rely on the freedom in lower courts have failed.[32] This means that hate speech laws in Australia are highly unlikely to infringe on the constitutionally secured implied freedom of political expression.

This demonstrates that speech-limiting hate speech laws are not generally hindered by the forms and extent of free speech protection in Australia. However, it does not yet answer the question of whether a selectively applicable speech-enhancing policy could be developed in the Australian context. Some further clarification on this question can be sought by examining one of the foundational cases for the freedom of political communication doctrine in the Australian High Court.

---

for determination with possible remedies including an order to apologise or retract, and/or a fine.

[31] In Western Australia, following a high-profile graffiti attack in which swastikas and slogans including 'Hitler was right' and 'Asians out' were painted on a synagogue and Chinese restaurant in July 2004, five men were successfully prosecuted for criminal damage (AAP 2005; Nott 2004). One of the men, Damon Paul Blaxall, was also charged with possession of racist material. In 2005 Blaxall was convicted on both counts, and sentenced to eight months in jail for criminal damage and four months for possession of the racist material (Rasdien 2005).

[32] See e.g., *Islamic Council of Victoria v Catch the Fire Ministries Inc* [2006] VSCA 284.

In *Australian Capital Television*[33] the High Court found invalid federal legislation[34] which sought to prohibit the broadcasting of political advertising during a period prior to a state or federal election or referendum. The legislation simultaneously imposed obligations on radio and television broadcasters to provide free air time to candidates in such elections, in a system whereby 90 per cent of time would be allocated to candidates of parties already holding seats in parliament (allocated in proportion to their votes in the previous election), 5 per cent or more to existing members of parliament not belonging to a political party, and the remaining proportion would be allocated by lot to candidates belonging to parties not yet represented in the parliament. The legislation contained exemptions permitting the broadcasting of news and current affairs, and permitting limited coverage of policy launches.

The legislation had been justified by the federal Labor government of the day in democratic terms, as safeguarding the integrity of elections, reducing the potential for corrupt influence by donors on political parties, and levelling the field by mitigating the extremely high cost of campaigning, which precludes all but the well-resourced from political advertising in the electronic media. It was also pointed out that similar legislation exists in other countries including the United Kingdom, France, Norway, Sweden, the Netherlands, Denmark, and Japan.[35] Nevertheless, the High Court found the legislation impermissibly infringed on the implied freedom of political communication.[36]

In the *Australian Capital Television* case, the legislation in question was perceived as speech-limiting, and moreover, speech-limiting in relation to public affairs. Speech in relation to elections and referenda is arguably at the core of what in the First Amendment environment is conceived as 'public discourse', and in Australia has been termed 'political communication' (noting that the former is far broader and more inclusive than the narrower Australian conception of 'political communication' as developed by the High Court). The speech-limiting aspect of the legislation, especially in the realm of political communication, contributed heavily to it being held invalid. Chief Justice Mason stated that 'freedom of speech or expression on electronic media in relation to public affairs and the political

---

[33] *Australian Capital Television v Commonwealth* (1992) 177 CLR 106.

[34] *Political Broadcasts and Political Disclosures Act* 1991 (Cth).

[35] *Australian Capital Television v Commonwealth* (1992) 177 CLR 106 at 129–31.

[36] Note the persuasive argument by Rosenberg and Williams (1997) that in making this finding the Australian High Court drew on US First Amendment jurisprudence, in particular the marketplace of ideas doctrine, to draw conclusions (about the effect of the legislation in supporting the status quo) which are not supportable by empirical evidence. They thus caution against the influence of First Amendment jurisprudence in this case.

process is severely restricted'[37] by the legislation. The legislation did not only restrict candidates or parties from advertising. Rather, it restricted all would-be interested parties from so doing. Impliedly this included non-government organizations and interest groups such as trade unions, employer organizations, or social welfare groups, and even politically motivated individuals.

In finding the legislation invalid, the High Court also argued that the regulatory regime imposed by the legislation skewed political debate in favour of political incumbents—candidates and parties already represented in parliament—through its mechanism for providing free air time as compensation for the general restriction. As Mason CJ stated, it 'favours the established political parties and their candidates without securing compensating advantages or benefits for others who wish to participate in the electoral process or in the political debate which is an integral part of that process'.[38] It is from this aspect of the case that some inferences can be gleaned regarding the potential fate of a speech-enabling policy. Although in this case the speech-enabling aspects of the legislation cannot be separated from its speech-limiting aspects (indeed the former were included as compensation for the latter), nevertheless there are instructive implications.

The High Court viewed the legislation's attempt to enact some speech-enabling elements with disfavour because it claimed they inherently favoured incumbents. Thus, new candidates, new parties, or new political views would be more easily kept out of political debate. This threatened the marketplace of ideas around election time, they argued, and impermissibly restricted the implied freedom of political communication. However, in a persuasive argument, Rosenberg and Williams conducted empirical research into the effects of the legislation in the brief period of time between its enactment and its invalidation. During this period, one State election, one Territory election, and one bi-election in a State were held (1997: 446). Their analysis shows[39] that, in empirical terms, the legislation enhanced rather than detracted from opportunities for participation in political debate. Evidence from a Tasmanian State election showed that candidates participated in more traditional, non-media-based, activities to convey their ideas including public gatherings, debates,

---

[37] *Australian Capital Television v Commonwealth* (1992) 177 CLR 106 at 132.

[38] *Australian Capital Television v Commonwealth* (1992) 177 CLR 106 at 132 per Mason CJ.

[39] They also convincingly reviewed the literature to argue that political advertisements by their nature (short, thirty-second bursts which are incapable of conveying complex policy ideas and are often negatively focused) act to the detriment of democratic deliberation, not its enhancement (1997: 465–75).

and grassroots campaigning. Moreover, the distribution of free air time benefited a party and an independent candidate who otherwise would not have had the financial means to advertise in the electronic media (1997: 479–81).

Thus, the stated aim of the policy as introduced by the legislature *was* achieved via its mechanisms for selectively enabling speech. The democratic foundations for the legislation's enactment were upheld in an empirical examination of events subsequent to it. However, the majority justices did not investigate these empirical events (Rosenberg and Williams 1997: 475) and drew conclusions as to the legislation's likely effects which were not borne out in practice.

What can be concluded from this? The fate of a speaking back policy in the courts may depend heavily on the extent to which the decision-makers in those courts recognize first, the context within which the policy is enacted, and second, the extent to which the policy could be considered to be speech-limiting.

In relation to the first point (the context within which the policy is enacted), the speaking back policy is designed to redress identifiable imbalances in the ability to speak. Should those imbalances not be recognized, it is possible that the policy could be found to constitute an unacceptable form of governmental control of speech opportunities. To such an argument I would respond as I have at length above in relation to the United States context. But the fate of a speaking back policy may depend in part on judges and decision-makers recognizing existing imbalances in opportunities to speak. The *Australian Capital Television* judgment examined here does not provide a strong basis for confidence that this is likely to occur. Judgments were made on the basis of presumptions about speech opportunities which were not subjected to evidentiary examination, nor was it considered that they needed to be.

In relation to the second point, for a speaking back policy to be looked upon unfavourably in the Australian courts on free speech grounds, it would have to be regarded as implicitly or indirectly (due to its selective application) speech-limiting, and as violating the requirement to be appropriately adapted to achieving a legitimate government end. However, existing hate speech laws, which are much more directly speech limiting than the speaking back policy, have not been held to be constitutionally invalid on these grounds. Therefore, it is highly unlikely that a policy providing support for engagement in speech opportunities would fall foul of the test. It is probable that if any hostility to a speaking back policy in Australia were to arise, it would derive not from free speech concerns *per se*, but from other, more general concerns about public policy implementation (such as cost, efficient allocation of resources, and so on).

V. Conclusions

Hate speech policy has typically been thought of in terms detrimental to the speech opportunities of the hate speaker. This binary conceptualization, where a gain in the dignity of hate speech targets must be offset by a loss in speech opportunities for the speakers, is ubiquitous, but ultimately not entirely helpful.

An alternative way of thinking through this dilemma is to imagine that the aim of hate speech policy is to ameliorate the effects of hate speech in such a way that the targets (broadly conceived) become able to respond by contradicting the messages contained within hate speech and counteracting its effects. Punishing hate speakers does neither of those things. Thinking differently about hate speech policy thus enables a new type of policy to be conceived, one with very different implications for how hate speech is responded to, but also one with very different fortunes when measured against justifiable and long-standing free speech concerns in both the United States and Australia.

One of the strengths of the idea that hate speech policy could serve to support engagement in speech, rather than limitations on speech, is that it appears robust enough to penetrate the constitutional environment which is most hostile to hate speech policies; that of the United States and the First Amendment. Additionally, in a constitutional context less hostile to hate speech laws but one in which political discourse still features as a distinct constitutional doctrine, it appears also to have potential for enactment. In short, the speaking back policy is conceptually and practically useful in combating hate speech, and also potentially robust in differing constitutional environments.

Bibliography

Austin, J. L. 1975. *How to Do Things With Words*, 2nd edn. Urmson and Sbisa eds. Oxford: Clarendon Press.

Australian Associated Press [AAP] 2005. 'Jail for Race-Hate Graffiti', *The Australian*, 20 May: 3.

Baker, C. Edwin 1992. *Human Liberty and Freedom of Speech*. New York: Oxford University Press.

Barendt, Eric 1994. 'Free Speech in Australia: A Comparative Perspective', *Sydney Law Review* 16(2): 149–65.

Barendt, Eric 2005. *Freedom of Speech*, 2nd ed. Oxford: Oxford University Press.

Chemerinsky, Erwin 1997. *Constitutional Law: Principles and Policies*. New York: Aspen Publishers, Inc.

Chesterman, Michael 2000a. *Freedom of Speech in Australian Law.* Aldershot: Ashgate.

Chesterman, Michael 2000b. 'When is a Communication Political?', *Legislative Studies* 14(2): 5–23.

Delgado, Richard 1993. 'Words That Wound: A Tort Action for Racial Insults, Epithets and Name Calling', in M. Matsuda, C. Lawrence, R. Delgado and K. Crenshaw eds. *Words That Wound: Critical Race Theory, Assaultive Speech, and the First Amendment.* Colorado: Westview Press.

Fiss, Owen 1996a. *The Irony of Free Speech.* Cambridge, MA: Harvard University Press.

Fiss, Owen 1996b. *Liberalism Divided: Freedom of Speech and the Many Uses of State Power.* Colorado: Westview Press.

Gelber, Katharine 2002. *Speaking Back: The Free Speech versus Hate Speech Debate.* Amsterdam: John Benjamins Ltd.

Gelber, Katharine 2003. 'Pedestrian Malls, Local Government and Free Speech Policy', *Policy and Society* 22(2): 22–49.

Gelber, Katharine 2007. 'Hate Speech and the Australian Legal and Political Landscape', in Gelber and Stone eds. *Hate Speech and Freedom of Speech in Australia.* Sydney: Federation Press.

Gelber, Katharine 2010. 'Freedom of Political Speech, Hate Speech and the Argument from Democracy: The Transformative Contribution of Capabilities Theory', *Contemporary Political Theory* 9(3): 304–24.

Habermas, Jürgen 1984. *The Theory of Communicative Action, Volume 1: Reason and the Rationalization of Society.* London: Heinemann.

Holmes, Stephen and Cass Sunstein 1999. *The Cost of Rights: Why Liberty Depends on Taxes.* New York: WW Norton & Co.

Lawrence, C. 1987. 'The Id, The Ego, and Equal Protection: Reckoning with Unconscious Racism', *Stanley Law Review* 39: 317–88.

MacKinnon, Catharine 1993. *Only Words.* Cambridge, MA: Harvard University Press.

Matsuda, Mari 1993. 'Public Response to Racist Speech: Considering the Victim's Story', in M. Matsuda, C. Lawrence, R. Delgao and K. Crenshaw eds. *Words That Wound: Critical Race Theory, Assaultive Speech, and the First Amendment.* Colorado: Westview Press.

McNamara, Luke 2002. *Regulating Racism: Racial Vilification Laws in Australia.* Sydney Institute of Criminology Monograph Series No. 16, Sydney.

Meagher, D. 2004. 'So Far So Good? A Critical Evaluation of Racial Vilification Laws in Australia', *Federal Law Review* 32: 225–53.

Nott, H. 2004. 'WA: Three Men Sentenced for Racist Graffiti', *AAP General News,* 5 August, Document AAP0000020040805e08500139, accessed 13/8/06.

Nussbaum, Martha 1990. 'Aristotelian Social Democracy' in R. Douglass and G. Mara eds. *Liberalism and the Good.* New York: Routledge.

Nussbaum, Martha 1999. *Sex and Social Justice*. New York: Oxford University Press.

Nussbaum, Martha 2000. 'Women's Capabilities and Social Justice', *Journal of Human Development* 1(2): 219–47.

Nussbaum, Martha 2003. 'Capabilities as Fundamental Entitlements: Sen and Social Justice', *Feminist Economics* 9(2–3): 33–59.

Nussbaum, Martha 2006. 'Reply: In Defence of Global Political Liberalism', *Development and Change* 37(6): 1313–28.

Patapan, Haig 2000. *Judging Democracy: The New Politics of the High Court of Australia*. Melbourne: Cambridge University Press.

Post, Robert 1995. *Constitutional Domains: Democracy, Community, Management*. Cambridge, MA: Harvard University Press.

Rasdien, P. 2005. 'Green Plea Fails to Save Graffiti Racist', *The West Australian*, 21 December, p. 41.

Rosenberg, Gerald M. and John Williams 1997. 'Do Not Go Gently Into That Good Right: The First Amendment in the High Court of Australia', *Supreme Court Review* 11: 439–95.

Schauer, Frederick 2003. 'Intentions, Conventions, and the First Amendment: The Case of Cross Burning', *The Supreme Court Review* 6: 197–230.

Schauer, Frederick 2005. 'The Exceptional First Amendment' in M. Ignatieff ed. *American Exceptionalism and Human Rights*. Princeton NJ: Princeton University Press.

Sen, Amartya 1992. *Inequality Re-examined*. Cambridge: Harvard University Press.

Stone, Adrienne 2001. 'Rights, Personal Rights and Freedoms: The Nature of the Freedom of Political Communication', *Melbourne University Law Review* 25(2): 374–418.

Stone, Adrienne and Simon Evans 2006. 'Australia: Freedom of Speech and Insult in the High Court of Australia', *International Journal of Constitutional Law* 4(4): 677–88.

Sumner, L. W. 2004. *The Hateful and the Obscene: Studies in the Limits of Free Expression*. Toronto: University of Toronto Press.

Sunstein, Cass 1988. 'Beyond the Republican Revival', *Yale Law Journal* 97(8): 1539–90.

Sunstein, Cass 1994. 'Academic Freedom and Law: Liberalism, Speech Codes, and Related Problems' in L. Menand ed. *The Future of Academic Freedom*. Chicago: University of Chicago Press.

Weinstein, James 1999. *Hate Speech, Pornography, and the Radical Attack on Free Speech Doctrine*. Colorado: Westview Press.

Williams, George 2002. *Human Rights Under the Australian Constitution*. Melbourne: Oxford University Press.

Williams, Patricia 1987. 'Spirit-Murdering the Messenger: The Discourse of Fingerpointing as the Law's Response to Racism', *University of Miami Review* 42: 127–57.

Beyond Belief: Pragmatics in Hate Speech and Pornography[1]

Rae Langton

1. Hate Speech and Pornography

1.1. *Game Plan: Scope*

Political theorists and philosophers of language are alike in wanting to know answers to certain questions about speech: What is speech for, and why does it matter? J. S. Mill took the primary function of speech to be our collective journey towards true belief, and he argued for a right to free speech that would allow it to fulfil this distinctive function.[2] Political theorists following in Mill's footsteps have wondered how far this goes. Some speech appears to offer dim prospects for helping us reach Mill's hoped-for destination. To take an example that will occupy us here, speech that promotes racial or sexual hatred is hardly friendly to the pursuit of true belief; and it is by no means obvious that freedom of speech stretches to freedom of hate speech.

Philosophers too are interested in speech and its relation to true belief. They ask how speech works. To answer these questions, they develop theories of meaning, and theories of speech acts and pragmatics. Robert Stalnaker gives voice to a crucial desideratum for such theorizing: it is desirable that 'the pragmatic notions developed to explain the linguistic phenomena be notions that help to connect the practice of speech with

[1] Early versions of this chapter have been presented at NYU, Oxford, Sheffield, Yale, Claremont McKenna College, MIT (Work in Progress Seminar, Workshop on Gender and Philosophy), and the APA (Vancouver, Spring 2009). I am grateful to all present for helpful discussion. Special thanks are due to Ishani Maitra, Mary Kate McGowan, Kai von Fintel, Bob Stalnaker, Christopher Peacocke, Steve Yablo, Seth Yalcin, Richard Holton, and Sally Haslanger.
[2] Mill 1859.

purposes for which people engage in the practice'. He has a certain paradigm in mind. The 'principal reason for speech', he says, is that 'people say things to get other people to come to know things that they didn't know before'.[3] Mill would surely have applauded.

This paradigm guides Stalnaker towards an emphasis on the special role of shared belief, for parties to a conversation. Speakers often rely on, or assume, a body of shared belief, a 'common ground' that provides the backdrop to the conversational moves they want to make. If I say, 'Even Sarah Palin could win', I rely on a shared belief that she is a less than stellar candidate. But more than that, it sometimes happens that I help to *create* that shared belief, if it was not shared before—and if nobody blocks my move with an indignant 'What do you mean, *even* Sarah Palin?' The beliefs of parties to a conversation tend to *accommodate* to whatever is needed to make sense of what is going on, thereby building up a ground of common belief that speakers can exploit in what they do next with their words.[4]

Can these stories told by philosophers shed light on hate speech? Can attention to hate speech return the favour, and help the philosopher's understanding of speech? The answer to both of these questions is probably, yes. This is already evident when one considers the interest philosophers have recently shown in the semantics and pragmatics of sentences that use epithets.[5] But speech need not use epithets in order to express and whip up hatred. Here, for instance, is an extract from Ernst Hiemer's 'The Holy Hate', in a 1943 issue of *Der Stürmer*:

Example 1:
We as a people will survive this war only if we eliminate weakness and 'politeness' and respond to the Jews with an equal hatred. We must always keep in mind what the Jew wants today, and what he plans to do with us. If we do not oppose the Jews with the entire energy of our people, we are lost. But if we can use the full force of our soul that has been released by the National Socialist revolution, we need not fear the future. The devilish hatred of the Jews plunged the world into war, need and misery. Our holy hate will bring us victory and save all of mankind.[6]

No epithets there, but this kind of anti-Semitic propaganda was effective, and considered grounds enough for its editor, Julius Streicher, to be tried

---

[3] Stalnaker 2002: 701–21, 703.

[4] Lewis 1983: 233–49; Atlas 2004: 29–52; von Fintel 2008: 137–70.

[5] Hom forthcoming; Williamson forthcoming; Richard 2008; Hornsby 2001: 128–41; Dummett 1973.

[6] Hiemer 1943; *German Propaganda Archive* 2009. While not containing epithets, the passage does, to be sure, contain the essentializing tag 'the Jew', and powerful use of generic constructions. For ground-breaking work on this topic, see Leslie forthcoming.

at Nuremberg and executed for war crimes.[7] There are plenty of reasons for philosophers to extend their interest beyond epithets. Here we shall be looking at politically problematic speech construed more broadly, with a focus on pornography and hate speech.

These forms of speech are hardly paradigms of what a political philosopher like Mill had in mind, when he argued that free speech could help us achieve true and justified beliefs. They are hardly paradigms of what a philosopher of language like Stalnaker has in mind, when he suggests that the principal reason for speech is to get people to know things they didn't know before. Nonetheless, I want to explore some possibilities for mutual illumination, which may prove the brighter if we are willing to consider some amendments that take us beyond the knowledge-oriented starting points of Mill and Stalnaker—amendments, in short, that take us beyond belief.

1.2. *What is Racial Hate Speech?*

The United Nations requires its member states to combat racial hate speech:

State Parties condemn all propaganda and all organizations which are based on ideas or theories of superiority of one race or group of persons of one colour or ethnic origin, or which attempt to justify or promote racial hatred and discrimination in any form, and undertake to adopt immediate and positive measures designed to eradicate all incitement to, or acts of, such discrimination and, to this end [. . .] shall declare an offence punishable by law all dissemination of ideas based on racial superiority or hatred, incitement to racial discrimination, as well as all acts of violence or incitement to such acts against any race or group of persons of another colour or ethnic origin.[8]

This proposal points us towards a conception of hate speech as, among other things, propaganda. Here are some more gems from the Streicher–Hiemer collaboration, this time aimed at a young readership:

Example 2. The Poison Mushroom, 1938:
Title Story. The illustration depicts a mother and young son in the woods, mushroom hunting. The caption reads, 'Just as it is often hard to tell a toadstool from an edible mushroom, so too it is often very hard to recognize the Jew as a swindler and a criminal.'

---

[7] See Altman this volume.
[8] *International Convention on the Elimination of All Forms of Racial Discrimination*, 1965, Article 4, http://www.hrcr.org/docs/CERD/cerd3.html, accessed June 3rd 2009. While many member states have implemented laws putting these principles into effect, the U.S. is an exception; its 1994 ratification was accompanied by a reservation pointing out that the requirement was incompatible with U.S. constitutional protection of speech.

The Experience of Hans and Else with a Strange Man. Large, ominous hook-nosed figure doles sweets to small blond children. 'Here, kids, I have some candy for you. But you both have to come with me . . .'

Inge's Visit to a Jewish Doctor. A doctor leers from a doorway at a young German woman. 'Two criminal eyes flashed behind the glasses, and the fat lips grinned.'[9]

Hate speech of this form has helped to make history, as the examples illustrate. In Rwanda, genocidal fervour was whipped up by a campaign of hate speech broadcast from a Hutu radio station. Here is a sample:

Example 3. Valérie Bemeriki, Rwanda, 1994:
They [the Tutsi] are all Inyenzi [cockroaches]. When our armed forces will get there, they will get what they deserve. They will not spare anyone since everybody turned *Inyenzi.*

The repeated slur, perpetually casting the Tutsi as vermin, paved the way for the murder of more than half a million fellow countrymen, in acts conceived as pest-eradication, as Lynne Tirrell aptly observes.[10]

What is going on, in hate speech, as described by the UN, and illustrated here? According to the UN description, racial hate speech *disseminates* ideas based on racial superiority; it *promotes* racial hatred and discrimination—'promotes' in a causal sense. It also *incites* racial discrimination and hatred, and *promotes* racial hatred and discrimination— 'promotes' in an advocacy sense. In terms that J. L. Austin made famous, there appear to be both illocutionary and perlocutionary dimensions to hate speech.[11] Austin distinguished the act performed in saying certain words, which he called the 'illocutionary' act, from the later effects achieved by saying them, which he called the 'perlocutionary' act. For example, 'In saying "Shoot her", Smith *urged* the man to shoot': that describes an illocutionary act. 'By saying "Shoot her", Smith *persuaded* the man to shoot': that describes a perlocutionary act.

Both these dimensions are visible in hate speech. It has effects on hearers' attitudes: they come to believe 'ideas based on racial superiority', as the UN puts it. The effects are on beliefs, and on other attitudes too. Some hearers begin to hate members of the target race, and desire to

---

[9] Hiemer 1938; *German Propaganda Archive* 2009. I describe the illustration, and quote its caption; the corresponding 'story' (along with others) is available at this site.

[10] Tirrell this volume. Note that 'Inyenzi' was at first a label self-ascribed by the Tutsi, so perhaps not initially pejorative. I am indebted to Tirrell for the quotation.

[11] Austin 1962; Langton 1993: 305–30; reprinted in Langton 2009.

avoid them.[12] The effects are there because of what hate speech is, as an illocutionary act: it incites hatred. The perlocutionary effects have their explanation in the illocutionary force. I take it that 'incite' is an illocutionary verb, in a class with others such as 'encourage', 'order', 'advocate', and 'legitimate'. 'Promote' is a verb that straddles both sides of Austin's distinction. The word has a perlocutionary, causal sense, and an illocutionary, constitutive sense. When smoking promotes cancer, it causes it. When tobacco companies promote smoking, they advocate it. By advocating smoking, they also cause it, since their advocacy brings about an effect, namely that people smoke. So hate speech 'promotes' hatred in both illocutionary and perlocutionary ways: it advocates and causes hatred.

Both aspects of hate speech were evident in the court's verdict, when Julius Streicher was tried at Nuremberg. He was condemned—

for his 25 years of speaking, writing, and preaching hatred of the Jews [...] In his speeches and articles, week after week, month after month, he *infected* the German mind with the virus of anti-Semitism, and *incited* the German people to active persecution.[13]

His speech was an illocutionary act: he 'incited' his countrymen to persecute the Jews. As a result, his speech was also a perlocutionary act, with effects on his hearers' mental states and actions, as they became 'infected' with anti-Semitism.

Besides working as a kind of propaganda, hate speech may sometimes work as a kind of assault. In the UN description, the envisaged hearers are other racists, or hoped-for racists, rather than members of the group targeted for hate. But some hate speech is used in a different way, to directly attack its target. Mari Matsuda's account of hate speech allows for this dimension, when she identifies three characteristics of racial hate speech: its 'message is of racial inferiority'; its message is 'directed against a historically oppressed group'; and its message is 'persecutory, hateful and degrading'.[14] The envisaged hearers, for Matsuda, include not, or not only, other racists, or hoped-for racists. The envisaged hearers are, or include, members of the target group. Matsuda's proposal draws on the idea of 'fighting words' in U.S. law, speech that assaults someone like a move in a physical fight. This expands not only our conception of the relevant hearers, but also of the relevant illocutionary force. When racial

---

[12] There is also the thought that hate speech has a certain *source*: it is 'based on' ideas or theories of superiority of one race. This might mean it has its causal genesis in those ideas, or is premised on those ideas, or presupposes those ideas.

[13] Gilbert 1995: 442.

[14] Matsuda 1993: 36.

hate speech is addressed directly to its targets, it directly 'persecutes', 'degrades', and 'assaults' them.

Consider the experience of Hank Aaron, who, in 1973, was poised to break Babe Ruth's record for career home runs. As his score crept closer and closer to matching the Babe's, he received a barrage of hate mail, of which the following is a sample:

Example 4. Letters to Hank Aaron, 1973:
'Dear Mr. Nigger, I hope you don't break the Babe's record. How can I tell my kids that a nigger did it?'

'Dear Nigger, You can hit all dem home runs over dem short fences, but you can't take dat black off yo face.'

'Dear Nigger, You black animal, I hope you never live long enough to hit more home runs than Babe Ruth.'

'Dear Nigger Henry, You are [not] going to break this record established by the great Babe Ruth if you can help it...Whites are far more superior than jungle bunnies...My gun is watching your every black move.'[15]

(How nice that the last correspondent was able to illustrate his 'far more superior' social status, with his far more superior command of language.) This is hate speech aimed directly at a member of the target race: speech that is not propaganda, but assault, insult, threat. The distinction here is a context-sensitive one. Propaganda aimed at turning its hearers into racists could also be used as an attack on an individual, just like these letters. Imagine a copy of *Der Stürmer*, featuring 'The Holy Hate', left deliberately where a Jewish colleague would find it. Assaultive hate speech is an important category, apparently not captured in the UN definition. My focus here, though, will be on speech directed towards hearers who are not members of the group targeted for hate. So having flagged it, I'm going to set it aside, for present purposes.

1.3. *What is Pornography?*

One answer to this question has nothing to do with speech. Pornography is 'in a sense, a substitute for a sexual partner', according to Anthony Burgess.[16] Another answer to this question has everything to do with speech, and with hate speech in particular. Pornography is 'the undiluted essence of anti-female propaganda', according to Susan Brownmiller.[17] It 'depicts women's degradation', and 'in such a way as to *endorse* the degradation', according to Helen Longino.[18] It is 'the graphic sexually

---

[15] Kennedy 2003: 20.
[16] Burgess 1970: 8; quoted in Feinberg 1985: 130.
[17] Brownmiller 1975: 443.
[18] Longino 1980: 29. (Longino has the whole phrase in italics.)

explicit *subordination* of women through pictures and/or words', according to Catharine MacKinnon.[19] It is 'a depiction of subordination' that '[tends] to *perpetuate subordination*', according to Judge Frank Easterbrook, who continued:

> The subordinate status of women in turn leads to affront and lower pay at work, insult and injury at home, battery and rape on the streets...but this simply demonstrates the power of pornography as speech.[20]

Putting Burgess and Easterbrook together, we confront the strange conclusion that ersatz sexual partners are words, covered by First Amendment protection of the U.S. Constitution. The idea that pornography is 'in a sense, a substitute sexual partner' has prompted some to conclude that pornography is not really *any* kind of speech, but should rather be kept in the same category as sex dolls and toys, not subject to the protection reserved for speech proper.[21] Anti-pornography feminists might be expected to welcome this approach, and some do. But many regard pornography as speech: as subordinating speech (MacKinnon) or propaganda (Brownmiller). Some have suggested that proscriptions on hate speech be extended to cover pornographic speech that incites 'sexual' as well as racial hatred.[22]

On this way of thinking, pornography is something to which speech act theory could apply, and with the same double Austinian aspects as its racial hate speech counterpart. Easterbrook picks up on a perlocutionary dimension: pornography causally 'perpetuates' subordination, and contributes to violence. Longino and MacKinnon pick up on an illocutionary dimension: pornography 'endorses' women's degradation, and 'subordinates' women. Note that misogynistic pornography may, like hate speech, sometimes function in an assault-like way, aiming directly at women: cases, for example, where it is used in a campaign of workplace harassment. But again, as for the case of racial hate speech, we shall focus on pornography that is not directed specifically to women as hearers.

1.4. *Game Plan: Limits*

We are going to be looking at what pornography and hate speech may have in common. This means we'll be leaving aside some interesting questions in the vicinity that deserve attention. For example: might

---

[19]   McKinnon 1987: 176.
[20]   771 F.2d 329 (7th Cir. 1985), italics added.
[21]   Schauer 1979: 899–933; Hornsby 1993: 38–45; reprinted in Dwyer 1995. See also McGowan and Maitra 2007: 41–68; Vadas 2005: 174–93.
[22]   Itzin 1993; Easton 1995: 89–104.

there be overlap between pornography and racial hate speech? Apparently yes. Some racial hate speech is also pornography, and some pornography is also racial hate speech. Streicher's main aim, in publishing *Der Stürmer*, was to stir up hatred towards Jews. One way he made it effective was by marrying hate speech to sex, filling the pages with lurid pictures offering the Adults Only equivalent of 'Inge's Visit to the Doctor', narratives of innocent German girls seduced and violated by Jewish men. Conversely, some pornography can be racist hate speech. While the main aim of pornographers is to make money by selling sex, they sometimes make more money if they marry porn to racism, providing options that create and cater to racial taste.

Besides the question of overlap between pornography and hate speech, there is the question of asymmetry between them. A simple case of racial hate speech, unmarried to pornography, will be different in many ways from a simple case of pornography, unmarried to racism. Here are three asymmetries worth noting: there may be differences of 'speech situation', differences of intention, and differences of apparent acceptability. The typical 'speech situation' of pornography consumption is, as Burgess noted, more like having sex than like reading the newspaper; indeed, it typically *is* a situation of having sex. Further, the typical intentions of hate speakers are often more consciously hateful than the typical intentions of pornographers. While one can think of exceptions, a rough rule is that most hate speakers are driven by hate, while most pornographers are driven by money. Finally, the status of pornography as propaganda is less visible than the status of its racial counterpart, not only because of the apparent differences in speaker intention, but because of the difference in perceptible hierarchy. For racial hate speech, hierarchy and subordination look like what they are—namely, hierarchy and subordination. For pornography, hierarchy and subordination look like what they are *not*—namely, the natural sex difference.

To sum up these caveats: in what follows, we'll leave aside these important differences between pornography and racial hate speech, and focus on what they might have in common. We'll also be assuming, rather than arguing, that pornography and hate speech have the effects critics claim for them, though that is of course a large topic in its own right.[23] On the assumption that pornography and hate speech sometimes work

---

[23] For an interesting evaluation and development of causal anti-pornography argument, see Eaton 2007: 674–715. For social science background: a meta-study by Malamuth, Addison, and Koss 2000: 26–91; Donnerstein, Linz, and Penrod 1987. Pamela Paul reviews and comments on social science evidence, and new data from interviews, in *Pornified: How Pornography is Transforming Our Lives, Our Relationships, Our Families*, 2005.

in similar ways, we'll be asking: what work do they do, and how do they work? The speech act story sketched above suggests that there are constitutive and causal aspects to a story about what work they do: hate speech can both incite hatred, and produce hatred. We'll be looking at constitutive and causal aspects of pornography and hate speech. In attending to causal effects, we'll be looking at changes not only in hearers' beliefs, but in other attitudes, including hatred and desire. And in thinking about *how* this sort of speech works, we'll begin with the thought that the speech act story has promise, but it is not the only contender.

2. Five Models

How, then, do pornography and hate speech work, when they do? Let me outline five different pictures of what is going on. We've already begun to look at the speech act model; in addition, I want to sketch an *argument* model; a *conditioning* model; an *imitation* model; and a *pragmatic* model. Some of these pictures are compatible; others compete.

2.1. *A Speech Act Model.* This is implicit, I suggested, in the UN description of hate speech, and the feminist description of pornography. According to this model, these forms of speech work, in Austin's terms, as *illocutionary* acts that can e.g. subordinate certain groups, legitimate attitudes and behaviours of discrimination, advocate violence, discrimination, and hatred; they may also work as *perlocutionary* acts, that cause subordination, and produce changes in attitudes and behaviour, including violence, discrimination, and hatred.

2.2. *An Argument Model.* On this picture, pornography and hate speech are a form of political speech, which present arguments for conclusions about how to live the good life. This is compatible with the illocutionary story, and can be viewed as offering an optimistic suggestion about what the illocutionary force of such speech is. Since political speech is especially likely to receive First Amendment protection, this model is of dialectical importance. I find at least the germ of it in Ronald Dworkin. He says that the pornographer, for example, contributes to the 'moral environment, by expressing his political or social convictions or tastes or prejudices informally'. Pornography, he says, 'seeks to deliver' a 'message' that 'women are submissive, or enjoy being dominated, or should be treated as if they did': it is comparable to political speech 'advocating that women occupy inferior roles'.[24] On this picture, the pornography consumer is presented

---

[24] Dworkin 1994: 13 and 1991: 104, 105. He suggests that pornography succeeds in persuading people when he concedes some of the effects claimed by MacKinnon: 'there is

with reasons for revising his normative beliefs. As normative beliefs alter in light of these new reasons, so too do desires, since one's desires follow one's conception of the good.

2.3. *A Conditioning Model.* At the other extreme, we have it that pornography or hate speech may work 'as primitive conditioning', with pictures and words being 'stimuli', as MacKinnon writes of pornography.[25] There is little scope here for argument, or the advocacy of political views. Pornography's status as speech is regarded as incidental, so this proposal, on the face of things, competes with the illocutionary account. It is like the story of Pavlov's dogs. Subjects associate some neutral stimulus often enough with an attractive one, and the previously neutral stimulus becomes a turn-on. Some social scientists appear to support the conditioning hypothesis for pornography. Consider this study (perhaps not about pornography in MacKinnon's sense) where an experimenter—

created a mild boot fetish in heterosexual male students by pairing slides of sexually provocative women with a picture of a pair of black knee-length women's boots. Not only did the boots become somewhat sexually arousing, but there was a slight tendency for this conditioned response to generalize to other footwear as well. The author concluded that there is little question that sexual responsiveness can be conditioned to external stimuli that initially fail to elicit any sexual arousal.[26]

Drawing on research of this kind, Danny Scoccia argues that violent pornography helps create violent desires by a process of conditioning, and he takes this to have implications for politics. Since the liberal principle 'does not protect speech insofar as it non-rationally affects its hearers' mental states' a ban on violent pornography is consistent with liberalism.[27] On this model, what initially changes is *desire*, sexual responsiveness; if there are changes in other attitudes, they probably arrive hanging on the coat-tails of desire.

2.4. *An Imitation Model.* In an elegant cross-disciplinary essay, Susan Hurley brings recent research on imitation to bear on questions about media violence and free speech.[28] Her argument has implications for the forms of speech that involve simulation and imitation, and so it will be

some evidence that exposure to pornography weakens people's critical attitudes toward sexual violence', 'Two Concepts', p. 105; Jennifer Hornsby comments, 1993: 38–45, reprinted with a postscript in Dwyer (ed.) 1995: 220–32.

[25] MacKinnon 1993: 16.

[26] Nelson 1982: 185, citing a 1966 study by Rachman 1966: 293–6.

[27] Scoccia 1996: 776–99. The quotation is from p. 777. Cass Sunstein argues that since pornography aims at arousal and affects propositional attitudes by a process akin to subliminal suggestion, it is non-cognitive speech, 1986: 589–627.

[28] Hurley 2004: 165–218.

relevant to some forms of hate speech and pornography. Drawing on current work in the cognitive and neurosciences, Hurley takes us through the evidence for (among other things) ideomotor theory, and the so-called 'chameleon effect'. Watching or imagining an activity in sufficient detail can help one perform it better. Subjects have a (defeasible) tendency to match their behaviour to the traits, actions, and stereotypes being modelled around them. Hurley proposes this as a possible explanation for the effects of media violence on behaviour, especially on children. Short-term priming effects are observed, the 'chameleon effect', and also longer-term 'cognitive scripting' effects. Sometimes scripting effects work via behaviour that is contrary to the agent's official values, so that a person who officially rejects violent norms can nonetheless find himself following a violent script.[29] Hurley rightly thinks there are significant implications here for debates about free speech. Perhaps we may decide that the value of free speech is worth the social cost of violent speech; but if we do go there, she says, we should go with our eyes open. The imitation model may well be compatible with the conditioning model, but offers different, perhaps supplementary, mechanisms for change.

2.5. *A Pragmatic Model.* On this picture, pornography and hate speech are not in the business of offering reasons or arguments, as the argument model would have it. Nor are they in the business of merely altering attitudes and behaviour via conditioning, or unconscious imitation.[30] In a development of Austin's speech act theoretic model, the pragmatic approach considers the question of how in more concrete terms pornography might have the illocutionary force of altering norms and social conditions, by legitimating, or advocating, certain beliefs, attitudes, and behaviour.

Unlike the speech of a legislator, hate speech and pornography are not usually spoken by officials uttering classic Austinian illocutions. Its speakers do not officially, and authoritatively say, for example, 'I hereby subordinate', or 'I hereby authorize you to discriminate'. Such speech acts work more subtly. They may implicitly *presuppose* certain facts and norms, rather than explicitly enacting them; but these implicit presuppositions may nonetheless work in ways that are comparable to classic Austinian

---

[29] Hurley p. 181, citing research by Huesmann and Taylor 2004; and Comstock and Scharrer, *op cit.*

[30] At least they're not explicitly doing that. If simulation theorists are right about our cognitive makeup though, it could be that all the ordinary processes of acquiring beliefs from each other involve something like imitation. I won't pursue this here.

illocutions.[31] Consumers then change their factual and normative beliefs by taking on board the 'common ground' (in Robert Stalnaker's phrase), or the 'conversational score' (in David Lewis's phrase) that is presupposed in the pornographic 'conversation'.[32]

Stalnaker and Lewis observed that conversational score, unlike the score of a baseball game, follows rules of accommodation: it tends to evolve in whatever way is required to make the play that occurs count as correct play. If I say, 'Even Palin could win', I add to the score not only the proposition I asserted, namely that Palin could win, but also what I presupposed, namely that Palin is an unpromising candidate. Unless of course I'm challenged ('What do you mean *even?*'). Drawing on these insights, Caroline West and I have argued that even if pornography does not explicitly say that women are inferior, or that sexual violence is legitimate, such propositions might be presupposed by what pornography explicitly says. Consider, for example, what the social scientists studying pornography describe as a 'favourable rape depiction'. In one example of such pornography, a woman is gang raped on a pool table in a bar, the men ignoring the woman's resistance, the woman eventually reaching a 'shuddering orgasm'. It may be stretching things to think of pornography in conversational terms, but in speech like this, rape myth propositions such as 'when women say "no", they mean "yes"', might become part of the 'score'—part of the 'common ground'— shared between speaker and hearer.[33]

Mary Kate McGowan's work on the 'conversational exercitive' can be seen as a development of the pragmatic model. Any conversational move that contributes to the score is also an illocution that alters normative facts about what is permissible, and even possible, in the conversation thereafter. She points out that conversational exercitives are different to paradigm Austinian speech acts. They work in covert ways: speakers don't need to be *intending* to alter any facts about permissibility, nor do they need the special *authority* that Austin attributed to speakers who enact norms.[34] In the conversation following an unblocked utterance of 'Even Palin could win', certain moves are impermissible later on (e.g. 'Hey, guess what, Palin

---

[31] I proposed this idea in a paper co-authored with Caroline West. Langton and West, 'Scorekeeping in a Pornographic Language Game', *Australasian Journal of Philosophy*, reprinted in Langton, *Sexual Solipsism*. Note that accommodation might sometimes fail even without challenges or blocks (perhaps the presupposition is clearly false, or there is a change of conversational topic).

[32] Stalnaker 2002; Lewis 1983.

[33] *Hustler*, January 1983, cited by Itzin, *Pornography*, discussed in Langton and West, 'Scorekeeping', pp. 184–5. Some social science data are collected in Donnerstein et al. 1987.

[34] McGowan 2003: 155–89; McGowan 2004: 93–111.

is an unpromising candidate'). Certain moves are permissible later on (e.g. mockery of Palin) that exploit a now-common belief about Palin's incompetence. The earlier conversational move changes facts about what is permissible, whether or not the speaker intends them to, and whether or not the speaker is especially authoritative.

The pragmatic story has promise, as a way to show how informal speech by ordinary speakers may change beliefs and alter norms, without needing to meet the strong felicity conditions typically required by traditional Austinian speech acts. And it can explain how speech can alter beliefs rather directly. If we think in Lewis's terms, we will say that, just as in a baseball game, the beliefs of players and spectators change in response to changes in the abstract score, in like manner the beliefs of speakers and hearers change in response to the abstract conversational score. If we think in Stalnaker's terms, the connection will be even more direct: altering the shared 'common ground' just *is* altering the shared 'common belief'. On an oversimplifying assumption, conversational score, common ground, and common belief are pretty much the same thing, in his framework. It's true that Stalnaker sometimes identifies common ground with common *acceptance*, a broader attitude that includes belief but also assumption and pretence.[35] But basically, on Stalnaker's approach the shared common ground is identified with certain belief-like propositional attitudes of the speakers; so there is no mystery about how altering common ground also involves altering such (belief-like) attitudes.

Five theoretical models, then, of how pornography and hate speech might work: a speech act model, an argument model, a conditioning model, an imitation model, and a pragmatic model. I give little credence to the argument model,[36] but the others each have something interesting and potentially important to offer. Do they all capture part of the story? Perhaps. For present purposes, I am going to place my bets on the pragmatic model.

3. Problem Cases: Desire and Hate

There is no mystery then, on the pragmatic approach, about how pornography and hate speech might alter factual and normative beliefs of consumers, in altering the 'conversational score' or 'common ground' shared

---

[35] Stalnaker 2002. A further caveat involves the issue of pretence in pornography, which may mean that we cannot move from common ground to belief quite so directly. The question of how beliefs about the world can be altered by fiction is another topic of our paper 'Scorekeeping in a Pornographic Language Game'.

[36] We attend briefly to it in Langton and West, 'Scorekeeping'.

between speakers and hearers. We can try to say that, even in the case of the fetishized boots, viewers, or 'hearers', are *accommodating* to what the material presupposes, namely that the boots are sexy. Only on that assumption does their inclusion in the series make sense. To say that the sexiness of the boots is 'presupposed' would gives us a change in the conversational score, in Lewis's terms; a change in the common ground, in Stalnaker's terms. Hearers, or viewers, take on board the presupposition that boots are sexy, and incorporate that into their beliefs.

But hold on a minute. *Believing* the boots are sexy is one thing. *Finding* them sexy is quite another. How on earth does that change in *desire* come about? There is something missing in this pragmatic picture of how norms and beliefs alter in response to conversational moves, and how pornography and hate speech shape them. In addition to changing beliefs, pornography and hate speech evidently change the desires of consumers. People who consume pornography come to find desirable things they did not find desirable before. They don't just believe something about boots: they desire something about boots. People who consume anti-Semitic propaganda don't just come to believe something about Jews: their desires also change—they want to avoid Jews, or destroy them. It's not just that consumers come to believe different descriptive or normative propositions. It's that they come to *want* different things than they did before.

What goes for desire also goes for hate. Hearers don't just believe differently than they did before, they *feel* differently than they did before. It is no mystery, on the pragmatic approach, how hearers come to believe something about Jews, for example, that good Germans hate Jews. But how do we get from the philosopher's story about belief acquisition, to these changes in desire and hate?

Evidently the psychological 'conditioning model' of how some speech works has no problem dealing with this question, giving us an easy non-rational account of how desire and emotion get changed. It is no mystery how desire gets 'conditioned' to a previously neutral 'stimulus' that happens to be speech, any more than there is a mystery understanding how Pavlov's dogs 'learned' to salivate when they heard the bell. The pragmatic model, by contrast, gives us an adequate story about how belief change can be achieved, through subtle conversational moves adjusting the 'common ground' or 'score'; but it seems inadequate to the task of addressing change in feeling and desire. Should we just throw up our hands at this point, and cede this territory to the psychologist?

Perhaps we can do a little better than that.

4. An Exploratory Proposal: The Accommodation of Desire and Hate

I want to propose, in an exploratory spirit, the idea that the phenomenon of accommodation might extend beyond belief—beyond conversational score, and common ground, as originally conceived—to include accommodation of other attitudes, including desire and hatred. My remarks here will inevitably be programmatic. But to convey the general idea: just as a hearer's belief can spring into being, after the speaker presupposes that belief, so too a hearer's desire can spring into being, after the speaker presupposes the hearer's desire; and so too a hearer's hatred can spring into being, after the speaker presupposes that hatred. Stalnaker's common ground can perhaps be extended to include not just common beliefs, and other belief-like attitudes, but common desires, and common feelings, as well. Speakers invite hearers not only to join in a shared belief world, but also a shared desire world, and a shared hate world. I am interested here in the implications of this for pornography and hate speech, but if my hunches are right, there are potential implications for a host of other ordinary speech situations as well, including, for example, advertising and jokes.

Recall that for Stalnaker, it is a desideratum that—

the pragmatic notions developed to explain the linguistic phenomena be notions that help to connect the practice of speech with purposes for which people engage in the practice.[37]

For Stalnaker, the paradigm case, embodying 'the principal reason for speech', is where 'people say things to get other people to come to know things that they didn't know before'. But there are many other reasons for which people engage in the practice of speech. The gaining of knowledge may be one principal reason for speech. But an alien arriving on earth might be as likely to conclude from his observations that the principal reason for speech was the gaining of money. More generally, a great deal of speech aims not at getting people to know things they didn't know before, but at getting them to want things they didn't want before, and feel things they hadn't felt before. While our topic here is politically problematic speech, hate speech, and pornography, it will readily be seen that the idea extends to a great deal of informal conversation, and presumably much advertising.

---

[37] Stalnaker, 'Common Ground', p. 703.

Let us see how our pragmatic story might be adapted to say something about the accommodation of desire and hate.

First, a little more thought about accommodation. One can think about the 'common ground' or 'score' that accommodates the moves speakers make in two importantly different ways: first as an *abstract structure*, analogous to the 'score' of a baseball game (which I take to be Lewis's approach); or as simply the *attitudes* of parties to the conversation, analogous to the beliefs of players and bystanders about the score of the baseball game (which I take to be Stalnaker's approach). These do not necessarily compete, and I find it helpful to see the phenomenon of accommodation as occurring at both of these levels. In baseball, a player makes a move. This then alters the abstract score of the game, and alters facts about what is normatively appropriate in the game. These alterations work, in Austin's terms, non-causally, in the way that illocutionary acts work. A player's move does not strictly *cause* the score to change: the score is an abstract structure, whose being is *constituted* by what the player has done. Just as smashing the bottle and saying the right words christens the ship, so hitting a home run changes the score.

As I see it, Lewis's account of 'conversational score' as abstract structure, is tracking change enacted 'straightway', at Austin's illocutionary level ('straightway' is Lewis's word, p. 240). Then the effects occur afterwards, among them effects on *attitudes* of parties to the game, effects that do not happen 'straightway', but as real-time psychological consequences. As I see it, Stalnaker's understanding of 'common ground' as attitude is tracking change brought about causally, at Austin's perlocutionary level. Bystanders come to believe that the player has hit a home run; they come to believe that the score has changed, and that the facts about what is normatively appropriate in the game have changed accordingly. We should welcome an understanding of accommodation that makes sense of change that occurs at both of these levels: first, abstract and illocutionary; second, attitudinal and perlocutionary.

How does the score-as-abstract-structure interact with the common-ground-as-attitude? It might work in the following way. The abstract score can be thought of as containing propositions (among other things). Looking at our earlier anti-Semitic example: a children's story might presuppose that 'Jews often kidnap children'; that 'It is appropriate to hate Jews'; that 'Good Germans hate Jews'; that 'Good Germans avoid Jews'. True, the story is presented as fiction, but as fiction that says something about the world, and says it by presupposing it. The abstract score incorporates the fact-claiming proposition that Jews often kidnap children, the normative proposition that it is appropriate to hate Jews, and the proposition (factual and normative) that good Germans avoid Jews. Then, if the conversation is a successful one, the attitudes of hearers change, just as the attitudes of bystanders change in response to the score of the baseball game. Abstract score accommodates to conversational move; psychological score accommodates to abstract score.[38]

How do the attitudes of hearers change? Let me make the following suggestion about how this might work, i.e. about how accommodation at the abstract level leads to accommodation at the attitudinal level. To insert these claims into the abstract score is to invoke a general *attitudinal appeal* to the hearer: '*Have attitudes that fit this score!*' This appeal may take the form of a quasi-pretence: the way to make the appeal is to go on as if the hearer had the relevant attitude already.[39]

The most straightforward one will be a *cognitive appeal*: 'Have the belief that fits this score!' To take up an earlier example, this might be: 'Believe that Jews often kidnap children!'; 'Believe it is appropriate to hate Jews!'; 'Believe that good Germans hate Jews!'; and 'Believe that good Germans avoid Jews!' The way a speaker makes these appeals is, often, to go on as if the hearers had these attitudes already. A speaker can invite someone into their belief-world by taking for granted that the hearer is already in that belief-world.

A psychological accommodation then follows, as a causal effect of the attitudinal appeal. Hearers come to believe that Jews often kidnap children; that it is appropriate to hate Jews; and that good Germans avoid Jews.

Besides a cognitive appeal, there may be appeals to other attitudes; and here we are attempting to extend the phenomenon of accommodation beyond belief. Speech may appeal to desire and to emotion. How it does so has traditionally been a topic for rhetoric, rather than pragmatics; but I see little reason for restricting our philosophical attention to purely cognitive attitudes.

So in addition to cognitive appeal there can be what we may call a *conative appeal*: 'Have the desire that fits this score!' For example, this may be: 'Desire to avoid Jews!' or 'Desire to be rid of Jews!'

Sometimes the conative appeal may be grounded in the cognitive appeal. For a hearer who antecedently desires to avoid kidnappers, the news that Jews are kidnappers can be offered as grounding a desire to avoid Jews. For a hearer who wants to be a 'good German', the news that good Germans avoid Jews can likewise be offered as grounding a desire to avoid Jews.

---

[38] These accommodations might come apart, e.g. in a case where a legislator enacts a law, and people fail to believe that he has done so.

[39] Stalnaker 2002; Atlas 2004: 29–52. I can't here address adequately the ways in which presupposition accommodation involves something like pretence.

I also want to suggest that the conative appeal may sometimes be direct, in a way that doesn't rely on antecedent desire. Speech can surely, sometimes, create a new desire directly, through an appeal not depending on what the hearer previously desired. Philosophers have, in Humean mode, said little about the origins of desire, rational or otherwise; but among its many possible wellsprings, speech is surely prominent. We have a multi-billion dollar advertising industry attesting to that fact, advertising which often makes a skilful direct appeal, aiming to create a desire to buy something, independent of anything the hearer might have desired before. As with advertising, perhaps too with anti-Semitic propaganda, there might be a direct appeal, aiming to create a desire to be rid of Jews, independent of anything the hearer might have desired before. And perhaps this direct conative appeal can be made, as in the case of a cognitive appeal, by going on as if the hearer had the desire already. A speaker can invite someone into their desire-world by taking for granted that the hearer is already in that desire-world.

A psychological accommodation then follows, as a causal effect of the attitudinal appeal. Hearers come to desire to avoid Jews.

In addition to cognitive and conative appeal, the abstract score may invoke an *emotional appeal*: 'Have emotions that fit this score!' For our example, this may simply be: 'Hate Jews!' As in the case of the conative appeal, sometimes the emotional appeal may be grounded in the cognitive appeal. For a hearer who is antecedently disposed to hate kidnappers, the factual news that Jews are kidnappers can be offered as grounding a hatred of Jews. For a hearer disposed to feel what he believes it's appropriate to feel, the normative news that 'It is appropriate to hate Jews' can be offered as grounding a hatred of Jews. For a hearer disposed to hate what he believes good Germans hate, the news that good Germans hate Jews might likewise be offered as grounding a hatred of Jews.

But again I want to suggest that the emotional appeal may sometimes be more direct, in a way that doesn't rely on antecedent attitudes. Speech can surely, sometimes, create a new emotion directly, through an appeal that does not depend on the hearer's antecedent attitudes, just as the frenzied, hateful rantings of *Der Stürmer* sometimes aimed to do. And, as for the cognitive and conative attitudes, perhaps this can sometimes be done by going on as if the hearer has the relevant attitude already. A speaker can invite someone into their hate-world by taking for granted that they are already in that hate-world.

A psychological accommodation then follows, as a causal effect of the attitudinal appeal. Hearers come to hate Jews.

5. Concluding Remarks

I have tried to suggest how the phenomenon of accommodation might be extended beyond belief, to take in attitudes that are of central importance to our political thinking about hate speech and pornography.[40] These extensions could be of interest to our thinking about speech in more mundane contexts too. I am painfully aware that these are mere gestures in a direction where I would like to see some more action; but something in this direction is, I think, sorely needed.

As political philosophers, and philosophers of language too, we tend to be god-like in our habit of creating man in our own image: of creating human beings who match a philosophical ideal, rather than a social reality. We create paradigm political agents, whose chief interest in speech is a search for truth. We create paradigm speakers, whose chief interest in conversation is the spread of knowledge. But if we want notions that, as Stalnaker put it, 'help to connect the practice of speech' with 'the purposes for which people engage in the practice', then let us try looking to the conversational score, and the common ground, to track whatever attitudes—whether beliefs, or desires, or feelings—are central to the kind of speech it is, in the all too messy world we live in.

References

Altman, Andrew, this volume. "Freedom of Expression and Human Rights Law: The Case of Holocaust Denial."

Atlas, Jay David 2004. "Presupposition," in Laurence R. Horn and Gregory L. Ward, *The Handbook of Pragmatics*. Malden, MA: Wiley Blackwell, pp. 29–52.

Austin, J. L. 1962. *How to Do Things With Words*. Oxford: Oxford University Press.

Brownmiller, Susan 1975. *Against Our Will: Men, Women and Rape*. New York: Bantam, p. 443.

Burgess, Anthony 1970. "What Is Pornography?" in *Perspectives on Pornography*, ed. Douglas A. Hughes. New York: St. Martin's, p. 8.

Comstock, G. and E. Scharrer 2003. "The Contribution of Meta-Analysis to the Controversy over Television Violence and Aggression," in D. Gentile (ed.), *Media Violence and Children*. Westport, CT: Greenwood Press.

---

[40] Other ideas in the literature which may provide some help here include, perhaps, Paul Portner's idea that common ground incorporates 'to do lists', in the case of imperatives, 'The Semantics of Imperatives within a Theory of Clause Types', 2004; see also Ninan 2005: 149–78; and Christopher Peacocke's idea that agents can build up together a 'mutually attended world' that includes facts and norms that merit certain reactions, 2005.

Donnerstein, Edward, Daniel Linz, and Steven Penrod 1987. *The Question of Pornography: Research Findings and Policy Implications.* New York: Free Press; London: Collier Macmillan.

Dummett, Michael 1973. *Frege: Philosophy of Language.* Oxford: Duckworth.

Dworkin, Ronald 1991. "Two Concepts of Liberty," in *Isaiah Berlin: A Celebration,* ed. Edna and Avishai Margalit. London: Hogarth Press, pp. 104, 105.

Dworkin, Ronald 1994. "A New Map of Censorship," *Index on Censorship* 1/2: p. 13.

Dwyer, Susan ed. 1995. *The Problem of Pornography.* Belmont, CA.: Wadsworth, pp. 220–32.

Easton, Susan 1995. "Pornography as Incitement to Sexual Hatred," *Feminist Legal Studies* 3: 89–104.

Eaton, A. W. 2007. "A Sensible Antiporn Feminism," *Ethics* 117: 674–715.

Feinberg, Joel 1985. *Offense to Others.* New York: Oxford University Press, p. 130.

German Propaganda Archive, trans. and ed. Randall Bytwerk, http://www.calvin. edu/academic/cas/gpa/thumb.htm, accessed June 3rd 2009.

Gilbert, G. M. 1995. *Nuremberg Diary.* Cambridge MA and New York: De Capo Press, p. 442.

Hiemer, Ernst 1938. *Der Giftpilz.* Streicher Verlag

Hiemer, Ernst 1943. "The Holy Hate," *Der Stürmer,* ed. Julius Streicher. Streicher Verlag.

Hom, Christopher, forthcoming. "The Semantics of Racial Epithets," *Journal of Philosophy.*

Hornsby, Jennifer 1993. "Speech Acts and Pornography," *Women's Philosophy Review* 10: 38–45.

Hornsby, Jennifer 2001. "Meaning and Uselessness: How to Think About Derogatory Words," in Peter French and Howard Wettstein (eds.), *Midwest Studies in Philosophy* 25, Oxford: Blackwell Publishers, pp. 128–41.

Huesmann, L. R. and L. D. Taylor 2004. "The Case against the Case against Media Violence," in D. Gentile (ed.), *Media Violence and Children.* Westport CT: Greenwood Press.

Hurley, Susan 2004. "Imitation, Media Violence, and Freedom of Speech," *Philosophical Studies* 117: 165–218.

International Convention on the Elimination of All Forms of Racial Discrimination, 1965, Article 4, http://www.hrcr.org/docs/CERD/cerd3.html, accessed June 3rd, 2009.

Itzin, Catherine ed. 1993. *Women, Violence and Civil Liberties.* Oxford: Oxford University Press.

Kennedy, Randall 2003. *Nigger: The Strange Career of a Troublesome Word.* New York: Vintage Press, p. 20.

Langton, Rae 1993. "Speech Acts and Unspeakable Acts," *Philosophy and Public Affairs* 22: 305–30.

Langton, Rae 2009. *Sexual Solipsism: Philosophical Essays on Pornography and Objectification.* Oxford: Oxford University Press.

Langton, Rae and Caroline West 1999. "Scorekeeping in a Pornographic Language Game," *Australasian Journal of Philosophy*, pp. 184–5.

Leslie, Sarah Jane, forthcoming. "The Original Sin of Cognition: Race, Prejudice and Generalization," *Journal of Philosophy*.

Lewis, David 1983. "Scorekeeping in a Language Game," *Philosophical Papers*, vol. I. Oxford: Oxford University Press, pp. 233–49.

Longino, Helen E. 1980. "Pornography, Oppression and Freedom: A Closer Look," in *Take Back the Night: Women on Pornography,* ed. Laura Lederer and William Morrow, p. 29.

MacKinnon, Catharine 1987. "Francis Biddle's Sister," *Feminism Unmodified.* Cambridge, MA: Harvard University Press, p. 176.

MacKinnon, Catharine 1993. *Only Words,* Cambridge, MA: Harvard University Press, p. 16.

Malamuth, Neil M., Tamara Addison, and Mary Koss 2000. "Pornography and Sexual Aggression: Are There Reliable Effects and Can We Understand Them?" *Annual Review of Sex Research* 11: 26–91.

Matsuda, Mari 1993. "Public Response to Racist Speech," in Matsuda, Charles R. Lawrence III, Richard Delgado, and Kimberle Williams Crenshaw, *Words that Wound: Critical Race Theory, Assaultive Speech and the First Amendment.* Boulder, CO: Westview Press, p. 36.

McGowan, Mary Kate 2003. "Conversational Exercitives and the Force of Pornography," *Philosophy and Public Affairs* 31: 155–89.

McGowan, Mary Kate 2004. "Conversational Exercitives: Something Else We Do With Our Words," *Linguistics and Philosophy* 27: 93–111.

McGowan, Mary Kate and Ishani Maitra 2007. "Limits of Free Speech: Pornography and the Question of Coverage," *Legal Theory* 13: 41–68.

Mill, J. S. 1859. "On Liberty" ch. 2, in *J. S. Mill: Utilitarianism and Other Writings,* ed. Mary Warnock 1962. New York: New American Library.

Nelson, Edward C. 1982. "Pornography and Sexual Aggression," in Maurice Yaffé and Edward Nelson (eds.), *The Influence of Pornography on Behaviour.* London: Academic Press, p. 185.

Ninan, Dilip 2005. "Two Puzzles about Deontic Necessity," in J. Gajewski, V. Hacquard, B. Nickel, and S. Yalcin (eds.), *New Work on Modality: MIT Working Papers in Linguistics* 51, pp. 149–78.

Paul, Pamela 2005. *Pornified: How Pornography is Transforming Our Lives, Our Relationships, Our Families.* New York: Henry Holt.

Peacocke, Christopher 2005. "Joint Attention: Its Nature, Reflexivity, and Relation to Common Knowledge," ch. 14 of *Joint Attention: Communication and Other Minds,* eds. N. Eilan, C. Hoerl, T. McCormack, and J. Roessler. Oxford: Oxford University Press.

Portner, Paul 2004. "The Semantics of Imperatives within a Theory of Clause Types," in K. Watanabe and R. Young (eds.), *Proceedings of Semantics and Linguistic Theory* 14. Ithaca, NY: CLC Publications.

Rachman, S. 1966. "Sexual fetishism: An Experimental Analogue," *Psychological Record* 16: 293–6.

Richard, Mark 2008. "Epithets and Attitudes," ch. 1 of *When Truth Gives Out*. Oxford: Oxford University Press.

Schauer, Fred 1979. "Speech and 'Speech'—Obscenity and 'Obscenity': An Exercise in the Interpretation of Constitutional Language," *Georgetown Law Journal* 67: 899–933.

Scoccia, Danny 1996. "Can Liberals Support a Ban on Violent Pornography?" *Ethics* 106: 776–99.

Stalnaker, Robert 2002. "Common Ground," *Linguistics and Philosophy* 25: 701–21.

Sunstein, Cass 1986. "Pornography and the First Amendment," *Duke Law Journal*, September: 589–627.

Tirrell, Lynne, this volume. "Genocidal Language Games."

Vadas, Melinda 2005. "The Manufacture-for-Use of Pornography and Women's Equality," *Journal of Political Philosophy* 13: 174–93.

von Fintel, Kai 2008. "What is Presupposition Accommodation, Again?" *Philosophical Perspectives* 22: 137–70.

Williamson, Timothy, forthcoming. "Reference, Inference and the Semantics of Pejoratives," in Joseph Almog and Paolo Leonardi (eds.), *The Life and Work of David Kaplan*. Oxford: Oxford University Press.

Subordinating Speech[1]

Ishani Maitra

1. Introduction

It is by now a familiar thought that words can be used to do many things. Famously, Catharine MacKinnon has argued that one of the many things that words can be used to do is subordinate.[2] Drawing upon MacKinnon's work, Rae Langton uses the following, by now well-known, example to illustrate the idea that speech can sometimes *constitute* subordination.[3] Langton asks us to imagine a legislator in apartheid-era South Africa enacting a law by saying in the appropriate circumstances, "Blacks are no longer permitted to vote."[4] That law deprives black South Africans of rights and powers they previously held. In doing so, it also ranks black South Africans as inferior to other South Africans, and legitimates discriminatory behavior against them. Since, as Langton argues, (unfairly) depriving individuals of rights and powers, (unfairly) ranking them as inferior, and legitimating discriminatory behavior towards them are all ways of subordinating said individuals, the South African legislator's words constitute a subordinating (speech) act.

Once we recognize that speech *can* subordinate—and further, that it can *constitute* subordination—we might ask which kinds of speech *in fact* do so. In part, this is an empirical matter, for whether a kind of speech

---

[1] Many thanks to Susan Brison, Mary Kate McGowan, audiences at SWIPshop and at Dartmouth, and an anonymous referee at Oxford University Press for feedback on earlier drafts of this chapter.

[2] See especially MacKinnon 1987 and 1993.

[3] Langton 1993.

[4] Langton 1993, pp. 302–3. The example is obviously stylized, for legislative bodies typically enact law by votes of their members, not by a single member producing an utterance of the sort envisioned here. Nevertheless, the example offers a particularly clear (though fictional) instance of speech constituting subordination. In actuality, as MacKinnon has noted, the legislator's utterance would constitute political speech (MacKinnon 1993).

subordinates depends upon various empirical facts. But in part, this is also a theoretical matter, for part of what we need to know to settle this question is what sorts of evidence bear on its truth. That is to say, we need to know, for any given kind of speech, what we would have to establish to show that speech of that sort constitutes subordination. As we shall see in what follows, this theoretical matter turns out to be more complicated than it may appear at first blush.

In this chapter, I focus on racist hate speech. More specifically, I am interested in the following questions. Can *ordinary instances* of racist hate speech subordinate in the way that the South African legislator's utterance subordinates in Langton's example? (I will say what I mean by 'ordinary instances' in § 3.) That is, can these instances of hate speech rank their targets as inferior, deprive them of rights and powers, and legitimate discriminatory behavior towards them, just as the legislator's utterance does? In other words, can ordinary instances of racist hate speech sometimes constitute subordination?

Even if we grant that Langton is right that the legislator's utterance constitutes subordination, there are several clear disanalogies between that speech act and ordinary instances of racist hate speech. The most glaring of these disanalogies has to do with authority, and gives rise to what I shall label 'the Authority Problem' (for ordinary instances of racist hate speech).[5] In brief, here's the problem. It's plausible to suppose that the South African legislator can subordinate in saying what he does only because he has the right kind of authority. A legislator in a democratic society has the authority to give or take away rights and powers from members of that society by enacting legislation. But an ordinary speaker— say, someone who accosts a person of color in the street with hate speech—does not appear to have any such authority. So, it is tempting to conclude that the ordinary speaker cannot subordinate in the same way as the legislator, and therefore, that the questions in the previous paragraph must be answered in the negative.

The Authority Problem has been extensively discussed in the literature on speech and subordination.[6] Some have taken it to be fatal to the claim that ordinary speech can constitute subordination.[7] Others have argued

---

[5] It should be clear that the Authority Problem arises for other kinds of speech as well. See also note 6.

[6] See, e.g., Langton 1993, 1998, this volume; Butler 1998; Green 1998; McGowan 2003, 2009, this volume; Sumner 2004; Bauer 2006; Wieland 2007. These writers have largely (though not exclusively) focused on the Authority Problem as it arises for pornography, not for racist hate speech.

[7] Green 1998; Sumner 2004; Bauer 2006.

that, contrary to initial appearances, authority isn't after all necessary for speech to subordinate.[8] In this chapter, I take a different tack. I argue that there are more ways in which speakers can come to have authority (and so, be in a position to subordinate) than have been generally recognized. In part, this is because authority has been taken to be too closely tied to social position. I present a series of examples which show that speaker authority needn't derive from social position at all. Moreover, and more controversially, these examples also show that a speaker can come to have authority even when they *lack* it prior to speaking. After distinguishing these different ways in which speakers can come to have authority, I argue that we have ample reason to think that even producers of ordinary instances of racist hate speech (call them 'ordinary hate speakers') can *sometimes* have authority in these ways.

Though my discussion in this chapter focuses mostly on speech and speaker authority, much of what I say will also apply to actions more generally, and to agent authority.

This chapter thus seeks to illuminate what it takes to have authority, and in virtue of that authority, constitute norms for others. It does not, however, purport to capture all the ways that this can happen. That is a much bigger project, in which this chapter can only make partial progress. My (more modest) aim here is to set aside some insufficient reasons for taking ordinary speakers to *lack* authority, and to highlight some further questions that need to be answered in order to settle when they *do* have authority.[9] The latter question, I hope to show, has received far less attention than it deserves.

2. Causing and Constituting Subordination

To say that speech *constitutes* subordination is a different (and more controversial) claim than to say that it merely *causes* subordination. Since this distinction will be central to my project in this chapter, it will be useful to begin by briefly outlining the difference between the two claims.

Speech can cause subordination in any of several ways. First, some speech can subordinate by causing physical and psychological harms to

---

[8] McGowan 2003, 2009, this volume.

[9] My discussion in this chapter is also intended as a contribution to a related project, namely, that of determining the status of racist hate speech vis-à-vis the First Amendment of the U.S. Constitution. I have argued elsewhere that if certain theorists (e.g. Charles Lawrence) are right about what some racist hate speech does, then such speech ought *not* be covered by the First Amendment (Maitra and McGowan 2010; Lawrence 1992, 1993). If I am right that ordinary hate speakers can have authority after all, then that's further reason to think that such speech does do what theorists like Lawrence have argued it does.

its targets that (unfairly) deprive them of significant rights, powers, and abilities. For example, if the speech causes its targets to feel extreme psychological distress, to the extent of preventing them from getting a decent education or keeping a job, that might be sufficient for subordinating members of the target group.

Second, speech can also subordinate by causing its hearers to form beliefs that, in turn, cause those hearers to treat others in ways that subordinate them. For example, if the speech causes hearers to believe that members of a particular racial group are inferior and so deserving of persecution, and those hearers act on those beliefs by violating members of the supposedly inferior group, then that may again be sufficient for subordination of the persecuted group.

Further, subordination needn't proceed via the *beliefs* of hearers. A third way in which speech can subordinate is by conditioning (or triggering) its hearers to act towards others in ways that subordinate them. In this case, the speech might cause subordination without altering the beliefs of the hearers, but by nevertheless altering their behavior via some non-doxastic route.[10] Note also that items on this list are neither exhaustive of the ways in which speech can cause subordination, nor mutually exclusive.

Critical race theorists like Mari Matsuda and Richard Delgado have argued that there is ample reason to think that racist hate speech does in fact cause a wide variety of physical and psychological harms to people of color, and that, in so doing, it causes their subordination. Matsuda, for one, has written that targets of such speech experience symptoms ranging from rapid pulse rate, difficulty breathing, nightmares, post-traumatic stress disorder, hypertension, psychosis, and suicide. Further, the damage to targets' sense of self-esteem and personal security can be devastating.[11]

More broadly, Matsuda argues that hate speech serves to divide its targets from even 'right-thinking' members of the hate speakers' group. Even those who object to hate speech may feel relieved that they belong to the dominant group (relative to the targets), and thus don't have to be subjected to similar abuse. Equally, being thus abused may cause targets to treat all members of the hate speakers' group with suspicion. Both dynamics serve to distance members of the targeted group and members of the hate speakers' group from each other.[12]

Delgado mentions several of the same effects in targets of hate speech. In addition, he emphasizes the dignitary affront that results from such speech,

---

[10] For discussion of the claim that some speech conditions its hearers, see Langton this volume.

[11] Matsuda 1993, pp. 24–6.

[12] Matsuda 1993, p. 25. I'll return to this point near the end of this chapter, in § 6.

that can work to keep targets compliant. Finally, Delgado also notes that racist hate speech can be particularly damaging to targets who are children, for whom it is especially difficult to reject the representations of people of color offered in such speech. If those representations are accepted, the speech can function as a self-fulfilling prophecy, further damaging its targets' prospects.[13]

Such claims about the effects of hate speech are, of course, controversial. But if they are true, that would seem sufficient to establish that racist hate speech *causes* the subordination of its targets (and perhaps, people of color more generally).

Let's turn now to the constitutive claim, namely, the claim that speech can *constitute* subordination. According to this further claim, subordination is not merely a downstream causal consequence of the speech in question. Rather, on the interpretation offered by Langton and others, to say that speech (of a given kind) can constitute subordination is to say that, under certain circumstances, the very act of producing speech of that kind just *is* a subordinating (speech) act.[14]

Langton appeals to speech act theory, and in particular, to J.L. Austin's notion of an illocutionary act, to develop this constitutive claim.[15] Simplifying a little, illocutionary acts for Austin are acts that speakers perform just in uttering the appropriate words in the appropriate circumstances. For example, suppose I say to you, "I'll bet you a bottle of wine that the United States will win the next World Cup." In saying what I do in these circumstances, I perform the (illocutionary) act of betting (and perhaps some other illocutionary acts as well). My words just *constitute* the betting act; there is nothing further I have to do, besides uttering those words, to perform that act.[16]

---

[13] Delgado 1993, pp. 90–6.

[14] It is worth noting that this is not the only possible interpretation of the constitutive claim. Here's an alternate interpretation: to say that speech can constitute subordination is to say that, under certain circumstances, the practice of producing speech of the kind in question is a subordinating *practice*. On the latter interpretation, unlike Langton's, the practice of producing racist hate speech (for example) may be subordinating, even though each particular act in that practice isn't a subordinating act. For a brief discussion of this possibility, see Maitra forthcoming.

[15] Langton 1993; Austin 1975.

[16] As I've noted, this is actually a simplification of Austin's view. For Austin, merely saying the right words in the right circumstances was necessary, but not sufficient for successful performance of an illocutionary act. However, since nothing in this chapter turns on whether a given act is an illocutionary one in Austin's sense, the details of his view need not detain us here. For more on Austin's notion, and for some of the problems with that notion, see Maitra 2009.

Examples of illocutionary acts abound. Asserting, warning, ordering, promising, christening, marrying, hiring, firing, acquitting, and of course, betting are all illocutionary acts. To this list, Langton adds another, namely, the illocutionary act of subordination.

To see how this is supposed to work, recall the example of the South African legislator from § 1. His utterance (unjustly) deprives black South Africans of rights and powers, (unfairly) ranks them as inferior to other South Africans, and legitimates discriminatory behavior towards them. Depriving of rights and powers (in the way that the legislator's utterance does), ranking, and legitimating behavior are all illocutionary acts. *Unjustly* depriving of rights and powers, *unfairly* ranking as inferior, and legitimating *discriminatory* behavior are all components of subordination, on Langton's view. Therefore, in doing what it does, the legislator's utterance (illocutionarily) subordinates black South Africans. His utterance just *is* an act of subordination.

This example shows vividly that there is no conceptual difficulty with the claim that speech can constitute subordination. On Langton's view, then, speech can subordinate illocutionarily—and thus, constitute subordination—by constituting norms that help to construct social reality for the subordinated group. More specifically, these norms determine, first, the (relative) social status of the subordinated group; second, what rights and powers members of the group possess; and third, what counts as acceptable behavior towards those members.

Langton relies on the picture just sketched to argue that, *contra* some commentators, there is nothing conceptually incoherent about Catharine MacKinnon's claim that *pornography* constitutes the subordination of women. Against MacKinnon (and Langton), critics have argued that there are conspicuous disanalogies between the South African legislator's utterance and acts of producing and distributing pornography, which render it implausible that the latter constitute subordination. As we shall see, some of the same disanalogies seem to also arise when we consider ordinary instances of racist hate speech. In the next section, I'll consider what I (and others) take to be the most important of these disanalogies, having to do with the role of authority in Langton's picture.

3. The Authority Problem

Langton labels as 'authoritative illocutions' those "actions whose felicity conditions require that the speaker occupy a position of authority in a relevant domain."[17] Ordering is a paradigmatic example of an authoritative

---

[17] Langton 1993, p. 305.

illocution. After all, a parent can order his child to go to bed because he has the authority to set rules about what the child can and cannot do, whereas the child's sibling or friend cannot (ordinarily) do the same, for they don't occupy any relevant position of authority.

Not all illocutionary acts are authoritative illocutions. Whereas ordering (as suggested above), christening, marrying, hiring, firing, and acquitting all do fall in this category, there are many other illocutionary acts—among them, betting, asserting, warning, suggesting, and promising—that don't seem to require any special authority on the part of the speaker. I'll return to some of these speech acts, especially asserting, later in this chapter (§ 6).

We've seen that, for Langton, ranking as inferior, depriving of rights and powers, and legitimating behavior are components of (illocutionary) subordination. Langton regards each of these as authoritative illocutions. From this, she infers that (illocutionary) subordination must also be an authoritative illocution. Consider ranking, for instance. A teacher, one might think, can rank the students in her classroom because she has the authority to do so in virtue of her position as teacher, but a mere passerby cannot do the same, precisely because he doesn't occupy any relevant position of authority. That seems to make ranking an authoritative illocution. Much the same can be said, it seems, about depriving of rights and powers, and of legitimating.

(In what follows, I will largely focus on the act of *ranking*. However, much of what I say about ranking, and what it takes to have the authority to perform that act, will apply, *mutatis mutandis*, to the other components of subordination mentioned above.)

In the case of the South African legislator, the subordination also seems to depend on the legislator's authority, since it's clear that not everyone can enact a law by uttering the words "Blacks are no longer permitted to vote." And the same, it seems, must go for ordinary instances of racist hate speech. That is, if such speech is to constitute subordination, it seems that the speakers must occupy social positions that furnish them with the authority necessary to perform that act.

Of course, *some* hate speakers do occupy social positions that furnish them with authority. But many more—indeed, most—clearly don't. Consider the following examples.

Example 1: Subway rider
An Arab woman is on a subway car crowded with people. An older white man walks up to her, and says, "F★★★in' terrorist, go home. We don't need your kind here." He continues speaking in this manner to the woman, who doesn't respond. He speaks loudly enough that everyone else in the subway car hears his words

clearly. All other conversations cease. Many of the passengers turn to look at the speaker, but no one interferes.[18]

Example 2: Political activist
At a political rally convened to protest the government's policies, many activists bring home-made signs with political messages. One activist holds up a sign bearing the legend, "Don't forget to pay your taxes . . . 21 million illegal aliens are depending on you," above a picture of four grinning Hispanic-looking men saying, "¡Muchos gracias!" The sign is clearly visible to other protestors, as well as to the cameras assigned to cover the rally.[19]

Example 3: Cross-burner(s)
A working-class black family has recently moved into an overwhelmingly white and relatively well-to-do community. Through a variety of small gestures, their neighbors make it clear that they are not welcome in the community. One night, the family wakes up to find that a cross has been left burning on their front lawn. Whoever left the cross is long gone, so the family has no way to know who the culprits might be.[20]

There is, unfortunately, nothing unusual about such examples of hate speech. But in each case, the speaker seems to occupy no position of authority comparable to that of the South African legislator. In the first and second examples, the speaker is an ordinary man off the street, not occupying any social position that bestows upon him the power to determine where others rank in any social hierarchy. The third example is even more problematic in this regard, for there, the identity of the speaker(s) is unknown. But where the speaker(s) are unknown, it seems impossible that their speech would subordinate in virtue of their occupying positions of authority.

This is enough to set up the Authority Problem. Let us say that an 'ordinary instance' of racist hate speech is one that is produced by a speaker (or speakers) who occupy no generally recognized position of authority comparable to the South African legislator's. Most instances of racist hate speech, it is plausible to suppose, are ordinary instances. Then, if speech can constitute subordination only when the speaker occupies a position of authority in some relevant domain, it seems to follow that such ordinary instances cannot constitute subordination.

[18] This is based on an incident I recently experienced on a train in New Jersey. For discussion of a similar example, see McGowan this volume.

[19] For an image of the sign described in this example, see Fogiv 2010. Variations on this sign are to be found at several locations around the web.

[20] For the purposes of this chapter, I will regard the posting of the burning cross as *speech*, at least in the sense relevant to principles of free speech generally, and the First Amendment in particular. This is in keeping with current First Amendment jurisprudence. See, e.g., *R.A.V. v. St. Paul.*

Following Langton, we can distinguish two aspects of the Authority Problem.[21] The first aspect has to do with *whether*, and *how*, a particular speaker has the authority to constitute norms for others in the first place. That is, does the speaker have the authority to, for example, rank certain individuals as inferior to others, or to legitimate discriminatory behavior against them? If so, how do they come to have that authority? The second aspect has to do with the *scope* of the authority involved. That is, *for whom* can the speaker constitute norms? Call the first aspect the 'constitutive aspect' of the Authority Problem, and the second its 'jurisdictional aspect'.

For ordinary instances of racist hate speech, the constitutive aspect of the Authority Problem seems the most pressing. Given that hate speakers lack generally recognized positions of authority, it seems that they cannot constitute norms for anyone else at all. Accordingly, in what follows, I focus mostly on that aspect, returning only briefly to the jurisdictional aspect at the very end of the chapter (§ 7).

Before turning to responses to the Authority Problem, it will be useful to consider how that problem has been pressed against MacKinnon's (and Langton's) claim that *pornography* subordinates, for some of the same concerns carry over to the analogous claim about hate speech.[22] In the remainder of this section, I will briefly consider two attempts to raise the Authority Problem for pornography, the first due to Leslie Green, the second to Nancy Bauer.

Green argues that pornography is not authoritative (and so, cannot subordinate) in societies like ours in which it is "low-status speech," and its message (about women) is contradicted by the message conveyed by more high-status speech, e.g. the speech of "the state, the family, and the church."[23] What might Green mean by 'low-status speech'? One interpretation is suggested by the following passage.

In a society that respects freedom of expression, pornography receives no imprimatur: it is simply *tolerated* speech—permitted although disapproved. Many more people now use pornography than admit to it; it is not reviewed in the Sunday papers; and it is, still, able to elicit embarrassment, disgust, and shame. These are signs that pornography is, for us, low-status speech.[24]

This suggests that speech is low-status in Green's sense if most members of the society in which it occurs disapprove of it, even if they tolerate it. But

---

[21] Langton 1998, p. 264.

[22] For discussion of the Authority Problem as it arises for pornography, see the references in note 6.

[23] Green 1998, pp. 296–7.

[24] Green 1998, p. 297.

that interpretation makes it implausible that pornography is low-status speech, given its extraordinarily widespread sales and use.[25] Other related interpretations run into similar problems. For instance, if speech is to be low-status if most members of the society at least *publicly* disapprove of it, then again, it's not clear that pornography would count as low-status speech, since many are perfectly willing to admit to and discuss their use of pornography.

A different, and more promising, interpretation is that speech is low-status if it is uttered by *speakers* who occupy low social positions within the social hierarchy. On this interpretation, we do get a contrast between the speech of pornographers and the speech of those associated with high-status institutions like the state, the family, and the church.

On this interpretation, in arguing that pornography is not authoritative because it is low-status, Green draws a connection between the authoritativeness of speech and the social positions of the speakers. This is, I think, a widely shared view, that pornography—and other kinds of speech, including racist hate speech—cannot be authoritative because the speakers in question occupy relatively low social positions. Nevertheless, as I shall argue in the next section, this view should be rejected.

Turning next to Bauer, we find that she argues that pornography is not authoritative (and so, cannot legitimate violence against women, for example) because *nothing* can do this. On Bauer's view, if pornography did "authorize" its consumers to be violent towards women, then it would absolve them of responsibility for their actions.[26] If such a consumer then attempted to excuse violence against his girlfriend by citing pornography, we would have to accept his excuse.

What we want to say is that *nothing* could authorize what he has done. This is not just because what he has done is horrific. It's not even just because, at the end of the day, we are loath to absolve rapists of their crimes on the grounds that our society is insidiously or even explicitly rape-friendly. It's because no person or institution that is not formally invested with the authority has such authority apart from individuals' granting it to them—because we understand human beings of a certain age as bearing responsibility for the way they see the world.[27]

Bauer thus draws a connection between the authoritativeness of speech and its excusing or absolving those who do as it suggests. A similar argument might be made for ordinary instances of hate speech: since we

---

[25] Johnston 2007. Of course, it's possible that those who buy and use pornography largely disapprove of it, but that doesn't seem very plausible.

[26] Bauer 2006, pp. 86–7.

[27] Bauer 2006, p. 87.

would not accept such speech as an excuse for someone's violent or abusive behavior towards persons of color, that means that hate speech is also not authoritative. In the next section, I shall argue that this view should also be rejected.

4. Conditions of Authority

What, then, does it take for a speaker to have the authority to constitute norms for others? I'll approach this question by looking again at the circumstances of the South African legislator's speech act. Then, I'll consider what features of the legislator's situation must be shared by other speech in order for the latter to also be authoritative.

Here are some relevant aspects of the legislator's situation. First, the legislator has authority to do what he does in virtue of occupying a particular *social position*, more specifically, a political office. Anyone occupying that office would possess the same kind of authority. Call authority in virtue of one's own social position 'basic (positional) authority', or 'basic authority,' for short.[28]

Second, authority is granted to occupants of that political office *formally*, via provisions in the South African Constitution. That is, that Constitution explicitly creates that office, and explicitly designates to its occupants certain powers.

Third and fourth, the legislator himself comes to occupy that office as a result of certain *actions* of others, namely, their voting actions in some election, and for a *clearly demarcated period*, once again determined by the South African Constitution.

With these aspects of the legislator's situation in mind, let's consider some further cases of speaker authority. I take each of the following to be a *clear case* of a speaker coming to have authority (to assign tasks to others). Making it the case that someone else should perform a task is one way of constituting norms for that person. Thus, a speaker who has the authority to assign tasks to others is able to constitute (some) norms for them.

The first case shows that it's possible for a speaker to have the authority to assign tasks to others even when his own social position does not endow him with the authority to do so, i.e. even when he lacks basic authority to do this. Here's the case.

---

[28] The phrase 'positional authority' is borrowed from Tirrell unpublished. Strictly speaking, someone has basic authority over certain others to perform certain actions. Thus, for example, the legislator has basic authority over South Africans, to deprive (or grant) them the right to vote.

Example 4: Teacher's helper
An elementary school teacher asks the students in her classroom to complete a project. The project involves each of the students performing a different task. Just as the teacher is about to assign tasks to students, she is called out of the classroom. She calls on Amma, one of the students in the class, and tells her to divide up the tasks among her classmates while she (the teacher) is out of the classroom. Amma does so, assigning each classmate a particular task.

A teacher clearly has basic authority to perform any number of actions regarding students in her classroom, including ranking them, granting or depriving them of rights and powers, assigning them tasks, and so on. But no student has the authority to perform these actions with respect to their classmates in virtue of their own social position. In the example above, however, the teacher confers upon Amma the authority to assign responsibilities for certain tasks. The authority that Amma comes to have as a result of this conferral is not *basic* authority, for it isn't authority in virtue of her own social position. But it is still positional authority, for it is authority in virtue of *someone else's* social position, namely, the teacher's. Call such authority 'derived (positional) authority,' or 'derived authority,' for short.[29]

In the case just considered, Amma comes to have derived authority as a result of a discrete action of the teacher, namely, the teacher's telling Amma to divide up the tasks. But it's also possible for a speaker to come to have derived authority as a result of an *omission*, rather than an action. Consider a variation on the previous case.

Example 5: Bossy student
Again, an elementary school teacher sets the students in her classroom to complete a project. The project involves each of the students performing a different task. Arlo, one of the students, is eager to get started, and generally very bossy besides. In full view of the teacher, Arlo begins to divide up the tasks among his classmates. Some of Arlo's classmates take exception at being ordered around (again!) by Arlo. They groan, and turn to look at their teacher, clearly hoping that she will intervene. The teacher holds her peace, and does not interfere.

In this case, Arlo seems to end up with derived authority to assign tasks to his classmates, just as much as Amma did in Example 4. But here, Arlo comes to have derived authority not as a result of any action of the teacher's, but rather due to the teacher's failure to interfere when he (Arlo) takes over. That failure to interfere is an omission. Accordingly,

---

[29] As with basic authority, someone has derived authority over certain others to perform certain actions. See note 28.

Arlo's derived authority (to assign tasks to his classmates) owes to an omission, rather than an action.

Note a further feature of Arlo's case. There, as perhaps in most other cases where authority is derived via an omission, there is no *formal* or explicit granting of authority. In fact, coming to have authority (derived or otherwise) without there being any formal granting of authority is common enough. For example, though some of the authority that parents have with respect to their children is formally granted to them, via various social institutions, much parental authority is not. Similarly for the authority of religious officials, teachers, and so on.

The two cases just considered involved positional authority, i.e. authority in virtue of someone's social position. But a speaker can have authority even when it isn't *positional* authority. Consider two further cases.

Example 6: Hike organizer
A bunch of friends want to go on a hike on the coming weekend. They begin to discuss the logistics of the hike: where to go, for how long, what to bring, how to get there, and so on. Some in the group express mild preferences for one or another of the available options, but no one expresses strong preferences. The discussion goes on, and on. In fact, it continues for so long that one of the group, Andy, begins to be concerned that nothing will get organized. He decides to take over, and begins to make decisions. He assigns each of the other group members a specific task: one is to pick a location, another is to buy enough food for the group, a third is to find some tents, and so on. No one objects. Everyone completes their tasks, and the hike takes place as Andy planned.

Example 7: Traffic marshal
There is a terrible traffic accident on a highway. Some of the cars involved end up skewed across the road, blocking most traffic in either direction. There remains open one narrow lane. Emergency personnel are on their way, but will take some time to arrive. Realizing that something must be done, one driver, Agnes, gets out of her car and begins to direct traffic. She clears some space around the accident, lets through a few cars in one direction, and then a few more in the other direction. The other drivers follow her instructions. Alternating in this manner, traffic begins to move through the accident site.[30]

In these cases, Andy and Agnes come to have authority to assign tasks to their friends and fellow drivers, respectively. Their instructions, moreover, are authoritative speech. But neither Andy nor Agnes comes to have authority in virtue of social position, their own or anyone else's. So, their authority in these cases is not positional authority.

---

[30] This example is based on one mentioned, in a different context, by Jeremy Waldron at the 2010 Connections between Moral and Political Philosophy Workshop at the Center for Human Values at Princeton University.

Several further observations about these cases are in order here. First, neither Andy nor Agnes would have come to have authority if their audiences had refused to go along. If, for instance, Andy's friends had objected as he issued his first instruction, if they had made clear that they had no intention of doing as he said, or if they had told him that he had no business telling them what to do, then he would not have come to have any authority. When speaker authority depends on (relevant) others refraining from challenging the speech, I shall say that the speaker (and the speech) is 'licensed' by those others. In the cases above, Andy is licensed by his friends, and Agnes is licensed by her fellow drivers.[31] Their instructions are licensed speech.

In the two cases being considered here, what authority the speakers come to have is granted to them by their audiences. Licensing, then, can be regarded as a kind of *granting* of authority, or (to borrow a term from Nancy Bauer) as a kind of *authorizing*, of a speaker by relevant others. In Examples 6 and 7, the relevant others are the speakers' intended audiences.

Second, and relatedly, neither Andy nor Agnes has authority from the very beginning, that is, from the moment that each speaker begins to issue instructions. Consider, for instance, Andy's very first instruction. When he makes this first assignment, it is not yet clear that his friends won't challenge him. By contrast, by the time Andy gets to his fifth or sixth instruction, it is (we can assume) pretty clear that no one is going to object, and that everyone is planning to do as he says. Thus, it seems that Andy comes to have authority sometime after the first instruction is issued, though it would be difficult to say precisely when this happens.

Third, licensing does not require that the licensors *agree* with the licensee in any substantive sense. For example, Andy can come to have authority even if his friends harbor private reservations about the wisdom of his plans, or about the effectiveness of his organizing. As long as they don't make those reservations public, this is compatible with Andy's coming to have authority.

The two cases just considered are importantly different from the South African legislator's, and, for that matter, from Examples 4 and 5 (the teacher's helper and bossy student cases), considered earlier in this section. In all the earlier cases, speakers had authority in virtue of their social positions, whereas, as I've been emphasizing, neither Andy's nor Agnes's authority stems from their own, or anyone else's, social positions. As such, neither has positional authority, basic or derived.

---

[31] As with both basic and derived authority, someone is licensed to perform certain actions that affect certain others. See note 28.

In fact, and interestingly, neither Andy nor Agnes has any (relevant) authority *prior* to their speech acts at all. Again unlike the earlier cases, their speech isn't authoritative *because* they already possess authority over the relevant domains at the moment of speaking. Rather, if anything, the explanation runs in the opposite direction: what authority Andy and Agnes come to have is theirs *because* their speech is licensed.

As in Example 5 (the bossy student case), neither Andy's case nor Agnes's involves *formal* granting of authority. Also as in Example 5, both speakers come to have authority as a result of omissions on the part of others, namely, their intended audiences. Finally, at least Andy's authority might extend open-endedly into the future, for we can imagine that his friends begin to rely on him to organize all their future hikes as well.

At this point, we've seen several distinct ways in which speakers can come to have authority. In light of this discussion, let's return briefly to the points made by Leslie Green and Nancy Bauer (discussed at the end of § 3) against the claim that *pornography* can be authoritative speech. The cases considered in this section show those points to be wrongheaded.

First, Green argued that low-status speech—which we took to be speech uttered by those in low social positions—is not authoritative speech. But once we abandon the view that speech can only be authoritative in virtue of a speaker's *own* social position, there is no obstacle to low-status speech being authoritative. As illustrated in several of the cases above, even if a speaker occupies a low social position, he may nevertheless have derived authority or be licensed. If so, his speech may be authoritative in spite of his social position.

Second, Bauer argued that speech that fails to provide an excuse to those who do as it instructs is not authoritative. But as may be clear from the cases discussed above, authoritative speech needn't work this way. Suppose, for example, that Amma (in Example 4, the teacher's helper case) thinks that the best way to complete the project is to steal ideas from a different class group. Accordingly, she sets her classmates to spying on the other group. If her classmates do as she says, her speech may give them a reason for their behavior, but it falls well short of an excuse. When their teacher finds out what they've done, they are unlikely to avoid blame by pointing out that Amma authorized them to do this. *Contra* Bauer, authorizing her classmates to steal ideas (as Amma does) may spread the blame to her, but it doesn't absolve the authorized.

There is, of course, much more that can be said about each of the notions of authority—basic (positional) authority, derived (positional) authority, and licensing—considered in this section. But as we shall see in the next two sections, even the sketch I've provided above will allow us to use these notions to begin to fashion responses to the Authority Problem.

5. Derived Authority

In light of the discussion in the previous section, let's return now to the three ordinary instances of racist hate speech described in § 3. It is clear that the ordinary hate speakers in each of those cases lack *basic* authority. But that doesn't settle the question of whether they have authority (and so, are in a position to constitute norms for others), for it is compatible with lacking basic authority that they have derived authority, and/or their speech is licensed. In this section, focusing on a version of Example 3 (the cross-burner(s) case), I'll briefly describe what it would take for a hate speaker to have derived authority. Then, in the next section, I'll consider how a hate speaker might come to be licensed.

To see how the cross-burner(s) in Example 3 might end up with derived authority, we need to add some details to the case.

Example 3 (extended version)
A working-class black family has recently moved into an overwhelmingly white and relatively well-to-do community. Through a variety of small gestures, their neighbors make it clear that they are not welcome in the community. One night, the family wakes up to find that a cross has been left burning on their front lawn. Whoever left the cross is long gone, so the family has no way to know who the culprits might be. Now, in this community, it is quite clear who the leaders are, i.e. who in the community has the authority to make decisions about matters that affect the community, to legitimate certain kinds of behaviors within the community, and to sanction other kinds. This may be an official body, such as a town or village council, or some unofficial group, like the elders of the community. When the cross-burning is brought to their attention, those leaders say nothing to denounce the act, or those who committed it. They fail, moreover, to express sympathy for the family that has been thus victimized.

The message conveyed by a burning cross is, of course, a matter of debate.[32] Nevertheless, at a minimum, it seems that an act of cross-burning seeks to mark its targets as undesirables, as unwanted and unwelcome in the place in question, and in doing so, to rank those targets as inferior to non-targets. If ranking is indeed an authoritative illocution (as Langton suggests), then to succeed in ranking their targets, cross-burners must occupy positions of authority in the relevant domain.

---

[32] See, e.g., *Virginia v. Black* for some of that debate.

In (the extended version of) Example 3, the situation of the cross-burners seems strongly analogous to Arlo's situation in Example 5 (the bossy student case). Both Arlo and the cross-burners clearly lack basic authority. But in both cases, those who do have basic authority, and thus are in a position to criticize or otherwise disavow their actions, clearly and markedly fail to do so. In both cases, this omission confers derived authority, on Arlo in the earlier case, and on the cross-burners here.[33]

If the cross-burners have derived authority in this way, then they are in a position to rank their targets, and, for that matter, to perform other authoritative illocutions as well.

Of course, in many actual contexts, things will be much more complicated than they are in the case described above. Some of these complications will make it hard to decide, in a particular instance, whether cross-burners do indeed have derived authority. For example, it may be unclear, in a given case, who the leaders of the community are, what they have authority to do, whether they are aware of the incident in question, and whether (and to what extent) what they say about the incident counts as a denunciation of it.

Nevertheless, these complications do not vitiate the main point I wish to emphasize here, namely, that at least for some ordinary instances of racist hate speech, the constitutive aspect of the Authority Problem can be resolved in the manner suggested above.

The kind of account suggested here cannot stretch to cover the speaker in Example 1 (the subway rider case). That's because in the setting of Example 1, there is generally no one present with basic or derived authority over the relevant domain. If the speech in that case is authoritative, there must be some other kind of authority at work.

---

[33] The idea that government action (or inaction) can send a message that supports certain private speakers is a familiar one. For example, Laura Beth Nielsen suggests that the existence of anti-begging ordinances conveys support for those who would speak back against beggars (Nielsen this volume). More strongly, Matsuda has written that allowing "an organization [such as the KKK] known for violence, persecution, race hatred, and commitment to racial supremacy to exist openly and to provide police protection and access to public facilities, streets, and college campuses for such a group means that *the state is promoting racist speech*" (Matsuda 1993, p. 43, emphasis added). I am arguing in this section that, under certain circumstances, government inaction (or, more generally, inaction of those with basic authority) can function as a conferral of *authority* on private speakers. Note that my claim is weaker than Matsuda's, for conferring authority on others to do something is importantly different from doing it oneself.

6. Licensing

In this section, focusing on Example 1, I'll consider a second line of response to the Authority Problem. For this line of response, we will need to look briefly at how certain speech acts work, beginning with assertions.[34]

Imagine that you and I are discussing the next soccer World Cup. This conversation, like any other, takes place against a background of shared information. Some of this is information that we both know or believe, including that this is 2012, that we are both in New York City, that it's about four-thirty in the afternoon, and so on. But the shared background may also include information that is not believed by either of us, but merely *accepted* by us for the purposes of the conversation. For example, if our purpose is to consider the prospects of the English team in the World Cup, we might include in the shared background something that we know hasn't yet happened, namely, that the English team will qualify for the finals in Brazil. To accept this for the purposes of the conversation is not to *endorse* it, in the sense of believing it to be true, or even to take it to be likely, or plausible.

Next, consider what happens when an assertion is made. Suppose I say, "England won't make it past the quarterfinals in Brazil." Typically, if my assertion is accepted by all participants in the conversation, it will become part of the shared background for the remainder of the conversation. That will mean, among other things, that the background will have to be updated to remove anything that is incompatible with the content of what I've just asserted.[35]

Note that an assertion may be accepted for the purposes of a conversation (and so added to the shared background) even if participants don't *believe* its content. For example, you (my hearer) may accept my assertion even if you think England will make it past the quarterfinals, if, e.g., you

---

[34] The picture I sketch below is a *very* simplified version of Robert Stalnaker's account of how assertions work (Stalnaker 1978, 2002). Others have used David Lewis's work (especially the framework described in Lewis 1979) to think about how speech acts—and in particular, acts of producing pornography and racist hate speech—work, what they say, and how they implicitly enact norms. See especially Langton and West 1999, Langton this volume, and McGowan 2003, 2009, this volume. Though there are important differences between the Lewisian and Stalnakerian frameworks, I don't take those to be crucial here. Rather, my interest is in what follows from these accounts, in light of the discussion in § 4, for the question about what it takes for a speaker to have authority.

[35] To see how this updating might work, see Stalnaker 1978.

would like to discuss the consequences of England losing in an early round.

But, of course, you needn't accept my assertion. You can challenge it (e.g. "Why not? They've improved a lot in the past couple of years") or reject it outright ("You're wrong! They're going to win it all this time"). If my assertion is rejected, I will still have asserted something, but the content of my assertion won't be added to the shared background.

What I've said thus far adds up to a simple and attractive picture of assertion. On this picture, we might say that the 'essential aim' of assertions is to make a difference of a particular kind to the shared background for a conversation, namely, to add its content to the shared background, and so to eliminate all possibilities incompatible with that content.

In principle, this picture can be extended to cover speech acts other than assertions. Consider, for example, the act of ranking. Rankings are related to assertions, in that a speaker can perform a ranking just *by* asserting something.[36] In fact, the very utterance that I used to introduce this picture—my saying "England won't make it past the quarterfinals in Brazil"—is one which, if accepted, *ranks* England lower than the eventual winner of the 2014 World Cup, whichever team that might be.[37]

The picture sketched above can be extended to cover rankings as follows. We can say that a ranking, just like an assertion, seeks to add its content to the shared background of the conversation. If none of the participants to the conversation objects, the content may be added. That means that the background must be updated to eliminate all possibilities incompatible with that content.[38] The ranking then becomes part of that shared background for the remainder of the conversation.

---

[36] I am here endorsing a kind of speech act pluralism, according to which a speaker can perform several distinct speech acts (such as asserting and ranking) by producing one utterance. For a recent and influential defense of (one version of) speech act pluralism, see Cappelen and Lepore 2005.

[37] There is, however, an important difference between assertions and rankings that is illustrated by the following example. Imagine a group of school friends, among whom there is no generally recognized leader. One day, one of the members of the group, Algy, tells another member, Zeno, "You're no longer welcome to hang out with us." If others in the group don't object to Algy's utterance, and moreover, begin to exclude Zeno because of what Algy has said, then it seems that Algy has both asserted that Zeno is no longer welcome, and ranked Zeno as an outsider. If, however, others in the group *do* object to Algy's utterance ("You can't say that to him!"), Algy *still* manages to assert that Zeno is no longer welcome, but doesn't seem to manage to rank Zeno as he intends. Thus, a speaker asserts something even when the assertion is challenged or rejected by his audience. But, at least in some cases (like the one just described), ranking something requires lack of challenge on the part of the audience.

[38] There are two tricky aspects to extending this picture of how assertions work to cover other speech acts, like rankings. One has to do with how to understand the *contents* of these

So far, so good. But this brings us to an important question. On the picture just sketched, are rankings still authoritative illocutions, as Langton had suggested? After all, in the case above, it did not seem that I needed any special authority to rank England lower than the eventual World Cup winner. For instance, it was not necessary that I be recognized as an expert on soccer. That seems to suggest that, on this picture, rankings are not authoritative illocutions.

We need to proceed carefully here. First, what happens in the case above (in which I rank England) seems strongly analogous to what happened in Examples 6 and 7 (the hike organizer and traffic marshal cases) in § 4. In all of these cases, the speaker lacks relevant positional authority. However, in each case, it is open to the audience in the case (Andy's friends, Agnes's fellow drivers, you) to object to or challenge the speaker's intended speech act. In all these cases, the failures on the parts of the audiences to do so licenses, and so, grants authority to, the speakers. Because of that licensing, the speakers are in a position to perform their intended acts.

Against this, it may be objected that the analogy between the earlier cases and my ranking England is not as strong as I have suggested. In the earlier cases, it might be said, Andy and Agnes came to have authority because others *acted on* their instructions. If, for instance, none of Agnes's fellow drivers in Example 7 had moved as she directed, then she couldn't be said to have any authority. By contrast, when I rank England, you don't act on my ranking. Therefore, so the objection goes, the analogy fails.

But *contra* this objection, if you do accept my ranking, you will be acting on it, in several ways. Most fundamentally, you will update your own beliefs about what has happened in the conversation thus far. You may also update your beliefs about my beliefs and other mental states. You may even decide to cancel the England shirt you had been planning to buy me as a present. All of these are ways of acting on my ranking.

Further, the notion of 'acting on' used in this objection is itself problematic. If, for example, Andy's friends in Example 6 do *some* (but not all) of what he instructs them to do, or if they perform tasks similar to (but not the same as) what he instructs them to do, have they acted on his

other acts, and the other has to do with how the updating of the shared background would work. Stalnaker understands the contents of assertions as sets of possible worlds, and updating as intersection of sets (Stalnaker 1978). But rankings, unlike assertions, purport not (merely) to describe the world, but to constitute norms. Whether this means that contents of rankings must be given a different treatment than contents of assertions I'll leave as an open question here. As long as the former can be thought of as sets of some kind (whether they be sets of worlds, or of world-norm pairs, or something else), updating can still involve intersection of sets. However, these technical details don't matter for my purposes in this chapter.

instructions? Nor is it clear that acting on these instructions is really necessary to Andy's (or Agnes's) coming to have authority. If, for instance, Andy's friends form the intention to act on his instructions, but are prevented from doing so by some unforeseen and catastrophic event, that might still be compatible with Andy's having authority in the case.

In light of these concerns, suppose we now put aside this objection, and grant that there *is* a strong analogy between the case in which I rank England and Examples 6 and 7. If my ranking depends on licensing, as this analogy suggests, and licensing is the granting of authority to the speaker, then my ranking depends on my being granted authority. Then, on this picture, ranking still seems to require authority.[39]

But next, recall (from § 3) that Langton characterized authoritative illocutions as "actions whose felicity conditions require that the speaker occupy *a position of authority* in a relevant domain."[40] Note that when a speaker is licensed, as in Examples 6 and 7, they may come to have authority, but they need not come to occupy a *position* of authority. In Example 6, for instance, the licensing invests *Andy* with authority. It does not invest authority in whoever occupies some given position. Therefore, if licensing is sufficient for ranking, then ranking isn't an authoritative illocution in Langton's sense, for ranking doesn't require that the speaker occupy a position of authority at all.

Nevertheless, even on the current picture, rankings are clearly closely related to authoritative illocutions in Langton's sense. That's because, on this picture, rankings still require that the speaker *have* authority in some relevant domain. However, as we've seen above, having authority isn't the same as occupying a position of authority.

Finally, much of what I've said about rankings here will also apply to other acts that are often thought to be authoritative illocutions, such as ordering. As with ranking, a speaker who lacks relevant positional authority can still succeed in ordering another, via licensing. It is an interesting question whether there are any illocutionary acts that require not merely authority, but *positional* authority, but I shall not pursue that question here.

We now have a picture of how rankings work, and we have seen that licensing can suffice for ranking. With this in mind, let's return to Example 1. Here's the case, once again.

---

[39] This is not to say that, on this picture, *all* illocutionary acts require authority on the part of the speaker. Consider assertion, for instance. As noted above (in note 37), a speaker can manage to assert something even if her assertion is challenged. So, assertions can be made even when they are not licensed. The same may be true of many other speech acts, such as suppositions, suggestions, warnings, and so on.

[40] Langton 1993, p. 305, emphasis added.

Example 1: Subway rider
An Arab woman is on a subway car crowded with people. An older white man walks up to her, and says, "F★★★in' terrorist, go home. We don't need your kind here." He continues speaking in this manner to the woman, who doesn't respond. He speaks loudly enough that everyone else in the subway car hears his words clearly. All other conversations cease. Many of the passengers turn to look at the speaker, but no one interferes.

In this case, all the passengers in the subway car can hear what the hate speaker has to say. Further, each passenger is aware that all the other passengers can hear the hate speaker as well. Under these circumstances, we can think of the passengers as (unwilling) participants in one conversation.

This conversation is one in which the speaker aims to mark his target as a terrorist and an undesirable, and in so doing, to rank her as inferior to others. No one challenges the speaker's claims. In light of the recent discussion, we can think of this failure as a licensing. Since licensing is sufficient for ranking, the speaker in this case succeeds in ranking his target as inferior.

It will be useful to consider some objections to what I have just argued. First, it may be objected that it's not right to regard all the passengers in the subway car as engaged in one conversation. Typically, in such settings, passengers are engaged in several distinct conversations, not in one car-wide conversation.

It is, of course, true that in a typical subway car, there are many ongoing conversations. But that isn't an impediment to there (sometimes) also being a car-wide conversation. After all, each person can be engaged in more than one conversation at once. Moreover, as we're all aware, whether we're drawn into a conversation isn't always up to us. Anyone can be pulled into a conversation that they would very much rather not be a part of.

Further, the main point I want to make here is that *sometimes*, a hate speaker can perform a ranking in the manner described above. Nothing I say requires that every subway car have a car-wide conversation. And, as far as I can tell, there is no reason to insist that such car-wide conversations are impossible.

This is not to deny that in some settings, it will be difficult to tell whether, and to what extent, there is a conversation in the relevant sense. Compare, for instance, the case above with Example 2 (the political activist case) from § 3. In the latter case, an activist holds a sign in a political rally, in full view of the other protesters. But especially in a sizeable rally, unlike in the (relatively enclosed) setting of a subway car, it will be much more difficult to tell who is aware of the sign in question. The kind of mutual awareness (of the fact that a speaker is speaking, and that other participants are aware of what he is saying) that characterizes a typical conversation may well be missing in such a setting.

Next, it may be objected that the case above (Example 1) differs from Examples 6 and 7 (the hike organizer and traffic marshal cases) in § 4 in that in the current case, there is no coordination problem that requires solution. It is only because there is such a problem in each of the earlier cases that the person who steps up to solve the problem ends up invested with authority. Given that that there is no such problem to be solved in Example 1, there is no granting of authority to the hate speaker.

But *contra* this objection, *any* conversation can be regarded as a coordination problem, at least in an extended sense (Lewis 1969). What this 'extended sense' amounts to is a hard question, and beyond the scope of the current discussion. For current purposes, it will suffice to note that there is reason to reject the disanalogy suggested in the objection above.

Finally, it may also be objected that silence on the part of the other subway passengers doesn't mean that they *agree* with the hate speaker's intended ranking, or with anything else he intends to convey. Therefore, silence shouldn't be regarded as a granting of authority to the hate speaker.

But here again, recall the discussion of Examples 6 and 7 (the hike organizer and traffic marshal cases) from § 4. As noted there, Andy and Agnes can end up with authority even if their friends and fellow drivers, respectively, have reservations about what they say, as long as they fail to share those reservations. The same holds true here. Even if the hate speaker's fellow passengers have strong reservations about what he says to the woman he targets, as long as they fail to speak up, the speaker can end up with authority.

This point has an important consequence. If staying silent in the setting of Example 1 licenses the hate speaker, then it seems to follow that the other passengers have some moral obligation to speak up. To put the point in other (and stronger) terms, if I am right about licensing here, then in staying silent, the other passengers are, to some extent, *complicit* in what the hate speaker does.

As in other instances of moral obligation, there may be considerations that tell against fulfilling the obligation, such as concern for personal safety. I'll leave as an open question whether such conflicting considerations override the moral obligation.

Against this, it may be objected that the other subway passengers shouldn't be blamed for having the bad luck to board a subway car with an abusive person. But arguably, it's possible for an agent to have moral obligations that they wouldn't have had if their circumstances had been different.[41]

Additionally, it is worth recalling here Matsuda's point (mentioned in § 2) that one of the harms of hate speech is that it divides targets from even 'right-thinking' members of the hate speaker's group. The account in this section captures one way in which this can happen. By putting the other passengers in the position of either licensing the abuse or risking (at least) drawing fire towards themselves, the hate speaker puts them in a double bind. At the same time, he puts his target in the position of wondering whether the other passengers agree with what he is saying to and about her. In doing these things, the hate speaker creates a situation in which his target and the other passengers are effectively divided from each other.

7. Conclusion

As we've seen, the Authority Problem, in both its constitutive and jurisdictional aspects, has been taken to pose a significant challenge to the claim that ordinary speech can constitute subordination. I have been arguing in this chapter that this is partly due to an unnecessarily impoverished view about speaker authority. Focusing on the constitutive aspect, I've presented a series of examples in which speakers come to have authority despite not occupying any exalted social position. Then, relying on analogies with some of these clear cases, I've sketched two ways of responding to the Authority Problem. On the first line of response, some ordinary hate speakers can constitute subordination via their hate speech in virtue of their coming to have derived (positional) authority, i.e. authority derived from someone else's basic (positional) authority. On the second line of response, some ordinary hate speakers can constitute subordination via their hate speech in virtue of being licensed by their audiences.

Each line of response suggests fairly natural answers to the jurisdictional aspect of the problem. In the first case, it is natural to say that the derived authority cannot have greater jurisdiction than that of the basic authority from which it is derived. In the second case, it is natural to say that the jurisdiction extends only to the parties to the conversation, and no farther. Accordingly, I have not argued that any ordinary instance of racist hate speech (directly) subordinates all people of color. Nevertheless, in a society in which racist hate speech is prevalent, the overlapping jurisdictions of various instances of such speech will be such as to reinforce the

---

[41] For more on moral luck generally, and circumstantial luck specifically, see Nagel 1979.

subordination that each instance separately contributes, and to thus pervade the lives of people of color.

As mentioned at the outset, this chapter is only one part of a larger exploration of what it takes for speakers (and agents more generally) to have authority. The larger project would consider both further questions about the notions of authority considered above, as well as questions about how those notions relate to other notions of authority. These questions include, among others, how the notions of authority considered above relate to what are sometimes called 'epistemic authority' (roughly, authority in virtue of being, or being considered, knowledgeable) and 'linguistic authority' (roughly, authority in virtue of being an author);[42] whether the latter are also non-positional notions of authority; and what becomes of the distinction between authority and social power once we recognize all these rather diffuse notions of authority. Only when we have answers to these questions will we have a full grasp of the different ways in which ordinary speakers can constitute norms for others, and (sometimes) thereby subordinate them.

References

Austin, J. L. 1975. *How to Do Things with Words*, 2nd edition, J. O. Urmson and M. Sbisá (eds.). Cambridge, MA: Harvard University Press.

Bauer, N. 2006. "How to Do Things with Pornography," in S. Shieh and A. Crary (eds.), *Reading Cavell*, 68–97. London: Routledge.

Butler, J. 1998. *Excitable Speech: A Politics of the Performative*. New York: Routledge.

Cappelen, H. and E. Lepore 2005. *Insensitive Semantics: A Defense of Semantic Minimalism and Speech Act Pluralism*. Oxford: Blackwell.

Delgado, R. 1993. "Words that Wound: A Tort Action for Racial Insults, Epithets, and Name Calling," in M. Matsuda, C. R. Lawrence III, R. Delgado, and K. Crenshaw (eds.), *Words that Wound: Critical Race Theory, Assaultive Speech, and the First Amendment*, 89–110. Boulder, CO: Westview Press.

Fogiv. 2010. "Racebook: Hate at the World's Most Popular Social Network." www.dailykos.com: *Daily Kos*. Available at URL = <http://www.dailykos.com/story/2010/03/07/843911/-Racebook:-Hate-at-the-Webs-Most-Popular-Social-Network>.

Green, L. 1998. "Pornographizing, Subordinating, and Silencing," in R. C. Post (ed.), *Censorship and Silencing: Practices of Cultural Regulation*, 285–311. Los Angeles, CA: Getty Research Institute for the History of Art and the Humanities.

---

[42] For discussions of linguistic authority, see Bauer 2006 and Wieland 2007.

Johnston, D. C. 2007. "Indications of a Slowdown in Sex Entertainment Trade." *New York Times*, 4 January 2007. Available at URL = <http://www .nytimes. com/2007/01/04/business/media/04porn.html>.

Langton, R. 1993. "Speech Acts and Unspeakable Acts." *Philosophy & Public Affairs* 22 (4): 293–330.

Langton, R. 1998. "Subordination, Silence, and Pornography's Authority," in R. C. Post (ed.), *Censorship and Silencing: Practices of Cultural Regulation*, 261–83. Los Angeles, CA: Getty Research Institute for the History of Art and the Humanities.

Langton, R. This volume. "Beyond Belief: Pragmatics in Hate Speech and Pornography."

Langton, R. and C. West. 1999. "Scorekeeping in a Pornographic Language Game," *Australasian Journal of Philosophy* 77: 303–19.

Lawrence, C. R., III. 1992. "Crossburning and the Sound of Silence: Antisubordination and the First Amendment," *Villanova Law Review* 37 (4): 787–804.

Lawrence, C. R., III. 1993. "If He Hollers, Let Him Go: Regulating Racist Speech on Campus," in M. Matsuda, C. R. Lawrence III, R. Delgado, and K. Crenshaw (eds.), *Words that Wound: Critical Race Theory, Assaultive Speech, and the First Amendment*, 52–88. Boulder, CO: Westview Press.

Lewis, D. 1969. *Convention*. Cambridge, MA: Harvard University Press.

Lewis, D. 1979. "Scorekeeping in a Language Game," *Journal of Philosophical Logic* 8 (3): 339–59.

MacKinnon, C. 1987. *Feminism Unmodified: Discourses on Life and Law*. Cambridge, MA: Harvard University Press.

MacKinnon, C. 1993. *Only Words*. Cambridge, MA: Harvard University Press.

Maitra, I. 2009. "Silencing Speech," *Canadian Journal of Philosophy* 39 (2): 309–38.

Maitra, I. Forthcoming. "Subordination and Objectification," *Journal of Moral Philosophy*.

Maitra, I. and M. K. McGowan. 2010. "On Racist Hate Speech and the Scope of a Free Speech Principle," *Canadian Journal of Law and Jurisprudence* 23 (2): 343–72.

Matsuda, M. 1993. "Public Response to Racist Speech: Considering the Victim's Story," in M. Matsuda, C. R. Lawrence III, R. Delgado, and K. Crenshaw (eds.), *Words that Wound: Critical Race Theory, Assaultive Speech, and the First Amendment*, 17–51. Boulder, CO: Westview Press.

McGowan, M. K. 2003. "Conversational Exercitives and the Force of Pornography," *Philosophy & Public Affairs* 31 (2): 155–89.

McGowan, M. K. 2009. "Oppressive Speech," *Australasian Journal of Philosophy* 87 (3): 389–407.

McGowan, M. K. This volume. "On 'Whites Only' Signs and Racist Hate Speech: Verbal Acts of Racial Discrimination."

Nagel, T. 1979. *Mortal Questions*. New York: Cambridge University Press.

Nielsen, L. B. This volume. "Power in Public: Reactions, Responses, and Resistance to Offensive Public Speech."

Stalnaker, R. 1978. "Assertion," in P. Cole (ed.), *Syntax and Semantics* 9. New York: Academic Press, 315–32.

Stalnaker, R. 2002. "Common Ground," *Linguistics and Philosophy* 25: 701–21.

R.A.V. v. City of St. Paul. 505 U.S. 377 (1992).

Sumner, L.W. 2004. *The Hateful and the Obscene: Studies in the Limits of Free Expression*. Toronto: University of Toronto Press.

Tirrell, L. Unpublished. "Authority and Gender: Flipping the F-Switch," paper delivered at 2010 American Philosophical Association Eastern Division Meeting, Boston, MA.

Virginia v. Black. 538 U.S. 343 (2003).

Wieland, N. 2007. "Linguistic Authority and Convention in a Speech Act Analysis of Pornography," *Australasian Journal of Philosophy* 85 (3): 435–56.

On 'Whites Only' Signs and Racist Hate Speech: Verbal Acts of Racial Discrimination[1]

Mary Kate McGowan

Imagine that an African American man boards a public bus on which all the other passengers are white. Unhappy with the newcomer, an elderly white man turns to the African American man and says, "Just so you know, because I realize that your kind are not very bright, we don't like niggers around here,...boy. So, go back to Africa...so you can keep killing each other...and do the world a favor!

1. Introduction

Although virtually everyone would deeply disapprove of what this elderly white man said, most would nevertheless defend his right to say it. After all, the First Amendment guarantees the right to free speech. Although speech can be false, impolite, offensive or even harmful (and the elderly white man's utterance is all of these things), we cannot really trust the government to decide what should and should not be said. To allow the government such control over us would clearly cause more harm than it would prevent. Consequently, our commitment to free speech seems to require granting the elderly white man (and others like him) the right to utter even such hateful racist speech.[2] Or, so goes the all too familiar liberal defense of racist hate speech.

---

[1] I thank Catharine MacKinnon and Ishani Maitra for helpful comments on an earlier draft of this chapter and I thank Fred Schauer for helpful discussions about these topics.

[2] Of course, some racist hate speech is already regulated, but such "fighting words" (*Chaplinsky v. New Hampshire*) are identified in terms of their *causal* effects. I am interested, by contrast, in racist hate speech that *constitutes* discrimination. For a discussion of problems with the fighting words doctrine, see Greenawalt 1995.

An additional reason to think that racist hate speech should not be regulated is that it (often) expresses a political opinion. Since a commitment to free speech is deeply incompatible with allowing the government to regulate the expression of political opinions, it seems that one cost of valuing free speech is the mandatory toleration of hateful speech. Thus, although racist hate speech conflicts with other deeply held liberal values (e.g. equality), our commitment to free speech nevertheless appears to require its toleration.

In this paper, I argue against this standard liberal defense of racist hate speech and I do so on at least two fronts. For starters, I reject the above conception of political speech. As we shall see, speech is complex in its functioning. Utterances often do several different things at once. As a result, the mere fact that an utterance expresses a political opinion cannot reasonably be treated as a sufficient condition of that utterance being political speech in the First Amendment sense (since that utterance may well do plenty of other things in addition). Thus, the mere fact that racist hate speech expresses a political opinion is not sufficient reason to view it as highly protected political expression.

I also take issue with the 'balancing of harms' approach implicit in the standard liberal defense. As one can see, according to the standard liberal approach, the harms *caused* by racist hate speech are outweighed by the harms that would be *caused* (to our system of free speech) were we to regulate it. Clearly, the focus is on the harms caused. My strategy here is importantly different. Rather than focus on the alleged harms caused by such speech, I instead focus on what the speech in question does (illocutionarily or otherwise).

Since this distinction (between the causal effects of an utterance and the acts actually constituted by it) is unfamiliar to many, an example may help. Consider apologies. Some speech causes apologies. When I said, "Gee, snugglebucket, when you called me a big fat cow, you kinda hurt my feelings," I caused my husband, Mike, to apologize. Contrast that with Mike's response: "I apologize for calling you a big fat cow." Mike's utterance constitutes the (illocutionary) act of apologizing. It doesn't merely cause an apology. It is one. Rather than focus on the causal effects of racist hate speech (as the standard liberal defense does), I focus instead on the actions constituted by such speech. In particular, I argue that some racist hate speech ought to be regulated because it constitutes an (otherwise illegal) act of racial discrimination.[3]

---

[3] First, not all acts of racial discrimination are illegal. It is perfectly legal, for example, to enact a racially discriminatory policy for one's own household. Second, I say that these acts of racial discrimination are *otherwise* illegal since the law currently does not regard them as such. I henceforth drop this qualification.

My strategy here (to extend anti-discrimination law) is familiar from, and owes much to, the work of Catharine MacKinnon. See, e.g., "Francis Biddle's Sister: Pornography, Civil Rights and Speech," 1987 and *Only Words*, 1993, where she also discusses racist hate speech.

Given the above, it should be no surprise that I also disagree with the above assessment of the elderly white man's utterance. As we shall see, even though this utterance expresses a political opinion, it should not count as political speech on my view. Moreover, I will argue that there is a compelling case to be made for the claim that this utterance ought to be regulated (under some circumstances anyway) because it does precisely what a 'Whites Only' sign does, i.e. it constitutes an illegal act of racial discrimination.[4] According to my analysis, the elderly white man's utterance is akin to an employer verbally enacting a discriminatory hiring policy. Suppose, for example, that the boss declares to his Human Resources Department, "From now on, we don't hire blacks. They're just too damn lazy." In so far as this utterance enacts a discriminatory policy, it is an illegal act of racial discrimination. In what follows, I argue that the elderly white man's utterance may well do the same thing and thus that it may well deserve to be illegal for the very same reasons.

The paper proceeds as follows. In § 2, some background on free speech theory is presented. Because an analogy with 'Whites Only' signs plays such an important role in the argument, a detailed discussion of the precise linguistic functioning of such signs is presented in § 3. Appealing to speech act theory, it is there demonstrated that 'Whites Only' signs constitute illegal acts of racial discrimination in virtue of enacting racially discriminatory permissibility facts in some (public) realm. Since a certain type of speech act (i.e. the exercitive) enacts permissibility facts, the focus here will be on exercitive speech. In § 4, the first model of exercitive speech (the standard exercitive) is presented. In § 5, the hypothesis that the elderly white man's utterance is a standard exercitive that does what a 'Whites Only' sign does (that is, enact racially discriminatory permissibility facts in some public realm) is explored and shown to be problematic. In § 6, a second model of exercitive speech (the covert exercitive) is presented and, in § 7, this model is applied to the case of the elderly white man's utterance. Here the case is made that the elderly white man's utterance may well do what a 'Whites Only' sign does. In § 8, yet another hypothesis (i.e. that the elderly white man's utterance is both a standard and a covert

---

Some critical race theorists have also argued that (some) racist hate speech constitutes acts of racial subordination. See, e.g., Lawrence 1993 and Matsuda 1993.

[4] MacKinnon was the first to point out that 'Whites Only' signs are *speech*; they are speech that constitutes discrimination and they are legally regarded as such. See her "Francis Biddle's Sister: Pornography, Civil Rights, and Speech": 194. See also her "Pornography: On Morality and Politics," 1989: 206 and her *Only Words*, 1993: 13. Lawrence also uses this example in his "If He Hollers Let Him Go: Regulating Racist Speech on Campus": 61–2.

exercitive) is explored and, in § 9, potential legal consequences are discussed. Various clarifications and objections are considered along the way.

2. Background on Free Speech

Free speech theory is not nearly as straightforward as one might suppose. Although contemporary American society fully embraces a free speech principle, that does *not* mean that we are free to say whatever we please. Plenty of speech is already regulated. What the First Amendment does, essentially, is shield speech from regulation by making it considerably more difficult to regulate. This is accomplished by requiring that the justifications for regulating speech meet raised standards of scrutiny.[5] Thus, although the First Amendment makes it especially difficult to regulate speech, it does not make it impossible. There are several well-known 'exceptions' to free speech. Defamation, for example, is one such exception. The reasons for regulating it are so powerful that they meet the raised standards of scrutiny relevant to the First Amendment. When this is the case (i.e. when the justifications for regulating a category of speech meet the raised standards), I shall say, following Schauer, that the speech in question is *unprotected*.[6]

Another category of regulated speech is not even considered 'speech' for the purposes of the First Amendment.[7] The regulation of such utterances is not subject to the raised standards of scrutiny relevant to the First Amendment. Such utterances are as regulable as any other non-speech action. Suppose, for example, that Sam verbally hires an assassin by saying (seriously and sincerely) to a known assassin, "I'll pay you $25,000 to kill my boss and hide his body so that the bastard is never found." When Sam says this, he is soliciting a crime and he is, therefore, breaking the law. Although his crime involves only the uttering of words, Sam cannot reasonably appeal to free speech in defending his behavior. This is because Sam's utterance is not even within the scope of a free speech principle. When an utterance is not even within the scope of the First Amendment,

---

[5] Different categories of covered speech are subject to different levels of raised scrutiny. So-called 'low value' speech (e.g. some commercial speech) is subject to lower standards than so-called 'political speech'. For a helpful discussion of this distinction, see Brink 2001: 119–57.

[6] This view of free speech doctrine is somewhat controversial. For an extensive motivation and defense of it, see Schauer 1982 and Schauer 2004: 2417–61. See also, Maitra and McGowan 2007: 41–68.

[7] It is an open and interesting question what makes something speech in the technical First Amendment sense. For a discussion of this question, see Greenawalt 1989 and Maitra and McGowan 2007: 41–68.

I shall say (again following Schauer) that the speech in question is *uncovered* by the First Amendment.[8]

As we shall see, 'Whites Only' signs are uncovered and they are uncovered because of what they do (i.e. constitute an illegal act of racial discrimination by enacting racially discriminatory permissibility facts in some public realm). Thus, if some racist hate speech does the same, it ought to be treated the same by the law. Therefore, if my argument here is successful, some racist hate speech is not even within the scope of a free speech principle and thus is a far cry from the status of highly protected political speech it is so routinely presumed to have.

3. 'Whites Only' Signs

Jimmy, a good old boy in the segregated South, hangs a sign in his restaurant that reads: 'Whites Only'. The hanging of this sign enacts a segregatory (and hence discriminatory) policy for his restaurant. What Jimmy does by hanging this sign is relevantly similar to what the boss does when he says (seriously and sincerely) to his hiring department, "From now on, we only hire whites." The boss's utterance puts a discriminatory hiring policy in place and is hence an act of discrimination. Because the hanging of the sign enacts a discriminatory policy for Jimmy's restaurant, the hanging of the sign is also an act of discrimination.[9]

Notice that although Jimmy and the boss are enacting policy (for their respective establishments), they are not thereby enacting law. When the boss said what he said, he thereby made it against company policy to hire non-whites, but he did not make it illegal to do so. This should not be a surprise since, after all, the boss does not have the power (or authority) to enact law. Moreover, the enacting of this discriminatory hiring policy is explicitly against the law (which is what makes the boss's utterance an *illegal* act of discrimination). The situation is similar with respect to Jimmy's posting of the 'Whites Only' sign. When he posted that sign, he enacted a policy for his restaurant and since the enacting of this segregatory policy is against the law, so too is the posting of the sign that enacts it.

Notice that, although the boss's utterance is speech in the ordinary sense, the regulation of this (sort of) utterance raises no free speech concerns at all. Since such utterances constitute acts of discrimination, they do not count as speech in the technical sense of the First Amendment. They are, and ought to be, entirely outside the scope of a free speech principle. Thus, in the terminology of the preceding section, such utterances

---

[8] Schauer 1982.   [9] See fn. 4.

are uncovered by the First Amendment. Since the posting of a 'Whites Only' sign also constitutes an act of discrimination, this too is uncovered by the First Amendment. As a result, the regulation of such signs raises no First Amendment concerns whatsoever. Moreover, this is as it should be. After all, neither Jimmy nor the boss ought to be able to appeal to the First Amendment in defending their behavior.

Although Jimmy clearly and forcefully expressed a political message when he posted the 'Whites Only' sign, the posting of that sign nevertheless is, and ought to be, outside the scope of a free speech principle. Thus, expressing a political message is not only *not* a sufficient condition for being highly protected political speech, it is not even a sufficient condition for being speech in the technical sense of the First Amendment. Consequently, the mere fact that racist hate speech expresses a political message is insufficient reason to view it as highly protected political speech. It's not even sufficient reason to view it as covered (that is, as within the scope of a free speech principle). Thus, if at least some racist hate speech is uncovered, then that subset of racist hate speech is not deserving of the special protections afforded by the First Amendment as the standard liberal defense tacitly assumes.

I have here argued that the posting of a 'Whites Only' sign is an illegal act of discrimination and this can be so even in cases where the sign is posted by someone other than the proprietor. Suppose, for example, that a certain regular at a certain establishment posts such a sign. So long as the proprietor is aware that the sign has been posted and does not remove it, the law will regard the posting of the sign as an illegal act of discrimination.[10] Moreover, this is also as it should be. After all, a racist proprietor should not be able to circumvent the law by arranging for a customer to post such a discriminatory sign on the proprietor's behalf.

Obviously, who posts the sign matters. If a misguided Aryan youth posts such a sign at the local coffee shop and it is immediately torn down by outraged patrons, no discriminatory policy is thereby enacted. When the proprietor posts such a sign, by contrast, the situation is quite different. Supposing that the proprietor is instituting new policy for his establishment, he commits a discriminatory act by posting such a sign.

When thinking about how one institutes discriminatory policies, it is helpful to appeal to the tools of speech act theory. Consider again the boss's verbal enacting of a discriminatory hiring policy. When the boss said, "From now on, we only hire whites," the boss performed what is

---

[10] I am here indebted to Fred Schauer.

called an exercitive speech act. Exercitive speech acts enact permissibility facts in some realm. In this case, the boss enacted permissibility facts for his employees, thereby making it impermissible (that is, against company policy) for them to hire non-whites. Because the permissibility facts enacted are of a certain sort (that is, they constitute an illegal discriminatory act), the utterance that enacts them is illegal too. The posting of the 'Whites Only' sign functions in the same way. It enacts permissibility facts for Jimmy's restaurant and those permissibility facts are discrimina-tory. Since the posting of the sign enacts those permissibility facts, the posting of the sign is an illegal act of discrimination.

3.1. *Clarifications and Potential Objections*

First, a rather obvious clarification. What the posting of a 'Whites Only' sign does depends on various contextual factors. Posting such a sign in a laundromat, for example, may well enact permissibility facts for that establishment, but if it merely renders it impermissible (or inadvisable) for patrons to wash non-white clothes, in a washing machine with an automatic bleach cycle, then the permissibility facts enacted are not dis-criminatory in the relevant sense. (It is also worth mentioning that, in such a case, 'whites' does not refer to members of a race.) Similarly, a curator at a museum may post such a sign as part of an exhibit of Americana and an historian may post such a sign as a reminder of our ugly past. In each of these cases, no discriminatory permissibility facts are enacted by the posting of the sign, thus no illegal act is committed by the posting of the sign. The posting of such a sign is illegal only when the posting of such signs constitutes an illegal act (of discrimination) and whether the hanging of such a sign does so depends on various contextual factors. Thus, I am certainly not committed to the highly implausible view that the law prohibits the hanging of *all* 'Whites Only' signage.

Second, one might think that the posting of the sign cannot enact the relevant permissibility facts in a context where segregation is explicitly illegal, but to think so is to confuse different sorts of permissibility facts with one another. It is prudent to keep in mind that there are various sorts of permissibility at play (i.e. legal, moral, and otherwise). Some permissi-bility facts constitute law (e.g. it is impermissible to drive faster than 40 miles per hour on the Neck Road in Mattapoisett, Massachusetts). Other permissibility facts constitute moral imperatives (e.g. it is impermissible to torture babies merely for the fun of it). Still others constitute policy for particular establishments. Thus, although segregation is illegal, a proprietor may nevertheless enact a segregatory (and hence discriminatory) policy *in his or her establishment.*[11] Therefore, just as an employer can enact a discriminatory hiring policy (without thereby making discrimination legal), so too these signs enact a segregatory seating policy without thereby making segregation legal. The permissibility facts in question are those pertaining to the establishment in question and not those of the law.

Thus, in what follows, I take it as an established legal fact that the proprietor's posting of a 'Whites Only' sign (in certain contexts anyway) is an act of racial discrimination. Moreover, this is so because the posting of such a sign enacts discriminatory permissibility facts in a public establishment. For this reason, I subsequently focus on speech that enacts discriminatory permissibility facts. Since it is exercitive speech that enacts permissibility facts, in what follows, I present two different models of exercitive speech. Each such type of exercitive speech affords a model for how other forms of speech might do what a 'Whites Only' sign does (i.e. enact discriminatory permissibility facts).

4. The First Model: Standard Exercitives

The first model of exercitive speech is already quite familiar from speech act theory and the work of J. L. Austin. Suppose that a coach says to his team, "I hereby impose the following rule: anyone who talks while I am talking will do ten laps." Since this utterance enacts a fact about what is permissible, this utterance is an exercitive speech act. By saying what he said (in the context in which he said it), the coach is enacting permissibility facts for the members of his team. He is making it impermissible for his players to talk while he is talking (without doing ten laps afterwards).[12] This is also an example of what I call a *standard* exercitive. Standard exercitives work *via the exercising of the speaker's authority* over the realm in which the enacted permissibility facts preside. Such utterances also typically communicate the content of the permissibility fact enacted.[13]

Clearly, standard exercitives are authoritative speech acts. The coach is able to enact the permissibility facts in question because, as the coach, he has the requisite authority over the members of his team. Had one of the players uttered the very same words under the very same circumstances (with all of the same intentions), the player's utterance would not have

---

[11] There was a time when segregation was the law (in southern states after abolition). Even in such a context, the posting of the sign enacts the *policy of the establishment* in question.

[12] He is also making it permissible (and otherwise appropriate) for him to demand ten laps from any player who does talk while he is talking.

[13] Note that this content can be communicated (via, e.g., implicature or presupposition) without being explicitly stated. See Grice 1989: 22–40 and Stalnaker 1973: 77–96.

enacted the corresponding permissibility fact (i.e. that it is impermissible for a member of the team to talk while that player is talking without doing ten laps afterwards). As one can see, standard exercitives require that the speaker have (and be exercising) his or her authority over the realm in which the enacted permissibility facts preside.[14] In fact, standard exercitives are a fairly familiar way in which permissibility facts change.

Note that standard exercitives are often quite subtle. Suppose, for example, that my son is about to fiddle with his father's brand new television antennae and I say, "I wouldn't do that if I were you!" Although my utterance is literally a claim about what I would do, it also indirectly enacts (permissibility) facts about what my son is permitted to do.[15] As such, it is an *indirect* exercitive. (Since the permissibility facts are enacted via the exercising of the speaker's authority, though, it is an indirect standard exercitive.) In addition, many exercitives are implicit. Suppose, for example, that my son writes all over an upholstered chair with a black felt tip marker and I respond, "No more markers for you, young man!" This utterance is an implicit standard exercitive. It is a *standard* exercitive because it enacts a new rule for my son via the exercising of my authority over him but it is *implicit* because the utterance (unlike the coach's) is not explicit about the fact that a new rule is being enacted. Had I said, instead, "I hereby decree that you are henceforth no longer permitted to use markers!" I would have uttered (the more formal and the more unusual) explicit (standard) exercitive. The possibility, and even prevalence, of implicit and/or indirect (standard) exercitives will be important in the following section when exploring the possibility that the elderly white man's utterance is a standard exercitive.

Consider again a 'Whites Only' sign. When the proprietor of an establishment posts such a sign, he is performing a standard exercitive speech act. In posting that sign, the proprietor is exercising his authority over the establishment in question and thereby enacting policy (i.e. permissibility facts) for that establishment. Since the signs are not explicit about the fact that a policy is being enacted, however, they are implicit standard exercitives.

In the following section, we reconsider the elderly white man's utterance. In particular, we explore the possibility that the elderly white man's utterance is an act of discrimination because, like a 'Whites Only' sign, it is

---

[14] Of course, the authority in question is limited to the domain over which the permissibility facts preside. Although the coach has the authority to enact certain permissibility facts for the members of his team, he does not have the authority to set the bedtime for my son.

[15] For a discussion of indirect speech acts, see Searle 1979: 30–57.

a standard exercitive that enacts discriminatory permissibility facts. As we shall see, although tempting, this hypothesis faces formidable challenges.

5. The First Model Applied

Consider again our earlier example of racist hate speech in which an elderly white man says to the only African American passenger on a public bus, "Just so you know, because I realize that your kind are not very bright, we don't like niggers around here, . . . boy. So, go back to Africa . . . so you can keep killing each other . . . and do the world a favor!" Imagine further that all the other passengers on the bus clearly indicate their approval of what the elderly white man said. Notice that if I can show that, in this case, the elderly white man's utterance does what a 'Whites Only' sign does, then I will have shown that *some* racist hate speech does what a 'Whites Only' sign does. I grant, at the outset, that both the utterance and the context of utterance are rather extreme.

Before exploring the hypothesis that this utterance is a standard exercitive (that enacts discriminatory permissibility facts just like a 'Whites Only' sign would), it makes good sense to first reflect pre-theoretically about the similarities between this utterance and such a sign. As I see it, there are several such similarities. First, both this utterance and such a sign make it abundantly clear that non-whites are not welcome on the public bus in question. Second, the sign and the racist utterance would generate some of the same effects. Both would discourage non-whites from riding the bus and both would make it extremely uncomfortable, to say the least, for any non-whites who did. Third, both the hanging of the sign and the uttering of racist hate speech are part of a broader system of racism. That whites can get away with doing such things is both a product and evidence of an antecedent unjust racial hierarchy. Even more than that, such actions perpetuate and even reinforce that hierarchy. In light of these similarities, one might begin to wonder whether there is much difference between posting a 'Whites Only' sign in a public place and uttering racist hate speech in such places.

Turn now to a direct consideration of our first hypothesis. According to our first model of exercitive speech, the elderly white man's utterance is a *standard* exercitive that enacts racially discriminatory permissibility facts. In other words, his utterance does what a 'Whites Only' sign would do and it does so via the same mechanism (i.e. via an exercise of the speaker's authority over the realm in question).

Of course, if the elderly white man's utterance is a standard exercitive, it seems that it must be both implicit and indirect. It must be implicit because the utterance does not explicitly state that it is enacting policy and it must be indirect because the utterance is literally (and thus directly) a statement about local preferences (and perhaps also a suggestion about where the addressee ought to be in the future). As we shall see, although tempting, this hypothesis (i.e. that this utterance is an implicit indirect standard exercitive that enacts illegal racially discriminatory permissibility facts for this public bus) faces several challenges.

First, as we have seen, standard exercitives are authoritative speech acts. The speaker must have authority over the realm in which the enacted permissibility facts preside. Note that this (speaker authority) condition is clearly met in the case of a proprietor hanging a 'Whites Only' sign. Recall that it is the proprietor who posts the sign and it is the proprietor who has the authority to enact policy for the establishment in question. Notice further that this condition does not appear to be met in the bus example. After all, the elderly white man is a mere passenger and it is unclear that he has the requisite authority to enact policy for the public bus on which he is riding.

Second, when a proprietor posts a 'Whites Only' sign, he intends to be enacting policy (that is, permissibility facts) for his or her establishment, but the same does not seem to be the case with the elderly white man. It is unclear that the elderly white man intended to do anything more than express an opinion about black people. Thus, if (as some maintain) intending one's utterance to enact permissibility facts is a necessary condition of an utterance enacting permissibility facts, then it seems that the elderly white man's utterance cannot be doing what a 'Whites Only' sign would do.

There are worthy responses to each of these two concerns. In fact, there are several ways to argue that the elderly white man does in fact have the authority to enact the relevant permissibility facts. One might argue, for instance, that the elderly white man has (derivative but effective) authority in virtue of having the entire history of institutionalized racism behind him.[16] Alternatively (or additionally) one might argue that, because everyone else on the bus accepts his utterance, the elderly white man has the authority of the majority. Finally, one might argue that since the government protects his right to say what he said, his utterance has the authority of the government behind it.[17] Thus, his words are akin to a 'Whites Only' sign hung by a patron (uttered by a citizen) but not removed by the proprietor (thus endorsed by the government). Of course, each of these

---

[16] Matsuda 1993: 17–51.
[17] This line of response is also suggested in Matsuda 1993: 17–51.

lines of response requires much more development than is offered here.[18]
I mention them only to point out that this issue of speaker authority is
considerably more complex than it might first appear and, for all we know,
it may be that the elderly white man does in fact have the requisite
authority.

Regarding the second concern, one might argue that one does not in
fact need to intend to be enacting permissibility facts in order to enact
them. After all, one might unwittingly enter into a verbal contract without
realizing that one is doing so and a proprietor might well post a 'Whites
Only' sign without consciously intending to enact policy.[19]

In sum, although such responses are available, they are by no means
decisive. As we have seen, there are considerable challenges to the hypothesis that the elderly white man's utterance is a standard exercitive. Despite
this, there is considerable intuitive pull to the idea that the elderly white
man's utterance does what a 'Whites Only' sign would do (i.e. enact
discriminatory permissibility facts). After all, our *main reason* for thinking
that the elderly white man's utterance might be a standard exercitive was
our sense of what the utterance in fact does in this context. For this reason,
another model of exercitive speech would be helpful and, in the following
section, another such model is presented.

6. The Second Model: Covert Exercitives

Elsewhere I have argued that norm-governed activities generate covert
exercitive force.[20] As we shall see, this enacting of permissibility facts is
covert since it is independent of either speaker intention or participant
awareness.[21] By norm-governed, I mean any activity governed by norms.
The norms in question need not be explicit, formal, exception-less, or
even consciously recognized. If at least some behaviors (as contributions to
the activity in question) would count as out of bounds or otherwise
inappropriate (as contributions to the activity in question), then that

---

[18] For an exploration of various forms of speaker authority, see Ishani Maitra's
"Subordinating Speech," this volume.

[19] Whether a speaker is held responsible for the action constituted by her utterance is, of
course, a separate question and that question seems to be especially sensitive to what the
speaker intended to do with her utterance.

[20] McGowan 2003: 155–89; McGowan 2004: 93–111; and McGowan 2009a: 389–407.
I have more recently argued that (what I am here calling) covert exercitives are not technically
an illocutionary phenomenon; they are instead (what I call) parallel acts.

[21] Other theorists use the term 'covert' to mean something else. See Bach and Harnish
1979: 97–102. Deceiving, for example, is covert in their sense since succeeding requires that
the addressee *fail* to recognize the relevant intention.

activity is norm-governed in the appropriate sense. Notice that all cooperative activities are norm-governed in this sense. Some such activities
have rigid norms (e.g. chess, checkers, and baseball) while others are
governed by less rigid norms (e.g. conversations, dancing, and playing
music). These less rigid norms are sometimes called rules of accommodation since the rules tend to accommodate what the participants collectively
and cooperatively treat as appropriate.[22]

To see that norm-governed activities generate covert exercitive force,
notice first that they are such that what is permissible depends on the
norms and what has already transpired in that particular norm-governed
activity. Whether it is permissible to walk to first base, for example,
depends on the norms (i.e. rules) of baseball and what has happened in
the game so far (i.e. whether four balls have just been pitched to the batter
in question). Similarly, whether it is permissible to start talking about
crayons, for instance, depends on the norms of conversation and what
has happened in the conversation thus far (i.e. whether crayons, or some
related thing, is already a topic of the conversation in question).[23]

Of course, not all actions involved in a norm-governed activity change
what is subsequently permissible. If a baseball player, for example, were to
scratch his nose while waiting in the outfield, for example, his doing so
would have no effect on the permissibility facts of the game. This is
because his doing so is not a proper part of the game. That is, his action
is not a move in the game. A *move* in a norm-governed activity is (just) a
contribution to, and thus a component of, that activity. As a result, moves
are governed by the norms of the activity in question. Swinging your bat
while at the plate during an at-bat, for example, is a move in baseball and
saying something relevant is a move in the norm-governed activity of
conversation.

Moves in norm-governed activities enact changes in what is subsequently permissible in that activity. When my opponent moved her
checker, for example, her doing so made it permissible for me to subsequently move mine. Similarly, when the receiver signaled for a fair catch,
he thereby made it impermissible for the defense to tackle him. Finally,
when my conversational partner started talking about her children, she
thereby made it appropriate for me to start talking about mine.

One might think that moves in norm-governed activities merely *cause*
the subsequent permissibility facts to change, but this is not correct. To see

---

[22] See Lewis 1983: 233–49.

[23] Of course, one is permitted to introduce new topics into a conversation (so long as one's
interlocutors cooperate). What one is not permitted to do, however, is make random
comments unrelated to the conversation in which one is participating.

this, consider the following. When a batter hits a home run, for example, his doing so does not cause the score to change, it actually enacts a change in the score. This is so even if his hitting a home run causes participants to *record* a change in the score and even if participants *realize* that there is a new score via causal mechanisms (e.g. perception and inference).

Now, here is the crucial insight. When speech constitutes a move in a norm-governed activity, it has exercitive force in virtue of enacting new permissibility facts for the activity in which it is a move. When a poker player says, "I call," she thereby makes it impermissible for anyone to raise the bet. Her utterance is an exercitive speech act. Similarly, when a conversational partner says something that successfully presupposes that she has a summer home, her utterance makes it subsequently inappropriate for her conversational partner to ask her if she owns any property.[24] Thus, although her utterance does not wear its exercitive force on its sleeve, it nevertheless enacts permissibility facts for the conversation and is therefore exercitive.[25]

In sum, when an utterance constitutes a move in a norm-governed activity, the utterance in question is exercitive. In virtue of being a move in a norm-governed activity, such an utterance triggers the norms of that activity and thereby enacts facts about what is subsequently permissible in that activity. Thus, although such an utterance may not appear to be enacting permissibility facts, it is.[26]

Of course, establishing that an utterance enacts permissibility facts does not establish that the enacted permissibility facts are discriminatory. Thus, in order for covert exercitives to afford an alternative model for how speech can enact *discriminatory* permissibility facts, it must sometimes be the case that the enacted permissibility facts are, in fact, discriminatory. In what follows, this issue is investigated in more detail.

6.1. *Discriminatory Permissibility Facts*

It is certainly *possible* for covert exercitives to enact discriminatory permissibility facts. To see this, imagine the following example. Suppose that, in a certain extremely racist society, whenever a white person says something, all non-white people, who are within earshot, must bow down in silence.

---

[24] The case of presupposition is a bit tricky. One successfully presupposes so long as one's interlocutor does not immediately question that presupposition (so long, that is, as one gets away with it). For a discussion of this complication, see Lewis 1983: 234.

[25] Again, the enacting of the permissibility facts is technically a parallel (as opposed to an illocutionary) act.

[26] For an interesting discussion of (the related phenomenon of) the action-engendering power of speech, see Lynne Tirrell's "Genocidal Language Games," this volume.

In such a society, a white person speaking is (whether it is intended to be or not) a move in the norm-governed activity of racism. As such, such utterances enact permissibility facts in that system and, in the case at hand, the enacted permissibility facts are discriminatory. This fictional example demonstrates that it is *possible* for covert exercitives to enact discriminatory permissibility facts.

Several clarifications are worth making at this point. First, I here assume that racism is a norm-governed activity. Since any practice or cooperative activity is norm-governed in the relevant sense, and since racism is clearly a human practice, it follows that racism is norm-governed. Racism is a structural phenomenon.[27] It is, at bottom, a complex social arrangement that systematically disadvantages some in virtue of their race (and hence systematically advantages others in virtue of theirs). As such, a system of racism involves complex norms of behavior. Moreover, some behaviors perpetuate the system and others (happily) undermine it. In other words, some behaviors (as contributions to the activity of racism) count as out of bounds or otherwise inappropriate (as contributions to that activity) and this is sufficient to show that racism is norm-governed in the relevant sense.

Second, one might think that the above analysis involves a problematic proliferation of discriminatory acts. After all, according to the above analysis, any utterance by a white person, in this fictional society, would be an act of discrimination because any such utterance would enact discriminatory permissibility facts. Although this result may seem counter-intuitive, on closer inspection, it is not. Just as a conversation involves the constant enacting and changing of permissibility facts for that particular conversation, so, too, a system of racism will involve the constant enacting and changing of permissibility facts at the micro-level of personal interaction.

Third, and perhaps more to the point for current purposes, not all acts of discrimination are on a par. To see this, suppose that Johnny, a staunch racist, declares that black people are not allowed in his home. Supposing that Johnny has the authority to enact this household policy, his utterance enacts discriminatory permissibility facts and is thus an act of racial discrimination. Although his utterance is an act of racial discrimination, it is not an *illegal* one. However regrettable his actions may be, they are not illegal. One has the right to ban certain people (and even certain sorts of people) from one's private home. As one can see, it is a separate question whether a particular act of racial discrimination is legally actionable.

---

[27] Young 1992: 174–95; Frye 1983: 1–16; Haslanger 2004: 97–123.

Finally, it is worth pointing out that a single utterance can be (and often is) a move in several different norm-governed activities at once. This fact is illuminated by the above example. Since whatever a white person says constitutes a move in the conversation to which it is a contribution, that utterance thereby enacts permissibility facts for that conversation. Since it is also a move in the norm-governed activity of racism, the white person's utterance also enacts permissibility facts in that system as well.

Although our fictional example demonstrates that it is at least *possible* for covert exercitives to constitute racially discriminatory acts, this clearly falls short of establishing that any actually do so. After all, one can always cook up some far out example whereby just about any utterance whatsoever constitutes the enacting of just about any permissibility fact whatsoever. Clearly what is needed is some reason to believe that actual utterances under actual circumstances covertly constitute acts of racial discrimination.

A moment's reflection, though, shows that we already have such reason. To see this, one need only realize that the uttering of racist hate speech constitutes a move in the norm-governed activity of racism. Recall that a move is (just) a contribution to, and thus a component of, the activity in question. Since uttering racist hate speech is one way to mistreat a person in virtue of her race, the uttering of racist hate speech is clearly and uncontroversially a move in the system. Of course, it will be controversial settling what else counts as such a move. (Some may believe racism to so saturate our way of life, that most social behaviors (e.g. one's speech patterns, comportment, and dress) would count as moves while others might maintain that only actions more directly connected to race are moves.) Fortunately for us, settling such complex questions is unnecessary since, no matter how such thorny issues are settled, the uttering of racist hate speech is a move.

It follows from this that racist hate speech is covertly exercitive. Since racism is a norm-governed activity, and since uttering racist hate speech is a move in that activity, racist hate speech covertly enacts permissibility facts for the activity of racism. As a result, the only remaining questions are: Which particular permissibility facts are enacted by such utterances? And, are they racially discriminatory? In order to address such questions, we return once again to the elderly white man's utterance on the public bus.

7. The Second Model Applied

Consider again our example of racist hate speech on a public bus. Although our first hypothesis (i.e. that the elderly white man's utterance is a *standard* exercitive that enacts racially discriminatory permissibility facts) faced formidable challenges, we turn now to the consideration of a different hypothesis. Perhaps, the elderly white man's utterance is a *covert* exercitive that enacts racially discriminatory permissibility facts. Perhaps his utterance enacts the very same racially discriminatory policy for the bus that the hanging of a 'Whites Only' sign would. As we shall see, this second hypothesis is quite promising.

Since the elderly white man's utterance is an instance of racist hate speech and since, as we saw in the previous section, racist hate speech is covertly exercitive, so too is the elderly white man's utterance. As a result, his utterance covertly enacts permissibility facts. This much has already been proven. What remains to be shown, however, is *which particular* permissibility facts are enacted by his utterance.

Concerning this issue, it certainly seems plausible to suppose that the utterance enacts the very same (racially discriminatory) permissibility facts that a 'Whites Only' sign would. After all, as we saw in § 5, the hypothesis that the elderly white man's utterance is a (racially discriminatory) *standard* exercitive had considerable intuitive appeal even though that utterance does not seem to satisfy certain important conditions of standard exercitives. This suggests that our primary reason for saying that the elderly white man's utterance may be a standard exercitive was our sense that the utterance did exactly what a 'Whites Only' sign would do (i.e. enact a racially discriminatory policy for that bus). In light of these considerations, it seems that a plausible hypothesis (regarding which particular permissibility facts are enacted) is that the utterance enacts the same racially discriminatory permissibility facts that a 'Whites Only' sign would.

Of course, such considerations are clearly insufficient to *prove* (i.e. establish with absolute certainty) that the covertly enacted permissibility facts are the very same racially discriminatory permissibility facts that would be enacted by a 'Whites Only' sign. For such a proof, we would need to *know*, with absolute certainty, something that we don't know (i.e. what *all* of the norms of racism are). Consequently, offering a highly plausible hypothesis is the very best one can do.[28] As a result, I henceforth assume that this hypothesis is correct. I henceforth assume that the elderly white man's utterance covertly enacts the same (racially discriminatory)

---

[28] Perhaps instead, the elderly white man's utterance makes non-whites merely unwelcome (rather than not allowed) on that public bus. Although distinguishing between these possibilities may seem like hair splitting, the difference may be relevant to law. After all, disallowing non-whites on a public bus is clearly illegal, but it is not so clear that making non-whites unwelcome is illegal too. That said, it's not clearly legal either! Since these hypotheses are so close and since I take the preferred hypothesis to be better supported, I henceforth overlook this complicating possibility.

permissibility facts that a proprietor's posting of a 'Whites Only' sign would.

7.1. *An Alleged Problem Over Speaker Authority*

As we saw in § 4, standard exercitives are authoritative speech acts. This means that the speaker must have the authority to enact the relevant permissibility facts. In fact, the mark of a standard exercitive is its mechanism of production: the enacted permissibility facts are generated via an exercise of the speaker's authority. Recall that this fact about standard exercitives raised a significant problem for our first hypothesis (i.e. that the elderly white man's utterance is a standard exercitive) since it seems that the elderly white man does not have the requisite authority to enact policy for a public bus. Since covert exercitives are not authoritative speech acts, our second hypothesis (i.e. that the elderly white man's utterance is a covert exercitive) appears to avoid this difficulty.

Or does it? Recall that being a covert exercitive requires that an utterance be a move in a norm-governed activity. Thus, the speaker of such exercitives must be capable of making the move in question and, arguably, this is a form of authority. To see this, consider some examples. If Shea and I are playing checkers and Nora moves one of my checkers, her action does not constitute a move in the game exactly because she is not one of the players. Moreover, some moves are not even open to some players. If it is not my turn, for example, I cannot legitimately move my checker even though I am a player in the game.[29]

All of this is correct, but it does not pose much of a challenge for our second hypothesis. To see this, notice that, in order for the elderly white man to have the 'authority' to make the move in question (that of uttering racist hate speech), two conditions must be met. First, he must be a player in the game (that is, a participant in a system of racism) and, second, he must be capable of making that move at that time. Clearly, each of these conditions is met. Since society is racist, there is a sense in which we are all players. We each contribute, in one way or another, to the complex human activity of racism.[30] We are each, therefore, 'players.' And, the elderly white man is obviously capable of making the move in question: the (mere) uttering of racist hate speech.

---

[29] I thank Ishani Maitra for suggesting that I respond to this objection.

[30] It hardly matters whether we say that we are only players when we make moves or that we are each always players.

7.2. *An Interesting Case*

Consider a modified version of our public bus example. Suppose that, instead of uttering racist hate speech, the elderly white man instead attempts to verbally enact a policy for the bus (by attempting to perform a direct standard exercitive). Suppose, that is, that the elderly white man had simply said "Whites only," as the African American man boarded the public bus. Further suppose that, in this case too, all of the other passengers nod in approval of what the elderly white man said. In such a case, what would the elderly white man's utterance manage to do? And, what, if anything, does that tell us about how racist hate speech functions?

It seems that there are basically two possibilities: either the elderly white man's modified utterance (i.e. "Whites only") does what a 'Whites Only' sign would do or it does not. Consider the former possibility first. Suppose, that is, that the elderly white man's (modified) utterance somehow succeeds as a direct standard exercitive so that it enacts a racially discriminatory policy for that public bus. Although this result may seem implausible, keep in mind that all of the other passengers visibly agree with what the elderly white man said (so that the enacting of a de facto discriminatory policy does not seem so very implausible).

Now notice that if the modified utterance (i.e. "Whites only") succeeds as a standard exercitive, then it seems that the elderly white man *does* have the requisite authority to enact such a policy after all. Furthermore, since the alleged failure of this speaker authority condition was the main reason for rejecting our first hypothesis, the motivation for our second hypothesis appears to be undermined. In other words, if the elderly white man has the requisite authority (to verbally enact policy for the public bus via a standard exercitive), then his original (hateful) utterance is best understood as a successful standard exercitive. And, if this is correct, then it seems that there is little reason to consider the second, more covert and more complex, hypothesis.

Consider now the latter possibility. Suppose, that is, that the elderly white man *fails* to enact a discriminatory policy for the public bus when he says, "Whites only." This seems perfectly reasonable. After all (and not withstanding the above considerations), on the face of it, it does seem that the elderly white man simply lacks the authority to enact the relevant policy for this bus. But, now notice this. If the elderly white man cannot enact the discriminatory policy overtly (when he says "Whites only"), isn't it especially outlandish to suppose, as we have done in this paper, that he can do so covertly (when he utters racist hate speech)? Thus, it seems that this second possibility also undermines the main argument of this paper.

Well, actually it does not. What the above reasoning overlooks is that the modified utterance ("Whites only") is a covert exercitive in addition to being at least an attempted standard exercitive. When the elderly white man says, "Whites only," he is at least attempting (via an exercise of speaker authority) to enact a discriminatory policy for the bus and, whether his utterance succeeds as a standard exercitive or not, his attempt to perform this speech act is a move in the norm-governed activity of racism. In other words, the mere attempt is a successful move. Consequently, his utterance is a covert exercitive and it follows from this that his utterance covertly enacts permissibility facts. Moreover, if the enacted permissibility facts are the same ones that would be enacted by a proprietor's posting of a 'Whites Only' sign, then his utterance covertly enacts a discriminatory policy for the bus.

That this modified utterance (i.e. "Whites only") is both a standard and a covert exercitive opens up a further possibility. It may be that the utterance fails as a standard exercitive (due to the failure of the speaker authority condition) but succeeds as a covert exercitive. In other words, it fails as an attempted exercise of speaker authority but succeeds as a move in the norm-governed activity of racism. If this is correct (and this is the hypothesis I favor for our modified utterance), then the elderly white man is *able to do covertly* what he *cannot do overtly*. This may seem to be an extremely surprising result but, in light of what we have here established, it should not be. As we have seen, speech is sneaky. It routinely does much more than we either realize or intend.

8. On Combining the Hypotheses

As we saw in the previous section, it is important to realize that a single utterance can be both a standard exercitive and a covert exercitive. Consider again the proprietor's posting of a 'Whites Only' sign. As we have seen, this is a standard exercitive that enacts (racially discriminatory) permissibility facts in virtue of the exercising of the proprietor's authority over his or her establishment. Notice that enacting that policy (i.e. those permissibility facts) is also a move in the norm-governed activity of racism and so the posting of the sign is also a covert exercitive! Thus, it seems that, in this case, there are two mechanisms involved in the enacting of the very same (racially discriminatory) permissibility facts.[31]

---

[31] Of course, it may also be that the covertly enacted permissibility facts are different from those enacted by the standard exercitive. In fact, this typically happens with conversational contributions.

Notice that the same may very well be the case with our original example of racist hate speech. As we saw in § 5, if certain conditions are met (or if they are not required), then the elderly white man's (original) utterance is a (successful) standard exercitive. Moreover, since his utterance is a move in the norm-governed activity of racism, it is also a covert exercitive. Thus, it may well be that this example of racist hate speech is a case where the same (racially discriminatory) permissibility facts are enacted via two distinct mechanisms. The first such mechanism is that of the standard exercitive (i.e. the exercising of the speaker's authority over the realm in which the enacted permissibility facts preside). The second such mechanism is that of the covert exercitive (i.e. the triggering of the norm-governed nature of the activity in which the utterance is a move).

9. Potential Application to Law

In this paper, I have argued that there is reason to believe that some instances of racist hate speech do what a 'Whites Only' sign does. Such utterances constitute acts of racial discrimination in virtue of enacting racially discriminatory permissibility facts. Since the posting of a 'Whites Only' sign is uncovered (by the First Amendment) exactly because of what it does (namely, constitute an act of racial discrimination), it seems that some racist hate speech ought to be uncovered as well. After all, if some racist hate speech constitutes illegal acts of racial discrimination, then such utterances should not count as speech in the First Amendment sense and so the regulation of such (uncovered) utterances should raise no free speech concerns at all.

No doubt that this is a bold and controversial position, thus raising a slew of objections and concerns. In what follows, I try to anticipate what some of those concerns and objections might be and offer what I can by way of response. First, I offer some clarifications.

9.1. Clarifications of Potential Application to Law

First, I am not here suggesting that all instances of racist hate speech ought to be regulated. Rather, I am claiming that certain instances of racist hate speech (namely, those that constitute an illegal act of racial discrimination) ought to be regulated. Although, on my view, all instances of racist hate speech are moves in the norm-governed activity of racism and are thus covertly exercitive, not all exercitives enact racially discriminatory permissibility facts. Moreover, as mentioned earlier, not all acts of racial discrimination are (or ought to be) illegal.[32] Suppose, for instance, that Sam enacts a household policy whereby no black people are allowed in his living room. Although Sam has thereby committed an act of racial discrimination, he has not broken the law. Sam has the legal right to be a racist in his own household. Had Sam, however, enacted a similar policy for a public bus (or for an employee lounge), his utterance would enact permissibility facts constitutive of an *illegal* act of racial discrimination. By way of clarification: I am here only interested in the free speech status of those instances of racist hate speech that constitute *illegal* acts of racial discrimination.

In sum, I have here argued that we have good reason to believe that some racist hate speech (that in the public bus example) constitutes an illegal act of racial discrimination. Even if the enacted permissibility facts are highly localized (pertaining only to that particular public bus), and, even if they are merely temporary (lasting only for a short while), the enacting of such permissibility facts nevertheless constitutes an illegal act of racial discrimination. The enacting of discriminatory policies for public places is no less illegal for being either bus-specific or short-lived.[33]

9.2. *Objections to Potential Application to Law*

Even if one accepts the theoretical claim made here (i.e. that some racist hate speech does what a 'Whites Only' sign does), one might nevertheless resist the suggestion that that subset of racist hate speech ought to be regulated. In other words, one might accept the theory and reject the suggested application to law. I have heard many different reasons for such resistance and I consider each in turn.

First, one might be concerned that it would be simply too difficult to draft legislation that would accurately identify the subset of racist hate speech in question. After all, there are many complex contextual factors involved in fixing which particular utterances constitute which particular acts. Thus, any legislation that attempts to specify all such contextual factors is doomed to fail. As a result, such legislation would inevitably misidentify the class of utterances (that constitute an illegal act of racial discrimination). Doing so would generate the unacceptable result that some speech that ought to remain protected is regulated (and some speech that ought to be regulated is not).

---

[32] Although not all such utterances ought to be regulated, all such utterances ought to be uncovered, on my view. For a discussion of this view, see Maitra and McGowan 2007: 41–68 and Maitra and McGowan 2010: 343–72.

[33] Of course, if the discriminatory policy is extremely short-lived, prosecution of this illegal act of discrimination may well be unlikely.

It is no doubt true that any attempt to specify the various contextual factors involved will ultimately fail. Fortunately, doing so is not required. The subset of racist hate speech in question can be identified in virtue of what it does (that is, constitute an illegal act of racial discrimination). After all, the law already identifies certain categories of speech for regulation *by identifying what such speech does* (e.g. insider trading, price-fixing, criminal solicitation, threats, and other verbal acts of discrimination). Of course, when applying such laws, one would need to know which utterances constitute which acts and this, in turn, requires a consideration of the various contextual factors. This is true, but the law already has this problem in virtue of regulating such contextually sensitive things as threats, criminal solicitation, and other verbal acts of discrimination. Thus, what I am suggesting here adds no additional burden. Furthermore, the law already makes sophisticated linguistic distinctions. Consider, for example, the distinction between an indirect request and an indirect order. This extremely subtle distinction is of legal significance, for example, when a police officer verbally seeks permission to conduct a search. Whether the subsequent search is consensual (and thus constitutional) depends on whether the driver intends to be granting permission and this, in turn, depends on whether that driver takes the police officer's utterance as an indirect order or as a mere request.[34]

Second, one might be concerned that any anti-hate-speech legislation would ultimately backfire and be used against those very people whom it was intended to protect (i.e. non-whites).[35] After all, this sort of thing has already happened. Obscenity law has been selectively used against rap music and some speech codes target the use of particular racial epithets, thereby prohibiting the re-appropriation of those terms. It is important to keep in mind, however, that I am not here advocating either of these approaches. Instead, I am suggesting that such legislation ought to target utterances in terms of what such utterances do (i.e. constitute illegal discriminatory acts). Thus, since the proposed strategy does not appeal to obscenity law, questionable judgments about the literary or artistic merit of, for example, rap music is beside the point.[36] Additionally, since I am not here suggesting that the proposed legislation target the use of particular words and since there is every reason to believe that plenty of uses of racial epithets (and perhaps especially those by people of color) do not constitute

[34] This particular example is discussed in Solan and Tiersma 2005: 35–46.

[35] Theorists from across the political spectrum have expressed this concern. See, e.g., Butler 1997; Green 2000: 27–52; Golding 2000; Bernstein 2003; and Carse 1995: 155–82.

[36] For a brief discussion of some of the ways that rap music is misunderstood, see Gates 1990: p. A23, 46.

discriminatory acts, such uses would not be targeted by the proposed legislation.[37]

Finally, one might be resistant to new legislation exactly because one does not believe that the proper remedy for harmful speech lies with the law. Many, for example, believe that counter-speech is the proper remedy. There are several things to say in response to this. First, it is not at all clear that more speech is the proper remedy for harmful speech. After all, one of the consequences of harmful speech is to disable the speech of the addressee.[38] Furthermore, the empirical evidence demonstrates that such counter-speech rarely, in fact, occurs and when it does it is ineffective.[39] Second, it seems obviously correct for the law to prohibit 'Whites Only' signs and other forms of verbal discrimination. Moreover, it seems plainly inadequate to expect counter-speech to remedy such verbal acts of discrimination. Since we are here targeting that subset of racist hate speech that does the same thing (as a 'Whites Only' sign), comparable legal treatment seems appropriate (at least in the absence of a persuasive argument to the contrary). Finally, in expecting counter-speech to remedy the harms of racist speech, it seems naïve to think that people can be counted on to do the right thing. After all, all too often we don't.

In sum, it is important to separate the theoretical claim explored here (i.e. that some racist hate speech functions like a 'Whites Only' sign) from its potential upshot for the law. There are, after all, further considerations involved in any such application. Despite this, it is also important to recognize that many of the reasons typically offered for resisting any such application do not stand up to scrutiny. Thus, if what I have argued here is correct (and some racist hate speech constitutes illegal acts of racial discrimination), then there are good legal grounds for regulating it.

10. Conclusion

Some naïvely believe that the First Amendment protects our right to say whatever we please. As we have seen, this is false. Some speech is not even covered (i.e. within the scope of the First Amendment) and plenty of

---

[37] The re-appropriation of terms such as 'queer' and 'nigger' is a fascinating, complex, and touchy subject. For an interesting discussion about the appropriate use of the word 'nigger,' see Kennedy 1999–2000: 86–96.

[38] There is now an extensive literature on silencing. See, e.g., MacKinnon 1993; Langton 1993: 293–330; Hornsby 1995: 127–47; West 2003: 391–422; Maitra 2004: 189–209; and McGowan 2009b: 487–94. For a discussion of how racist hate speech, in particular, may silence, see Caroline West "Words that Silence? Freedom of Expression and Racist Hate Speech" this volume.

[39] Nielsen 2004. See also her "Power in Public: Reactions, Responses and Resistance to Offensive Public Speech," this volume.

covered speech is regulated anyway. Some naïvely believe that speech is merely a mechanism for making (true or false) claims about the world around us. As we have seen, this is false too. Speech does things and some of the things it does are quite powerful. Furthermore, the law is already well aware of this power of speech. Many verbal acts are already illegal and it is speech, after all, that enacts the law itself.

In this paper, we have focused on a fairly specific thing that speech can do (i.e. constitute an illegal act of racial discrimination). I have here argued that there is a compelling case to be made for the claim that both 'Whites Only' signs and some racist hate speech constitute such discriminatory acts. Our discussion highlights several important points. First, the mere fact that an utterance expresses a political opinion is not sufficient reason to view it as highly protected political speech. A consideration of 'Whites Only' signs makes this clear. As we have seen, such signs are not even covered by (i.e. within the scope of) the First Amendment. Second, since 'Whites Only' signs are uncovered exactly because of what they do, and since we have reason to believe that some racist hate speech does the very same thing, we have reason to place that subset of racist hate speech outside the scope of a free speech principle. Third, if that subset of racist hate speech ought to be uncovered, then it ought to be regulated. That is, once such discriminatory racist speech is no longer regarded as speech in the technical sense of the First Amendment, there is no good reason to tolerate its harms. If it isn't even speech in the free speech sense, its regulation poses no such threat to our commitment to free speech. Thus, just as the regulation of 'Whites Only' signs raises no free speech concerns, the way ought to be clear for the regulation of (some) racist hate speech in our public spaces.

References

Bach, Kent and Robert M. Harnish 1979. *Linguistic Communication and Speech Acts.* Cambridge, MA: MIT Press, pp. 97–102.

Bernstein, David 2003. *You Can't Say That: The Growing Threat to Civil Liberties From Anti-discrimination Law.* Washington, DC: CATO Institute.

Brink, David 2001. "Millian Principles, Freedom of Expression, and Hate Speech," *Legal Theory* (7): 119–57.

Butler, Judith 1997. *Excitable Speech: A Politics of the Performative.* New York: Routledge.

Carse, Alisa 1995. "Pornography: An Uncivil Liberty?" *Hypatia* 10 (1): 155–82.

Frye, Marilyn 1983. "Oppression," in *The Politics of Reality.* Freedom, CA: The Crossing Press, pp. 1–16.

Gates, Henry Louis Jr. 1990. "2 Live Crew, Decoded," *New York Times*, June 19, p. A23, 46.

Golding, Martin 2000. *Free Speech on Campus*. Lanham, Maryland: Rowman & Littlefield Publishers.

Green, Leslie 2000. "Pornographies," *The Journal of Political Philosophy* 8 (1): 27–52.

Greenawalt, Kent 1989. *Speech, Crime and the Uses of Language*. Oxford: Oxford University Press.

Greenawalt, Kent 1995. *Fighting Words: Individuals, Communities, and Liberties of Free Speech*. Princeton, NJ: Princeton University Press.

Grice, H. Paul 1989. "Logic and Conversation," in *Studies in the Way of Words*. Cambridge, MA: Harvard University Press: 22–40.

Haslanger, Sally 2004. "Oppression: Racial and Other," in *Racism in Mind*, ed. Michael P. Levine and Tamas Pataki. Ithaca, NY: Cornell University Press, pp. 97–123.

Hornsby, Jennifer 1995. "Disempowered Speech," in Haslanger (ed.) *Philosophical Topics* 23: 127–47.

Kennedy, Randall 1999–2000. "Who Can Say 'Nigger'? And Other Considerations," *The Journal of Blacks in Higher Education* 26: 86–96.

Langton, Rae 1993. "Speech Acts and Unspeakable Acts," *Philosophy & Public Affairs* 22: 293–330.

Lawrence, Charles III 1993. "If He Hollers Let Him Go: Regulating Racist Speech on Campus," in M. Matsuda, C. R. Lawrence, R. Delgado and K. Crenshaw (eds.), *Words that Wound: Critical Race Theory, Assaultive Speech, and the First Amendment*. Boulder, CO: Westview Press: 53–88.

Lewis, David 1983. "Scorekeeping in a Language Game," *Philosophical Papers Volume I*. New York: Oxford University Press: 233–49.

MacKinnon, Catharine 1987. "Francis Biddle's Sister: Pornography, Civil Rights and Speech," in *Feminism Unmodified: Discourses on Life and Law*. Cambridge, MA: Harvard University Press.

MacKinnon, Catharine 1989. "Pornography: On Morality and Politics," in *Towards a Feminist Theory of the State*. Cambridge, MA: Harvard University Press, p. 206.

MacKinnon, Catharine 1993. *Only Words*. Cambridge, MA: Harvard University Press.

Maitra, Ishani 2004. "Silence and Responsibility," *Philosophical Perspectives* 18: 189–209.

Maitra, Ishani and Mary Kate McGowan 2007. "The Limits of Free Speech: Pornography and the Question of Coverage," *Legal Theory* 13: 41–68.

Maitra, Ishani and Mary Kate McGowan 2010. "On Racist Hate Speech and the Scope of a Free Speech Principle," *Canadian Journal of Law and Jurisprudence* 23 (2): 343–72.

Matsuda, Mari 1993. "Public Response to Racist Speech: Considering the Victim's Story," in M. Matsuda, C. R. Lawrence, R. Delgado and K. Crenshaw (eds.), *Words that Wound: Critical Race Theory, Assaultive Speech, and the First Amendment.* Boulder, CO: Westview Press: 17–51.

McGowan, Mary Kate 2003. "Conversational Exercitives and the Force of Pornography," *Philosophy & Public Affairs* 31 (2): 155–89.

McGowan, Mary Kate 2004. "Conversational Exercitives: Something Else We Do With Our Words," *Linguistics and Philosophy* 27 (1): 93–111.

McGowan, Mary Kate 2009a. "Oppressive Speech," *Australasian Journal of Philosophy* 87 (3): 389–407.

McGowan, Mary Kate 2009b. "On Silencing and Sexual Refusal," *Journal of Political Philosophy* 17 (4): 487–94.

Nielsen, Laura Beth 2004. *License to Harass: Law, Hierarchy and Offensive Public Speech.* Princeton, NJ: Princeton University Press.

Nielsen, Laura Beth "Power in Public: Reactions, Responses and Resistance to Offensive Public Speech," this volume.

Schauer, Frederick 1982. *Free Speech: A Philosophical Enquiry.* Cambridge: Cambridge University Press.

Schauer, Frederick 2004. "The Boundaries of the First Amendment: A Preliminary Exploration of Constitutional Salience," *Harvard Law Review* 144: 2417–61.

Searle, John 1979. "Indirect Speech Acts," in *Expression and Meaning.* Cambridge: Cambridge University Press: 30–57.

Solan, Lawrence and Peter Tiersma 2005. *Speaking of Crime.* Chicago, IL: University of Chicago Press, pp. 35–46.

Stalnaker, Robert 1973. "Presupposition," *Journal of Philosophical Logic* 2: 77–96.

Tirrell, Lynne "Genocidal Language Games," this volume.

West, Caroline 2003. "The Free Speech Argument Against Pornography," *Canadian Journal of Philosophy* 33 (3): 391–422.

West, Caroline "Words that Silence?: Freedom of Expression and Racist Hate Speech," this volume.

Young, Iris Marion 1992. "Five Faces of Oppression," in *Rethinking Power*, ed. Thomas Wartenberg. New York: SUNY Press, pp. 174–95.

Power in Public: Reactions, Responses, and Resistance to Offensive Public Speech

by Laura Beth Nielsen

Everyone who has spent time in public places has been part of a speech interaction initiated by a stranger. White women and people of color regularly encounter offensive racist and sexually suggestive speech in public places (Davis 1994; Duneier 1999; Feagin and Sikes 1994; Gardner 1980; Gardner 1995; Nielsen 2002; Nielsen 2004). Empirical evidence proves and commentary suggests that such speech is harmful to its targets (Delgado 1993; Feagin and Sikes 1994; Feagin 1991; MacKinnon 1993; Nielsen 2002; Nielsen 2004). This chapter considers the claim that offensive public speech, like other forms of "undesirable" speech, is "best" countered with more speech.

Despite notable exceptions (Delgado and Stefanic 1994; Delgado and Yun 1995; MacKinnon 1993; Matsuda et al. 1993; Meiklejohn 1948), many legal scholars advocate unfettered free speech, claiming that individuals who are offended or harmed by speech can (and should) counter these bad effects with various kinds of "more speech" (Abel 1998; Chevigny 1988; Post 1990; Post 1993; Volokh 1992). But what exactly might that entail? And how realistic is it to expect the target to engage the speaker?

The popular and jurisprudential preference for "more speech" places the burden of response on the individual target of such speech—but, as we shall see, only for *some* forms of speech and not others.[1] In this essay,

---

[1] For a discussion of potential justifications for state-supported speaking back, see Katharine Gelber's "Speaking Back: The Likely Fate of Hate Speech Policy in the United States and Australia," this volume.

I argue that the jurisprudential preference for more speech has serious flaws. The *first* section of this chapter demonstrates that not all public speech is created (or protected) equally. Various forms of offensive and threatening speech, including begging, are quite often legally regulated, and those regulations withstand judicial scrutiny. Although I am not here arguing in favor of more restrictions on street begging, I do aim to show that legal regulation of speech between strangers occurs routinely, and courts tend to uphold these statutes when begging (as opposed to racist or sexist hate speech) is the kind of speech at issue. Thus, when the targets of problematic public speech are more privileged members of society, the state seems quite willing to intervene to protect them. Where courts reject speech restrictions, they often do so with a prescription for "more speech." In the *second* section, I demonstrate that the "more speech" solution relies on faulty empirical assumptions. That is to say, for reasons that are entirely credible, targets of some sorts of problematic public speech do not in fact "talk back" because, for example, they fear violence or even government intervention on behalf of the harasser. The *third* section argues that it is easier to respond to begging because there are already a variety of formal mechanisms in place that discourage it. I *conclude* by arguing that the law protects the powerful from harassment in public places while placing on its less privileged members an unrealistic duty to respond or accept their own subordination.

1. All Speech is NOT Protected Equally

At first blush, begging may seem like an odd comparison for racist and sexist speech. I include the study of begging (or panhandling) in my research primarily to show that all public speech is *not* protected (or conversely, restricted) equally. By including begging with sexist and racist speech, I make no *normative* judgment about begging's relative harm or offense to ordinary citizens in public. However, law's treatment of begging provides insight into the legal and social construction of public places. Moreover, law's treatment of begging raises a number of theoretically driven, but empirically unexamined, questions. Unless we consider a form of unsolicited street speech that tends to target white men, we could not compare the treatment of more or less privileged groups in First Amendment jurisprudence. Also, by including begging, we can gain some leverage in examining how law defines "offensive" public speech and consider what individuals consider "offensive" in their everyday lives.

Hate speech, especially in public places, continues to pose a fundamental jurisprudential problem in American society. Law itself, in the form of judicial opinion and political debate, and most legal scholars largely view the problem of street harassment acontextually—that is, for the most part, the social context (public space) in which such interactions occur is absent from consideration and analysis. Attempts to regulate race-related speech, including racist hate speech, generally have met unsympathetic responses by the courts and by advocates of free speech. Restrictions on sexually suggestive or sexually explicit speech are largely accepted in the workplace and in education, but are not considered viable for public spaces. Meanwhile, restrictions on begging in public places are constitutionally ambiguous but continue to be upheld. These conflicts continue to unfold in legal battles over hate speech codes, restrictions on begging and loitering, as well as other restrictions on public speech and behavior.

A full doctrinal analysis of this disparity is beyond the scope of this paper, but it is important to understand that courts largely allow (with some notable exceptions) the regulation of begging, but strike down restrictions on racist speech and have provided little guidance on sexist speech outside the workplace. Although speech in public spaces enjoys the highest degree of First Amendment protection by the courts (*Hague v. CIO*, 1939), many cities and states have and enforce laws which specifically prohibit begging and which routinely survive constitutional scrutiny. Restrictions on begging in "public" places have been upheld in the Second,[2] Seventh,[3] and Eleventh Circuits.[4] In the Sixth Circuit there has been no ruling, but there has been an indication by the court that an ordinance restricting "reckless interference with pedestrian or vehicular traffic" likely would be upheld.[5]

One notable example is the New York City Transit Authority's prohibition on begging within the confines of the New York City Transit Authority (including Grand Central Station). When challenged by homeless advocates and civil libertarians, the Second Circuit Court of Appeals upheld the restriction. The *Young* Court determined that the ordinance restricted a type of speech that does not merit full constitutional protection and went on to articulate a compelling state interest in protecting commuters who must use this space for transportation. Relying on a survey

[2] *Young v. New York City Transit Authority*, 903 F.2d 146 (2d Cir.), cert. denied, 498 U.S. 984 (1990) (holding that begging and panhandling could be prohibited in the New York City subway system because the subway system is not a public place for purposes of First Amendment analysis. See below for more discussion of *Young*).

[3] *Gresham v. Beterson*, 225 F.3d 899 (7th Cir., 2000) (upholding a city ordinance on panhandling as a reasonable time, place, and manner restriction).

[4] *Smith v. Ft. Lauderdale*, 177 F.3d 954 (11th Cir., 1999) (upholding order of summary judgment in favor of city's ordinance restricting begging, soliciting, and panhandling on beaches as an acceptable time, place, and manner restriction).

[5] *Greater Cincinnati Coalition for the Homeless and Charles Godden v. Cincinnati*, 56 F.3d 710 (6th Cir., 1995) (denying standing to Godden, a beggar cited with an infraction on the basis of the ordinance).

conducted by the Transit Authority, commuters felt annoyed and some-times threatened by the beggars in "the *very real* context of the New York City subway," in which people with *legitimate* business are intimidated, harassed, and threatened (*Young*, p. 159; emphasis added). In a populist appeal, the Court asserted that the subway is the "primary means of transportation for literally millions of people of modest means, including hard-working men and women, students and elderly pensioners" (*Young*, p. 153). Moreover, ample alternative channels were left open to beggars in New York City, according to the *Young* Court, because panhandlers could beg in any of the streets and sidewalks of the city.

Other jurisdictions have allowed the regulation of begging in public places on the grounds that states have an interest in "providing a safe, pleasant environment and eliminating nuisance activity on the beach" (*Smith v. City of Ft. Lauderdale*, 1999, p. 956), and "ensuring public safety and order, in promoting the free flow of traffic on public streets and sidewalks" (*Madsen v. Women's Health Center*, 1994).

Despite these examples of courts allowing restrictions on public beg-ging, it is important to note that some courts have struck down legislation restricting begging on First Amendment grounds, including the Ninth[6] and Second Circuits.[7] Begging is thus regarded as a contentious free speech issue in American jurisprudence.

In contrast, laws, ordinances, and codes aimed at restricting racist speech have been passed in a variety of settings, but they have also been struck down. Hate speech regulation has been written into city ordinances (e.g. St. Paul, Minn., Legis. Code § 292.02 (1990), workplace environ-ments (Post 1990), as well as both public (*Doe v. University of Michigan*, 1989, or *UMW Post Inc. v. Board of Regents of the University of Wisconsin System*, 1991) and private institutions of higher learning (*Corry v. Stanford*, 1995). Only restrictions on racist speech in the workplace have been upheld, although not every situation has been legally tested. Restrictions on racist speech in institutions of higher learning and city ordinances have been struck down on the grounds that they are content-based, which the courts treat as a fundamental constitutional flaw.

In perhaps the most famous of the opinions on the subject, *R.A.V. v. City of St. Paul*, the Court overturned a St. Paul, Minnesota ordinance that

---

[6] *Blair v. Shanahan*, 775 F. Supp. 1315 (N.D. Cal. 1991) (striking down state statute criminalizing aggressive panhandling. *Blair* suffers a complex subsequent history in which portions of the opinion were vacated, but not the decision as to the unconstitutionality of the statute on First Amendment grounds).

[7] *Loper v. New York City*, 999 F.2d 699 (2nd Cir., 1993) (striking down a law which prohibited loitering for the purposes of begging throughout all of New York City).

prohibited "fighting words" that provoked violence, "on the basis of race, color, creed, religion, or gender" (1992), including cross-burning. More recently, the Court upheld an ordinance prohibiting cross-burning, but made very clear that the "speech" or expression embodied in the cross-burning remains protected. It is merely the "threat" embodied in cross-burning that can constitutionally be regulated (*Virginia v. Black*, 2003). A relatively unnoticed Supreme Court opinion, in *Black*, six justices agreed that the component of intimidation transformed the regular communicative cross-burning protected in *R.A.V.* into something that could be legally prohibited. The only disagreement among the six justice majority was whether or not cross-burning could presumptively be said to be threatening. Interestingly, the only African-American Supreme Court justice was also the only one who thought that cross-burning could be presumed to be threatening. Nonetheless, a statute prohibiting cross-burning done with the intent to intimidate is constitutionally valid so long as a judge or jury makes the determination about the intent to intimidate.

As one can see, the constitutional status of laws restricting racist hate speech is clearer than the constitutional status of laws prohibiting begging. It is definitely *not* permissible to merely prohibit the racist or sexist subset of hate speech (since such restrictions are likely to be regarded as content-based). However, it *may* be permissible to prohibit *all* forms of hate speech, and it certainly *is* permissible to restrict hate speech when done "with the intent to intimidate." Begging is somewhat more complex because the Supreme Court has not definitively ruled on whether begging is protected speech. Thus, depending on federal court jurisdiction, it may be possible to limit begging using time, place, and manner restrictions.

Of the three types of public discourse that concern me here (begging, race-related public speech, and gender-related public speech), gender-related public speech is the least doctrinally developed. Although verbal harassment on the basis of sex is prohibited by federal anti-discrimination laws in the workplace by Title VII of the Civil Rights Act of 1964, restrictions on gender-related speech in public have not been passed or challenged at the Supreme Court level. Although speech restrictions in the workplace now are widely accepted (but see Volokh 1992), the idea that women should not suffer unreasonable sexual advances by people with power over them was, until very recently, not widely accepted. In recent years, however, prohibitions on sexual harassment in the workplace have become accepted in the law, and even in society more generally. But harassing gender-related speech in public remains a novel and untested legal issue.

First Amendment doctrine about unsolicited speech between strangers in public places is confused at best. Statutes that are clearly content-based which mention "asking for money" are treated as though they are content-neutral (and therefore are subjected to a less burdensome constitutional standard as in *Smith v. Ft. Lauderdale*, 1999). Statutes designed to prohibit various kinds of speech that might disturb public order including racist speech are universally struck down (as content-based and therefore unjustifiable as in *Corry v. Stanford*, 1995). Why?

I suggest that the difference embodies judgment about the perceived social value of the target of the speech in question. What happens in fact is that speech which targets people of higher social status (e.g. begging) is successfully regulated, and speech that targets people on the basis of their race and/or gender is struck down. My perhaps simplistic, but factually accurate, analysis of this is that the law protects people from harassment and annoyance only when they are of a certain social status. As I see it, the law favors the powerful, and courts are hostile to the claims of people of color.

Scholars of Critical Race Theory have posited a more subtle version of this argument, according to which judges are sympathetic to claims they can understand (Delgado and Stefancic 1997; Delgado and Yun 1995; Lederer and Delgado 1995). Unfortunately, the relatively homogenous composition of the judiciary prevents those who have actually experienced the harms of hate speech (e.g. white women and people of color) from being in a position to decide such matters. The *Black* opinion only bears out this argument. In *Black*, Justice Clarence Thomas, the only African-American member of the Supreme Court, wrote separately from the majority in concurrence to deride the majority for the proposition that cross-burning could ever be done without the intent to intimidate. By contrast, and with respect to begging, the *Young* Court recognized that, "begging in the subway often amounts to nothing less than assault, creating in the passengers the apprehension of imminent assault" (*Young*, p. 157). Life experiences and a visceral understanding of harm, offense, and threat affect how justices understand the ramifications for targets of allowing offensive speech.

To observe that courts tend to give cursory treatment to some harms or subjective experiences of threat and not others is not necessarily to advocate for a different outcome. Rather, it merely points to the ways in which life experience frames how individual decision-makers decide that some words are *merely* offensive, while others are obviously and necessarily threatening. As I have argued, in the United States, we treat our problematic public speech differently. When it is targeted toward those with more social capital, courts are more likely to intervene.

And what advice do judges give to targets of unsolicited speech they abhor? More speech. In legal opinion and commentary, the remedy to troubling speech (when law does not intervene) is for the deliberative process to take place. We are supposed to engage in a "free trade in ideas" (*Abrams v. U.S.*, 1919) saying, "the best test of truth is the power of the thought to get itself accepted in the competition of the market" (*ibid.*). The idea that more speech is the answer to some forms of troubling speech also was famously declared by Justice Brandeis in his concurring opinion in *Whitney v. California* (1927). Brandeis wrote, "[i]f there be time to expose through discussion the falsehood and fallacies, to avert the evil by process of education, the remedy to be applied is more speech, not enforced silence" (at 377). Indeed, both formal law and ordinary citizens claim that it is not proper for law to intervene in offensive public speech encounters, at least those that revolve around racist and sexist speech (Nielsen 2004). The jurisprudentially preferred solution for the problem of offensive speech (of some varieties) is *more speech*.

This formulation of the problem (that an offensive idea has been inserted into the marketplace of ideas) crowds out other formulations of what precisely may be problematic about being the target of racist or sexist speech in public places. For example, a target might feel threatened, objectified, or dehumanized. In the course of day-to-day life, targets of racist or sexist speech are reminded of their subordinate social status or their status as sex objects. Framing the problem of offensive speech as skewing a "marketplace of ideas" makes the remedy of more speech seem sensible. After all, markets are thought to run well when they are unregulated and the power of a good product/idea will prevail in the end. Thus, rather than looking to the courts to prevent the offensive speech from entering the marketplace, consumers of ideas are expected to reject the bad ones, insert the better ones, and eventually prevail.

Unfortunately, judicial prescriptions for more speech are typically vague. Should a target of offensive speech (or consumer of ideas in a marketplace) respond immediately? Should she hold a protest or rally at a later time to condemn the idea? We do not know precisely what is imagined by the judiciary's instruction to engage in "more speech," but in what follows, we see what some individual targets think and do when unexpectedly confronted with offensive speech in public places.

In some contexts, more speech may be just what is called for. Organized counter-speech is documented and advocated as a remedy in the face of organized racist hate speech as when the Nazis march through Skokie (Abel 1998; Downs 1985), and in a policed public environment, counter-speech may be effective and safe. But what of the victim of individual, targeted hate speech in public? What kind of speech effectively counters the "truth" of a racial epithet or sexual slur? And how likely are those who are made its target likely to respond? I'll consider some of these questions in the next section.

2. "More Speech" Relies on Faulty Empirical Assumptions

This section of the paper uses empirical data to answer the question: (How) do ordinary citizens respond when they are made the target of offensive public speech?[8] In other words, does the judicially recommended response actually happen on the streets? If so when, and if not, why not? In what follows, I consider race-related public speech, gender-related public speech, and begging, in that order.

Before proceeding, it may be useful to note the following about my use of race and gender categories, and their relation to axes of privilege/subordination. In what follows, I do not mean to essentialize the individuals in these interactions to their race or gender. All people lie at different axes of privilege and subordination at different times and in different places. Hierarchies are not static and people are simultaneously privileged and burdened by complex and competing hierarchies. For example, in her privileged racial status, a white woman may make a racist comment to a man of color. Similarly, invoking his privileged status as a man, a man of color may make a sexually suggestive comment to a white woman. Finally, with begging, the power in the interactions is embedded in the classes of the parties involved. Unlike racist or sexist speech, begging is a request made by the more disadvantaged to the more privileged.

Responding to Race-Related Speech in Public Places

Race-related speech may be the most troubling kind of public speech, but, for the most part, targets of racist speech do not counter it. By far the most

---

[8] The research involved ethnography of public places and in-depth interviews with 100 subjects drawn from public places including a suburb, a small city, and a large city in California. I conducted the ethnography in subway stations, public thoroughfares, and outside places of business, varying the time of day and night and day of the week when I conducted observations. I then randomly chose people from the public places where I conducted observations to interview at a later time. Those interviews, lasting about an hour each, were tape-recorded, transcribed, and analyzed using NVivo, a qualitative data analysis software program. The final sample was 63% women and 37% men; 51% white, 27% African-American, 6% Hispanic, and 16% Asian/Pacific Islander. Over 50% of subjects were between the ages of 18 and 34, but the sample includes people in their 50s, 60s, and 70s. The research is described in detail in Nielsen, Laura Beth. 2004. *License to Harass: Law, Hierarchy, and Offensive Public Speech*. Princeton: Princeton University Press.

common response to problematic race-related public speech (e.g. racist speech, racist hate speech) between strangers in public is to ignore it. Targets say they typically, "do nothing," "laugh it off," "ignore it," or, "ignore it and leave" when they are targeted. This woman's story about being called a "white bitch" was common; she was subjected to a race-related comment and ignored it.

And there was a strike somewhere . . . and we had taken a boat ride, and when we got off, the strikers . . . didn't accost us physically, but verbally. And they hollered at us about all being white rich bitches who were supported by their husbands who never worked a day in their lives.

Q: And how did you respond to that?

A: . . . I didn't respond . . . you know.

Q: Just keep walking?

A: I just keep walking and acting like I'm deaf [laugh] (54-year-old white woman, homemaker, interview #05).

There are a variety of reasons why targets report that they are unwilling to engage in counter-speech. Many report being fearful for their safety, as these quotations illustrate:

And I was at a gas station, and a guy came out, didn't talk to me directly, but I knew he was talking about me. I was seated in the car, and the driver who was beside me was white, and the guy just said, kind of in the air, "I can see the driver's the only human being around here." Implying I was not a human being.

Q: Uh huh. And did you respond to that in any way?

A: No, I didn't, because I was afraid (21-year-old Filipino woman, student, interview #75).

[W]ith racist comments, I think it combines more things. You feel threatened . . . (24-year-old white woman, child advocate, interview #51).

Another subject noted that he does not have the option of responding (negatively) to racist speech due to fear. He said,

I can move away from the race-related comments, or I can adjust to it . . . I don't raise my voice at people. You know, you call me a black bastard, I'm going to say, "Thank you very much," and I'm gonna keep on moving if I can. I'm just going to keep moving (44-year-old African-American man, stockbroker, interview #29).

Fear is not the only reason to ignore such speech. A number of interviewees reported ignoring such speech because the speaker is ignorant, and targets believe that it is not their job to educate or debate with speakers. This is combined with the idea that such an interaction would ultimately not change the attitudes of the speaker at all, as this woman elaborates:

It [being the target of a racist comment] hurts my feelings, and you don't know if you want to stoop down to their level or just ignore it. There's really nothing you can do about it—I mean, they're ignorant (18-year-old African-American woman, interview #54).

It's not a problem if they do it [make racial comments], because that's just their own ignorance that they have to deal with—it's a problem that they haven't been educated enough to know that's not something that you do . . . If someone calls me a name, I try not to let it affect me, because that's their own ignorance . . . it's no reflection on me (37-year-old African-American woman, interview #94).

Unlike some gender-related public speech (e.g. sexually suggestive speech), which some may argue serves the quasi-legitimate purpose of allowing men and women to approach one another for courtship purposes, there is far less ambiguity about the redeeming social value of racist or race-related speech between strangers in public places. The vast majority of subjects agree that it is never socially appropriate for a stranger to comment on another person's race (Nielsen, 2004). The clarity of this norm makes the target of racist comments able to assess the situation quickly. Despite this, subjects reported mixed feelings and difficult decisions in determining how to deal with such race-related comments. This woman's response was typical of targets of race-related public speech.

I was at a gas station . . . [and] . . . two cars were trying to get into the same pump . . . My friend pulled in really fast and got it. And the guy [in the other car] jumps out and he's like, "Well that's my pump, and you guys better move." And we're like, "No," and he's like, "You fucking people need to go back where you came from. I'm sick of this, you guys come over here, think you can take everything away from us . . .". So I've had several situations like that. I've had in school, where people wrote in the books and they would spray paint on the wall "nigger exterminator" and things of that nature.
Q: Uh huh. And how did you respond to the guy at the gas station, or people— how do you typically respond to an incident like that?
A: *Now*, I try to calm myself and just ignore them because whatever their problem is, it's *their* problem, and it's not going to go away until *they* fix it regardless of what I do. But [sometimes I'd like to] . . . act as ignorant as they would and scream back and holler back, you know, "What are you going to do about it?" . . . *I just try not to escalate them*. Whatever. However they feel they feel, and there's nothing I can do about it, so I just pretty much try and ignore it and let it go (29-year-old African-American woman, account representative, emphasis mine, interview #79).

This woman's stories demonstrate the difficulties associated with the prescription for more speech to counter race-related speech in public.[9]

---

[9]   It is genuinely unclear what advocates of the "more speech" response have in mind. It sometimes seems that "more speech" requires a reasoned response to the content of the

Most notably, she indicates that she would like to try to use counter-speech when she says she would like to "act as ignorant as they are and scream back," indicating that there is a powerful competing force of civility or intelligence that prevents her from engaging in more speech. She also externalizes the problem. She says, "whatever their problem is, it's *their* problem . . ." (*ibid.*). By saying the speaker (and not the target) has the problem, she attempts to distance herself from the interaction, making it easier to deny that such interactions affect her at all.

More speech does, of course, occur, though rarely. In fact, only 16 of 100 respondents indicated that they had *ever* responded verbally to a racist comment.[10] The evidence suggests that men are more likely to respond verbally, though one woman talked about how she "corrects" people who make racist or race-insensitive remarks.

I don't like hearing racist remarks. You know, and I don't tolerate them. If I hear them, I say something . . . I'm . . . not gonna let shit slide, excuse my French. I feel strongly, you know, that if people stop tolerating racist remarks, people would stop making them. Now, I think I'm a perfect example, because those van drivers, for example, . . . they know better. They know that if they say—start—if they say, "Chink," I'm going to call them on it, if they even say, "Oriental," I'm going to educate them. I'll say, "Excuse." I'll do it very diplomatically . . . —"Chinamen," for example, I'll say, "You shouldn't do that, it's just [like] . . . somebody black being called a nigger. Don't do that. It's offensive. Maybe you don't know that," or I'll say something like that. Or I'll say, "You shouldn't call Asians oriental—there are oriental rugs and vases, but not people." You know? And people will usually accept it. They'll say, "Oh, oh, I didn't know that," or something like that (59-year-old African-American woman, volunteer worker, interview #85).

Other people responded less politely:

A: . . . [T]hree friends and I were all walking, and then this guy said, "Oh, one more of you and you're a gang," or something like that. Or whatever.
Q: And how did you respond to that?
A: I—I really—I didn't really care. I—but my friends . . . responded with some vulgar language (18-year-old African-American man, gas station attendant, interview #31).

problematic speech. But it is often hard to tell what such a reasoned response might look like. For example, consider a person who is targeted with a racial epithet. What is the content of such an epithet, and how would the target offer a reasoned response to that content? As we have seen, even when targets do respond, they are exceedingly unlikely to engage in this way.

[10] Of these, two were white men. That means that although 43 of the 47 respondents of color (92%) experienced such comments, only 12 of them (28%, or just slightly more than a quarter) ever responded directly.

These are classic examples of what happens when targets respond verbally. But it is hard to imagine that these interactions are changing the mind of the original speaker. After all, hurled epithets are probably not intended to start meaningful dialogue.

Perhaps the most adamant interviewee about responding to racist speech was a white man. When people responded to him, making note of his whiteness, he was quite offended, and said he would always respond, trying to "educate" the speaker (always a man of color) about his own racism. He said:

I was in a BART station in San Leandro, and uh—this dude asked me for a cigarette and [when I gave him one], he said, "Thanks, whitey, I appreciate that," and I said, "You know, man, I do have a name . . .". I'm pretty comfortable around people, enough to the point where I take that stuff and turn it into a conversation and try to gear them away from doing that in the future . . . (22-year-old white man, security officer, interview #56).

Another white man recounted similar stories, including this one:

Okay. The other day, again walking on Telegraph, further on Telegraph, um, I had a letter in my hand that I was looking to mail all day, and there was a little mail truck there with the mail guy in it . . . I handed him the letter and I said, "Hey, man, do you mind posting this for me?" He said, "No, not at all." He takes them and puts them in his little box. And he's talking to two guys standing around the truck, and the mailman in the truck was a black guy, and the two guys on the street . . . I gathered from his accent that he was Persian or Greek or something like that—he says to the mailman, "Why you want to help the white man out?" So—I turned around, and got an eyeful of him, and kind of wandered back over and [said], "Probably because he's a decent chap and because I put my $.32 stamp on it (28-year-old white man, student/disk jockey, interview #76).

Since men are less likely to be physically vulnerable, it may not be surprising that they are more likely to be willing to engage in a conversation that could potentially escalate into something more threatening. Moreover, this speaker, who did respond, is white (and thus, a member of the racially dominant group).

Some people of color said they felt an obligation to say something in the face of racist speech. It was simply something that they could not ignore.

Um. I don't know—they [race-related comments] just sort of seem to hit me personally, I guess. I really don't know why—but it's just when something racially comes up, I just take it more like it's sort of my duty to correct it. Or sort of try to deal with it (25-year-old Chinese-American man, service industry, interview #28).

Another subject spoke of her "obligation" to respond to individual acts of racism. As a light-skinned Hispanic mother, this respondent often is questioned about her relationship to her darker-skinned son. She told me,

[T]he most common comment that we received when he was a young, young child in arms, was—or when he was a little toddler, was, "Who's your mommy?" or "How come you're black and she's white?"... They see such a difference in our races, that they can't conceive on first glance that I'm his mother. And I got it so much, I got pretty used to fielding it from all races.... [One time], the remark was made like, "How come you're black and she's white?"And he said—he turned around and in his little bell-like three-year-old voice—he said, "It's because of my DNA."

She went on to explain her philosophy about why she responds when people question her or her son about race.

So, what I do is I educate people. You know. Both white and black. Hey—you may not know who you're talking to—is what I use with white people, and with black people I say, "Is that how your mother or grandmother taught you to deal with this issue?" and, "What kind of family are you from? Didn't you have a grandmother that taught you the right way to talk to folks?" ... And then with Christians you use, "Everybody's blood is red," and with politicians you go, "You don't know who you're talking to—it might be a voter that's on your side." There's a lot of ways to respond, and the best way is to get—to get past the personal point of being offended and educate people, because if they're even discussing it, they are dealing with these racial issues, and they're seeking some kind of resolution (51-year-old multiracial woman, laborer, interview #43).

In sum, overt verbal responses are more likely to be made by men, but overall, very few people (< 5%) respond verbally. Moreover, when you exclude white males, who after all have a different motivation for resisting racist speech targeted at whiteness, the number of overt responders is even lower. Some of those who respond do so rudely, while others attempt to use such interactions as an opportunity for educating others about the complexities of race and race-relations. The nature of the overt response depends on the nature of the comment, the place where the comment is made, as well as a determination about the violent tendencies of the speaker, among other things. The main point is that well under a third of those who have been targets of problematic race-related public speech have ever overtly responded.

Reactions to Gender-Related Speech in Public Places

Women repeatedly make the point that they are capable of dealing with some problematic gender-related public speech—in particular, offensive sexually suggestive speech—on their own. But how do women actually handle such speech? Do they, for example, follow the recommendations of legal scholars about combating such speech with more speech?

Women had a number of reactions to offensive sexually suggestive speech. In what follows, I describe how women react and respond to offensive sexually suggestive speech in public places. As we shall see, like targets of problematic race-related speech, targets of offensive sexually suggestive speech most commonly do not respond at all. When they do respond, the responses vary, depending on various features including the nature of the comment itself.

Although all 63 women interviewed claimed to have been the target of offensive, sexually suggestive speech by a stranger in a public place, the most common response was to simply ignore it. Of the 63 women interviewed, 27 (about 43%) said that ignoring offensive sexually suggestive speech was their primary response, although there were many reasons given for ignoring the speech.

Some women ignore such speech because they fear the consequences of any other response.

I know just last week, I was in the BART Station at Montgomery and there was, um, I think a homeless man who came up to me and said, "I hate women, they're all sluts" ... That probably sticks in my mind the most. . . .
Q: Um, what did you say to the guy who, um, informed you that all women are sluts?
A: Um, I just turned around; I didn't say anything. I was pretty scared of him (24-year-old white woman, student, interview #10).
A: [Men will say things] like, "Hey, baby, you look real good," or "Ooh, come back here and talk to me," or you know, "Let's go somewhere and be alone," that kind of stuff.
Q: And how do you typically respond to this type of comment?
A: It depends. *If I don't feel threatened, then I usually say something* like, you know, "Does your mother know you're here—talking to women this way?" or "How would you feel if someone talked to your girlfriend this way?" or something like that. *If I feel threatened, I just pretend like I didn't hear it and I keep going* (29-year-old white woman, interview #16, emphasis mine).

Notice that both respondents here make a calculation about their personal safety, and the second respondent also makes a reference to the women in the speaker's life. The reference to women close to the speaker is an attempt to embarrass the speaker by calling attention to shared social norms that the speaker has, at least for the moment, disregarded.

Occasionally, however, women's decision to ignore comments is a form of hidden resistance, or at least defiance. For example, some women ignore these comments because they think that the man seeks a response.

By ignoring such speech, these women are doing what they believe is the most effective thing to thwart the speaker's true desire.

> But that actually happens to me a lot when I'm running. Actually, I run at Fort Point, I live on the Peninsula, and when I go there by myself, someone always approaches me and talks to me—a man.
> Q: Mm hm. And how do you typically respond?
> A: Again, it sort of depends on the situation. Sometimes I ignore people. I rarely . . . give back any response, because that's what they're looking for, so I usually just ignore them (21-year-old Filipino-American woman, student, interview #74).

Women also fail to respond because they are ashamed. When a man shouted loudly that one woman had nice legs, she "Just kept on walking. I acted like I didn't hear it. I was embarrassed" (43-year-old African-American woman, project manager, interview #45). Women are ashamed because they feel they should be able to control being the target of offensive public speech by altering the way they dress, talk, and interact (Bowman 1993; Nielsen 2004).

The severity of the comment bears little relation to the response (or lack thereof). Both aggressive, offensive comments and subtle, pervasive ones are ignored, though for different reasons. Women often ignore the offensive, aggressive comments because they fear escalating the situation. They ignore the subtler and pervasive comments because to deal with all of them would be too time-consuming.

> Um. One time I was in Spain, and it was about two years ago, and I was walking down the street with a loose shirt and no make-up on. Trying to look, as blending-inable as possible. And um, from like, 100 feet down the street, this man started shouting in Spanish that I was a bitch and a whore—shouting it over and over. And following me down the street.
> Q: How far did he follow you?
> A: Probably about—I don't know—another 200 feet. . . .
> Q: . . . And how did you respond?
> A: I ignored him (26-year-old white woman, unemployed, interview #30).

Of the 63 women interviewed, well under half (26 or 41%) reported that they *ever* had verbally responded to offensive sexually suggestive speech in public. Furthermore, of the 24 women who did respond verbally, only 9 (14% of all the women interviewed) reported assertive responses, in the sense that they engaged the speaker and complained about being made a target in this way.

Among the women who responded verbally, the most unusual case came from a woman who seemed afraid of nothing. Although her story is the aberration, it exemplifies the kind of speech that seems to be imagined by scholars who advocate "more speech."[11]

I was walking down this street toward my house, and this drunk Mexican drove up and asked me to turn a trick, and I had just gotten off work . . . I weigh 250 pounds, and I'm 50 years old, and I had like this orange striped reflective vest on and everything. And blue jeans and work boots and glasses, and my hair was all—and I was dirty, and . . . I raised so much hell about it—not because he asked me for a trick, [but] because he was too drunk to tell I wasn't a hooker. I'm a grand-mother—a fat, old working grandmother, and he's asking me to turn a trick. "Man," I said, "what is wrong with you? You are drunk—you better take a good look at who I am!" . . . So anyway, I'm liable to go off on them. It's just—it depends on what's appropriate. You get a sense for—if you've been in the streets a long time yourself, you know when to just shine somebody on, or when to talk to them like you're one of them (51-year-old multiracial woman, laborer, inter-view #43).

This woman's bravado in this particular situation belies the fact that she too seeks to avoid such situations, and she recognizes that there are some times when a response is just not a good idea. Although she responds assertively here, this does not mean that she thinks that "more speech" is always the appropriate response. She also has a recipe for avoiding being made a target in the first place. She went on to say:

I mean, if you look gorgeous, you better wear big old loose clothes and big jackets. Don't walk around with no clothes on. That's stupid . . . lots better to protect yourself than to be a target. And if you don't want people to say stuff to you— don't give them anything to talk about. Or you know, carry a body guard. Get some big old bad guy, or obviously a boyfriend or a husband, wear a wedding ring. Walk in a certain kind of protective camouflage. You know. It's easy enough to get a big ole puffy coat or loose wrapping stuff that hangs down to your ankles, and wear it . . . people out there are crazy and they're messed up and they're deranged, and they're all loose. Police can't protect you—the courts aren't on your side. You know—you better learn how to handle your shit. That's just the way it is. And if you don't want people to make suggestive comments, look them right in the eye, and just dare them to. And then talk about their *Mama. And who raised them* (51-year-old multiracial woman, laborer, interview #43, emphasis mine).

When this woman does respond to offensive speech, her response is also designed to embarrass the speaker. By calling the offender's family into question ("talk about their Mama"), she draws attention to the fact that his remarks are not socially acceptable.

---

[11] See note 9.

As we've already seen, when asked how they respond to sexually suggestive speech from strangers in public places, the vast majority say that they do not respond at all. Those who do respond typically do not respond as colorfully as the woman quoted above.

Some women respond to offensive sexually suggestive speech non-verbally, but with a communicative message nonetheless—an obscene gesture. Of the 63 women interviewed, 3 (less than 5%) reported making such a gesture, and one of them indicated that this response escalated the situation.

I was taking a walk with a friend, it was when I lived in the beach flat, and I was walking along that street where like all the cars go out, and it was just a bunch of white teenage boys, and they—and we were just really wanting to be—we were like having an intense talk, and we didn't want to deal with a bunch of asshole guys shouting out, "Hey—blah blah blah," you know—like stupid shit. And so um, and so—I don't even remember what they first said, but I flipped them off, and then they shouted out that I had a fat ass (26-year-old white woman, unemployed, interview #30).

Far more common responses include glaring or "acting rudely" to those who targeted them. Although it may require a perceptive speaker to notice, by responding this way these women attempted to communicate their message to those who made them targets. Of course, it is impossible to know if the speakers actually received the intended message.

Oh, I was coming from my brother-in-law's office in Downtown Oakland. Um, walking—actually, I was walking back to his office in Downtown Oakland, and some person got directly into my face and said something totally out of place as far as wanting to . . . screw me.
Q: Mm hm. And is that the word he used?
A: Uh . . . "[I] want some of that ass."
Q: Mm hm. And how did you respond to that?
A: I looked at him like he was crazy and kept walking (43-year-old African-American woman, office administrator, interview #63).

Sexually suggestive speech in public often begins as something more benign. Women are more likely to respond to men who make benign or friendly conversation, only to have the conversation take a turn for the offensive. These perpetrators start seemingly polite conversations with women in public places, counting on the woman to respond as is socially appropriate. When the woman indicates that she is uninterested in the man, the situation degenerates.

When approached as though for a date, 8 women reported being rude or mentioning a boyfriend or husband. Sometimes this is sufficient to make the men go away.

Yeah, actually, I was buying some flowers on the cart out at Market Street, and had a gentleman come up and say, "You know, I'd really like to take you out." It was really interesting, he didn't introduce himself or say anything else; he just started with that one statement. So I chuckled kind of at first, and said, "No thank you, I have a boyfriend." And then he continued to hang around, and then one of the last comments, and again I was wearing a skirt, which is interesting, but he said, "Wow, your legs go from your ass to the ground" (23-year-old white woman, marketing manager, interview #59).

Some women acknowledged that they lied about boyfriends and husbands in order to discourage unwanted amorous attention.

It was a man, and he complimented me on my smile.
Q: Mm hm. And how did you respond to that?
A: I smiled and said, "Thank you."
Q: Mm hm. And how did you feel when he said that?
A: Well, I was a little bit uneasy. You know, I was flattered, but . . . was kind of expecting him to take it further, and he did. You know.
Q: Uh huh. And what did he say after that?
A: Well, he asked me out for coffee. Well, he started a conversation, and then later on he asked me out. And I told him I was engaged.
Q: Uh huh. And is that true?
A: No. That's a lie (19-year-old East Indian woman, interview #71).

Referring to a boyfriend or husband to thwart unwanted sexual attention is a tactic about which feminists may well be ambivalent. Although effective in some circumstances, it does not communicate any of the messages that women said they would like to convey—that men do not have unfettered access to them simply because they are in a public place. Nor does it convey the message that it is legitimate for the woman to resist such attention simply because she does not want it. For example, the woman whose legs go from her ass to the ground went on to say, "It made me angry. I was like, 'Who are you to speak to me that way?' You know, I didn't invite this conversation whatsoever." But her response did little or nothing to convey that message. The underlying message when she refers to her male partner is that such comments might be welcome if she were unattached, despite most women's claim that there is virtually no chance they would make plans with a stranger they met in a public place. Rebuffing unwanted sexual attention by mentioning a husband or boyfriend conveys a false message to the man. And it plays to the idea that unattached women are somehow open prey for men at all times.

As we have seen, most women who are made targets of sexually suggestive speech in public places just ignore it, though they do so for a variety of reasons. Some are afraid, some are refusing to give the speaker what he wants (e.g. a reaction), and some are ashamed. Of course, just because the majority of respondents ignore such speech does not mean that they simply accept its message. In fact, many women report a number of hidden actions they take when they are made the target of offensive sexually suggestive speech. These hidden actions include leaving the situation (reported by 19% of the women interviewed), deciding the speaker is stupid (reported by 3% of the women interviewed), "laughing it off" (reported by 6% of the women interviewed), externalizing (deciding the speaker has the problem, reported by 3% of the women interviewed), and "denial" (reported by 3% of the women interviewed).

When women do respond to offensive sexually suggestive speech in public places, their responses often are ambiguous. Some report offering an obscene gesture; some glare or act rudely; and others mention having a husband or boyfriend. These responses do not critically engage with the (offensive) message of the speech in question. This is not to suggest that women have an obligation to be more forthcoming and to jeopardize their safety for the sake of combating sexism. Instead, the purpose of illustrating women's reactions, responses, and resistance is to demonstrate that the seemingly simple "more speech" solution is not so simple after all. Targets have a difficult time "handling it" when it comes to responding to such speech.

Begging

In contrast to the other types of problematic public speech, targets of begging are not reluctant to respond to panhandlers. When the initial speech is deemed appropriate, targets often respond by saying something benign such as "no thank you" or, "not today." Even when the initial speech is perceived to be inappropriate, targets are nevertheless considerably more likely to respond verbally than are targets of race-related or gender-related public speech. Of course, the same considerations about personal safety are present in targets' calculations about whether to respond to begging. However, respondents do not report as many complicated, calculated ways of dealing with it as they do with the other forms of offensive public speech. Far more subjects simply respond to begging, indicating that this type of speech is less intimidating than the other forms of street speech discussed above.

As with the other forms of speech, a very common reaction to begging is to ignore the request for money. But, although this response is common, it is not the most common reaction. Surprisingly, the most common response to begging is actually to respond to the person speaking to resist the idea that the target should give money to the speaker. For example, one man says:

At the BART station . . . there's this gentlemen, you know, I don't know him, but he keeps coming up to me . . . and I ain't never seen him before, and he puts on this little friendly act like you know him and stuff, but you don't know him . . . It's really very uncomfortable for me. . . . Basically I will tell him, "No, I don't have any [money]." He says, "Aw, come on, come on, brother." I say, "Brother, I don't have any, I'm trying to go to work and get it myself." And he'll just go about his business (34-year-old African-American man, laborer, interview #35).

Another respondent told a similar story:

Most of the time, I just don't say anything, I keep going, and then if they get persistent, then I just really tell them . . . "Just go elsewhere." You know, one time I was in San Francisco and a young boy came up, a young man, dressed really well, and he said he didn't have any money, and gave me this big story, and I said, "Well, there's places you can go eat if you're hungry, I don't have any money on me" (59-year-old white woman, interview #60).

But, many people are not as assertive; they just politely say they are unable to give money. The polite response that beggars receive is indicative of the fact that targets do not take offense at begging in the same way they do for race-related or gender-related public speech. Evidently, targets think that beggars deserve a respectful response. As we have seen, this is not the case with the other forms of public speech considered here.

There is also a certain nonchalance when targets discuss begging. Although they report occasionally being afraid of a panhandler, these interactions mostly are described as trivial and unthreatening. This comports with the data presented elsewhere which shows that respondents view begging as the least serious personal and social problem of these forms of speech (Nielsen 2000; Nielsen 2004).

There may be multiple reasons for this. First, with begging, the target is identified for his or her more powerful position in the interaction. This may partly account for why targets of panhandlers may feel less threatened by it. Second, as we shall see in the following section, there are a number of formal mechanisms to eliminate or reduce begging in public places. Thus, unlike race-related and gender-related public speech, which encounter no such mechanisms of formal resistance, there are many processes by which begging in public places is discouraged. This difference may also give respondents confidence in responding to begging, but not to the other kinds of public speech. More on the latter point in the next section.

3. How State Action Supports "More Speech" in Response to Begging

As we have seen, targets of begging are considerably more likely to speak back than targets of either race-related or gender-related public speech. While there may be many reasons for this, I suggest that one reason is the existence of various formal mechanisms that discourage begging. I shall argue that these mechanisms support speaking back in the case of begging. Furthermore, the absence of such mechanisms in the cases of race-related and gender-related public speech actually function to discourage speaking back in those cases.

Most large cities in the United States have ordinances prohibiting begging. In fact, in its 1996 report on "anti-homeless" laws, litigation, and alternatives, the National Law Center on Homelessness and Poverty documents that of the 50 largest cities in the United States, at least 36 (75% of those reporting) had city ordinances of one variety or another prohibiting begging (data unavailable for 2 cities) (Poverty 1994; Poverty 1996; Poverty 1999). More specifically, 10 cities have city-wide bans on begging, 20 cities prohibit begging in particular public locations, while 20 cities have ordinances prohibiting "aggressive panhandling" (Poverty 1996 at 8–9). In a 1999 update of this study, the National Law Center on Homelessness and Poverty documents that 43 (86% of those reporting) of the nation's 50 largest cities had laws against begging (data unavailable for 1 city) (Poverty 1999 at ii).

In some of the nation's largest cities, at least, these ordinances and others like them are designed to prevent homeless people from annoying other citizens, and are enforced with vigor and regularity. In addition to an increase in the number of cities that have ordinances preventing panhandling in one form or another, the National Law Center reports that over a third of these cities instituted "crackdowns" on panhandling in the year studied (Poverty 1999). Indeed, mayoral campaigns are won and lost on campaigns to reduce or eliminate panhandling in public. And, as explained above, these ordinances often are upheld in the face of First Amendment challenges because restrictions on begging tend to be interpreted as content-neutral.

In addition to formal legal mechanisms designed to combat begging, informal mechanisms to resist begging also exist. These programs fall into three categories: voucher, competition, and education programs. Voucher programs enable potential givers to purchase vouchers in very small increments to hand to panhandlers in lieu of change. The benefit of the voucher is that it can be used only for approved expenses (not drugs or alcohol, in theory).

In the summer of 1991, a partnership between the University of California Berkeley, local businesses, homeless service agencies, and the City of Berkeley was formed to establish the "Berkeley Cares" voucher program. Approximately 100,000 25-cent vouchers were sold from some 100 businesses annually. Over 95% of the vouchers sold were redeemed at over 200 businesses (Fagan 1994; Boot 1991). Given its success, Berkeley's voucher program served as a model for more than a dozen other voucher programs in the United States (Fagan 1994; Boot 1991).

Some cities also employ "competition" programs that are designed to "compete" with individual panhandlers by collecting the donations of generous pedestrians in coin boxes rather than allowing them to go to panhandlers. Some cities employing this type of program include Buffalo, New York (Childress 1995), Santa Monica, California (City News Service, 1997), and Durham, North Carolina (Herz 1994). The money collected is then used for homeless programs and support. Cities erect colorful and compelling containers such as mock parking meters (Herz 1994) or dolphin-shaped banks (Herz 1994) to attract and educate pedestrians. In some cities, local merchants or merchant associations who display signs encouraging potential donors to refrain from giving cash to the homeless also match the funds collected.

Finally, other formal, extra-legal mechanisms designed to resist begging in public places include awareness and education programs. These programs provide referrals to homeless people in the form of pamphlets listing locations of soup kitchens, homeless shelters, as well as city, county, state, and federal aid agencies. Similar pamphlets are distributed to potential donors to educate them about the options available for charitable donation, including donations to non-profit and religious groups that help the homeless. For example, in New York City, part of the anti-panhandling movement was to convince targets that by giving cash to panhandlers, they would be preventing the person from getting help (Lessig 1995).

That there are such formal and informal state policies prohibiting (or discouraging) begging suggests that such policies are necessary and this, in turn, suggests that it is simply not viable to expect the targets of such speech to combat it with "more speech". Moreover, by formally discouraging begging, these policies send a social message that begging is inappropriate and this, in turn, supports those inclined to refuse the panhandler's request for money.

These formal and informal mechanisms set up by the state (in the form of speech regulations) and by business and business interests (such as voucher and competition programs) support targets in speaking back if they are troubled by begging. Although there are these formal mechanisms that support speaking back in the case of begging, there are no such mechanisms for those seeking to resist race-related and gender-related public speech. In such cases, we are on our own.

4. Conclusion: Law and Power in Sidewalk Social Encounters

As we have seen, reactions and responses to both race-related and gender-related street speech are the product of complicated calculations made by the targets of such speech. While some targets speak back and convey a message to the speakers (and to everyone else who witnesses such interactions), it is far more common for targets to ignore the speech altogether (or to have a hidden response).

One interpretation of these data is that targets respond to problematic public speech when they are really offended by it. Some First Amendment scholars whose model for combating racist and sexist speech involves "more speech" may take heart in these results, claiming that they are evidence that simply allowing more speech is effective. Those who really are bothered by such speech will respond.

This interpretation, however, ignores the effects such speech has on many of its targets. All targets, whether they reported responding to such speech or not, said that they weighed their options very carefully when deciding how and whether to respond, and that the most important factor that determined their response was their own safety in the situation. So, these comments engender fear for physical safety, just as many critical race scholars have claimed (Delgado and Yun 1995). And since women are more likely to fear for their physical safety when they are made targets of sexually suggestive speech than are man-targets, "more speech" disproportionately burdens women by requiring that they overcome their fears for their safety more often than men. This is in addition to the burden placed by the "more speech" idea in the first instance.

A second interpretation of these data is that there is very little resistance on the part of the targets. By failing to contradict such comments, the targets of offensive public speech might be accused of tacitly participating in their own subordination. This interpretation belies the complicated processes that underlie targets' decisions about protesting such comments. The data show that targets *are* inclined to respond, but often are precluded from doing so because they fear for their safety. Targets' options are limited.

Those who do engage in active forms of resistance by talking back to their harassers may be doing something serious to combat prevailing power relations, including racism and sexism, by managing to "redefine positively their general social position relative to the dominant group" (McCann and March 1996). The problem is that this is rare. Only certain members of the targeted group (i.e. more often whites, and more often men) have the luxury of resisting by talking back. Even they are more likely to choose not to do so.

Overt state power may seem absent in these fleeting but pervasive street encounters, but it is not. State power, through law, works to normalize and justify such interactions when they are race- or gender-related. The false but tacit assumption that "more speech" is both easy and simple, coupled with the assumption that any proposed regulation of problematic race- or gender-related speech would not survive judicial scrutiny, provides powerful normative reasons for people to oppose the legal regulation of such speech. When the offensive public speech is begging, and the targets include the more privileged members of society, by contrast, the state intervenes. Thus, state power is implicated because for certain kinds of public speech (problematic gender- or race-related speech), but not others (begging), the judicially preferred solution, "more speech," requires the burden to be borne by the target, with no help from the state. Law, as an institution and as official ideology, treats such offensive public speech as a problem with which its targets must live.

References

Abel, Richard L. 1998. *Speaking Respect, Respecting Speech*. Chicago, IL: University of Chicago Press.

Boot, Max 1991. http://articles.latimes.com/1991-05-07/news/mn-1306_1_ voucher-program.

Bowman, Cynthia Grant 1993. "Street Harassment and the Informal Ghettoization of Women," *Harvard Law Review* 106.

Chevigny, Paul 1988. *More Speech: Dialogue Rights and Modern Liberty*. Philadelphia, PA: Temple University Press.

Childress, Steven Alan 1995. Appeal and Error in First Amendment Adjudication, Doctoral Dissertation for University of California at Berkeley, UMI Dissertation Services, Inc., Microform No. 9602509.

Davis, Diedre 1994. "The Harm That Has No Name: Street Harassment, Embodiment, and African-American Women," *U.C.L.A. Women's Law Journal* 4.

Delgado, Richard 1993. "Words That Wound: A Tort Action for Racial Insults, Epithets, and Name Calling," in *Words That Wound: Critical Race Theory,*

Assaultive Speech, and the First Amendment, edited by Charles R. Lawrence, Mari J. Matsuda, Richard Delgado, and Kimberle W. Crenshaw. Boulder, CO: Westview Press.

Delgado, Richard, and Jean Stefancic 1997. *Must We Defend Nazis? Hate Speech, Pornography, and the New First Amendment*. New York: New York University Press.

Delgado, Richard, and Jean Stefanic 1994. "Hateful Speech, Loving Communities: Why Our Notion of 'A Just Balance' Changes So Slowly," *California Law Review* 82.

Delgado, Richard, and David Yun 1995. "'The Speech We Hate': First Amendment Totalism, the ACLU, and the Principle of Dialogic Politics," *Arizona State Law Journal* 27: 1281.

Downs, Donald 1985. *Nazis in Skokie: Freedom, Community, and the First Amendment*. Notre Dame, IN: University of Notre Dame Press.

Duneier, Mitchell 1999. *Sidewalk*. New York: Farrar, Straus, and Giroux.

Fagan, Kevin. 1994. "Berkeley Finding Vouchers Work: Program to Help Homeless Being Used More and More," *San Francisco Chronicle. Berkeley*, p. A21.

Feagin, Joe R. 1991. "The Continuing Significance of Race: Antiblack Discrimination in Public Places," *American Sociological Review* 56: 101–16.

Feagin, Joe R., and Melvin P. Sikes 1994. *Living with Racism: The Black Middle-Class Experience*. Boston, MA: Beacon Press.

Gardner, Carol Brooks 1980. "Passing By: Street Remarks, Address Rights, and Urban Women," *Sociological Inquiry* 50.

Gardner, Carol Brooks 1995. *Passing By: Gender and Public Harassment*. Berkeley, CA: University of California Press.

Herz, Richard 1994. "No Homeless People Allowed: A Report on Anti-Homeless Laws, Litigation and Alternatives in 49 United States Cities," pp. 1–120. Washington, DC: National Law Center on Homeless & Poverty.

Lederer, Laura, and Richard Delgado (eds.) 1995. *The Price We Pay: The Case Against Racist Speech, Hate Propaganda, and Pornography*. New York: Hill and Wang.

Lessig, Lawrence 1995. "Understanding Changed Readings: Fidelity and Theory," 47 *Stanford Law Review* 395.

MacKinnon, Catharine 1993. *Only Words*. Cambridge: Harvard University Press.

Matsuda, Mari J., Charles R. Lawrence, Richard Delgado, and Kimberle Williams Crenshaw 1993. *Words That Wound: Critical Race Theory, Assaultive Speech, and the First Amendment*. Boulder, CO: Westview Press.

McCann, Michael W., and Tracey March 1996. "Law and Everyday Forms of Resistance: A Socio-Political Assessment," *Studies in Law, Politics, and Society* 15: 207.

Meiklejohn, Alexander 1948. *Free Speech and Its Relation to Government*.

Nielsen, Laura Beth 2000. "Situating Legal Consciousness: Experiences and Attitudes of Ordinary Citizens about Law and Street Harassment," *Law and Society Review* 34: 201–36.

Nielsen, Laura Beth 2002. "Subtle, Pervasive, Harmful: Racist and Sexist Remarks in Public as Hate Speech," *Journal of Social Issues* 58: 265–80.

Nielsen, Laura Beth 2004. *License to Harass: Law, Hierarchy, and Offensive Public Speech*. Princeton: Princeton University Press.

Post, Robert 1990. "Racist Speech, Democracy, and the First Amendment," *William and Mary Law Review* 32.

Post, Robert 1993. "Meiklejohn's Mistake: Individual Autonomy and the Reform of Public Discourse," *University of Colorado Law Review* 64.

Poverty, National Law Center on Homelessness & 1994. "No Homeless People Allowed: A Report on Anti-Homeless Laws, Litigation and Alternatives in 48 United States Cities," pp. 1–120. Washington DC: National Law Center on Homelessness & Poverty.

Poverty, National Law Center on Homelessness & 1996. "Mean Sweeps: A Report on Anti-Homeless Laws, Litigation and Alternatives in 50 United States Cities," pp. 1–71. Washington DC: National Law Center on Homelessness & Poverty.

Poverty, National Law Center on Homelessness & 1999. "Out of Sight—Out of Mind: A Report on Anti-Homeless Laws, Litigation and Alternatives in 50 United States Cities," pp. 1–84. Washington DC: National Law Center on Homelessness & Poverty.

Volokh, Eugene 1992. "Freedom of Speech and Workplace Harassment," *University of California Law Review* 39: 1791.

Genocidal Language Games[1]

Lynne Tirrell

The road to genocide in Rwanda was paved with hate speech.

—*William Schabas*[2]

Words have killed my country.

—*Naasson Munyandamutsa*[3]

What makes power hold good, what makes it accepted, is simply the fact that it doesn't only weigh on us as a force that says no, but that it traverses and produces things, it induces pleasure, forms knowledge, produces discourse. It needs to be considered as a productive network which runs through the whole social body, much more than as a negative instance whose function is repression.

—*Michel Foucault*[4]

1. Introduction

The power of language to shape social being is clearly displayed in the workings of derogatory terms for human beings. The normative power of derogatory terms is most obvious in their negative force, but they also exert positive power, giving social and material strength to those who wield them. Using such terms helps to construct a strengthened 'us' for the

[1] I would like to thank Catherine Z. Elgin, Ishani Maitra, and Mary Kate McGowan for their insightful comments on an earlier draft of this chapter. I am deeply indebted to Robert Gakwaya for his invaluable research assistance, and strength of heart.
[2] Schabas, William 2000, p. 144.
[3] Naasson Munyandamutsa, speaking at "The Language of Genocide" symposium, Harvard University, March 27, 2007.
[4] Foucault 1980, p. 119.

speakers and a weakened 'them' for the targets, thus reinforcing or even realigning social relations.[5] As we shall see, such speech acts establish and reinforce a system of permissions and prohibitions that fuel social hierarchy. The changing linguistic landscape of Rwanda in the early 1990s illustrates how linguistic practices eroded protective norms, and thus opened the door to previously prohibited actions. In this and other twentieth-century genocides, the majority population was made ready to kill their minority neighbors, first by getting them talking amongst themselves as if these neighbors were not really people at all, using derogatory terms for these others that spread fear and disgust. Then the derogatory terms were used openly and publicly, increasingly targeting individuals. As people get used to this new disregard, non-linguistic disregarding actions become more widely accepted. It is not a short route from derogating speech acts to murder, but it is crucial to understand the power of speech to facilitate the growth of both linguistic and broader social norms that make murder and mayhem come to be accepted.

The use of derogatory terms played a significant role in laying the social groundwork for the 1994 genocide of the Tutsi in Rwanda. Linguistic practices and the norms that govern them do not operate alone; they shape and are shaped by collateral social practices and norms. These norms and practices produce social possibilities, granting power to some participants while denying it to others. In Rwanda, the genocide was preceded by an increase in the use of anti-Tutsi derogatory terms, at first primarily amongst Hutu, who used these terms not as epithets hurled directly at Tutsi, but as in-group ways of referring to Tutsi. Use of these derogatory terms marked the Hutu as 'us' and the Tutsi as 'them,' during "animation sessions" which drummed up anti-Tutsi fervor.[6] As these linguistic practices took hold amongst the Hutu, the terms became more openly and directly aimed at Tutsi. Then, during the 100 days of the genocide, derogatory terms and coded euphemisms were used to direct killers to their victims, urging them to "finish the work," "clear the tall trees," that is, to kill. Understanding these speech acts helps to illuminate important ways that power is enacted through discourse, how speech acts can prepare the way for physical and material acts, and how speech generates permissions for actions hitherto uncountenanced. Studying the role of speech acts and linguistic practices in laying the groundwork of the genocide illuminates how patterns of speech acts become linguistic practices that constitute permissibility conditions for non-linguistic behaviors. Understanding

---

[5] See Jacques Semelin (2003), "Toward a Vocabulary of Massacre and Genocide," *Journal of Genocide Research* (2003), 5(2): pp. 193–210, especially p. 201.

[6] Des Forges 1999, p. 39, 45.

this action-engendering force can make sense of thinking that words can destroy a people and a nation.

Linguistic violence is violence enacted or delivered through discursive behaviors, that is, through speech acts that would ordinarily constitute social or psychological damage to the targeted person, as well as through speech acts that generate permissions for physical damage, including assault and death. Like physical violence, linguistic violence uses its force to injure or abuse, and the varieties of harms it can cause are as multiplicitous as the functions of speech. Just as violations come in degrees, so too do the damages of linguistic violence. In Rwanda, as in any society marked by civic struggle, people often disregarded the power of linguistic violence; avoiding physical violence, torture, and death were higher priorities. Nevertheless, linguistic violence, itself constituting psychosocial and cultural harm to its targets, also created permissions for the very acts of physical violence they sought to avoid. If we take seriously Wittgenstein's view that a language is a way of life, then we must examine the broader Rwandan social context in understanding how linguistic practices contributed to the genocide.

This paper offers a philosophical analysis of genocidal language games, with a focus on the role that language played in setting the social conditions for the 1994 genocide in Rwanda. By analyzing the role that derogatory terms played in Rwanda, we can see that these derogatory terms are action-engendering—that is, they license non-linguistic behaviors. The most commonly used derogatory terms included '*inyenzi*' (Kinyarwanda for 'cockroach'), and '*inzoka*' (Kinyarwanda for 'snake'). In addition to altering beliefs and licensing inferences about those against whom the terms are used, the use of such terms can also make actions like assault and even murder seem legitimate. Few cultures like snakes, but in Rwanda, boys are proud when they are trusted to cut the heads off snakes. There are significant actions associated with '*inzoka*', so it is not trivial to use this term for the Tutsi. I shall argue that the widespread use of such terms played a significant role in bringing about the Rwandan genocide. Because of the action-engendering force of derogatory terms, actions hitherto unthinkable (i.e. the extermination of a people) came to be regarded as socially appropriate and even required. In short, I will be supporting Schabas's claim that "the road to genocide in Rwanda was paved by hate speech."[7]

---

[7] Schabas 2000. Neither Schabas nor I maintain the absurd view that speech alone *caused* the genocide. Speech acts were a key mechanism for reshaping social norms, and it was the confluence of linguistic and non-linguistic behaviors that promulgated genocide.

The paper proceeds as follows. In § 2, I offer some historical background about Rwanda, to aid unfamiliar readers in sorting out the key events and processes at work, focusing on the late twentieth-century changes leading up to the genocide. The distinction between horizontal and vertical ethnic systems is used here to help frame questions about the changing social landscape in Rwanda. Then, in § 3, I introduce key elements of my analysis of derogatory terms, focusing on deeply derogatory terms like '*inyenzi*' and '*inzoka*'. I set out five features of deeply derogatory terms, and offer an apparently derogatory case that is in fact an illustrative near-miss. In § 4, I further develop this theoretical framework, showing how '*inyenzi*' meets the criteria set out in § 3, and argue that the widespread linguistic practice of using '*inyenzi*' and similar derogatory terms to refer to Tutsi individuals played a crucial role in licensing the 1994 genocide. This section includes a brief exposition of the inferential role of '*inyenzi*' (cockroach) and a sketch of relevant aspects of the inferential role of '*inzoka*' (snake). Then, in § 5, I return to the concept of genocidal language games, arguing for the important action-engendering aspect of the inferential roles of deeply derogatory terms as used in Rwanda. In closing, I consider some reflections, offered after the genocide, about the role that language played in laying the genocidal groundwork.

2. Rwanda Before the Genocide: Some Basic Background

Imagine a society of multiple ethnicities all living in peace and relative equality. Ethnic groups are fluid, members intermarry, and children are not shunned. Ethnic identities, while often recognized, are not a determining force in one's life prospects. Pascasie, a Tutsi woman born in 1959, who suffered many horrors of the genocide, says that growing up in Nyanza, "Ethnicity didn't seem to matter to the ordinary Rwandan; it seemed to matter only to the people who wielded power."[8] Within Rwanda, there is one language, one cuisine, shared songs and dances, common marriage rituals, shared customs of all sorts. Thus, ethnic boundaries are vague and do not fit anthropological categories.[9] In fact, for a long

---

[8] Pascasie Mukasakindi, in deBrouwer and Hon Chu, 2009, p. 74. See also Gourevitch 1998, pp. 54–5 for early Belgian observations of Rwandan unity.

[9] See Mamdani 2004, chapters 2 and 3, for a thoughtful critique of assimilating 'Hutu' and 'Tutsi' to ethnicities at all. Instead, Mamdani urges us to think of these as state-enforced "bipolar" political identities (p. 73). Rwanda also includes a people called the 'Twa,' whose presence in Rwanda is said to pre-date the arrival of both the Hutu and the Tutsi. The Twa are a tiny minority, left out of this bipolar power play.

time, people could move from one ethnicity to another, simply by having more or fewer cows. Applying Charles Mills' distinction between horizontal and vertical racial systems, we might call this a *horizontal ethnic system*.[10] There are many who would describe pre-genocide Rwanda this way, more or less.[11] A *vertical ethnic system*, in contrast, makes identity features relevant to one's life prospects, marking amongst ethnic groups a clear hierarchy determining access to power, resources, and opportunities.

The *Horizontalist* view describes Hutu and Tutsi living in harmony, playing soccer, sharing a drink of banana wine or Primus at the end of the day, intermarrying, and generally looking after each other.[12] Neighbors might bring neighbors soup, but not lend each other money. Some Tutsi survivors, and Hutu *génocidaires* as well, suggest a relatively horizontal society that erupted into violence to create hierarchy. Even before colonization in the late nineteenth century, Joseph Sebarenzi says, "Rwandans spoke one language—Kinyarwanda—worshipped one God, and answered to one King."[13] Sebarenzi argues that although Tutsi had more "power, social status, and influence" than Hutu, for centuries under Tutsi monarchies, and then under colonial rule after the 1880s, nevertheless, the people lived peacefully together following an ancient Rwandan saying, "*Turi bene mugabo umwe*," meaning "we are all sons and daughters of the same father."[14] This Horizontalist view emphasizes a general social unity and fluid social categories. Evidence of shared social customs is strong, as is evidence of intermarriage, and ethnic boundary crossing, which supports the Horizontalist thesis, but is not conclusive.

There is also, however, ongoing evidence of ethnicity shaping life prospects, which supports the Verticalist thesis. The *Verticalist* view holds that there was always hierarchy between the groups, with Tutsi ruling

---

[10]   Mills 1998, p. 43.

[11]   Jean Hatzfeld describes it thus: "Black Africa is a formidable medley of willingly assumed ethnic identities of a diversity equaled only by the spirit of tolerance that keeps them in equilibrium. And when a seemingly ethnic disturbance breaks out, the conflict is usually in fact chiefly regional (north versus south; interior plateau versus the coast), religious (Christians against Muslims), economic (about the appropriation of mines), or social (residential neighborhoods against the business district); *the ethnic group is not the true source of violence and misunderstanding but only a mode of defensive assembly.* So we must emphasize both the normality in Rwanda of identifying oneself as Hutu or Tutsi and the anomaly, the deviation represented by the anti-Tutsi propaganda during the regime of president Habyarimana." Hatzfeld 2005, pp. 209–10, italics added. See also Sebarenzi 2009, pp. 6–9; Sebarenzi carefully illustrates the mixture of what I am calling horizontal and vertical dimensions of life in Rwanda before 1994. See Gourevitch 1998, pp. 232–6 who argues that Hutu power created a bipolar 'us'/ 'them' world, but that great complexity of identities lay just below the surface.

[12]   Prunier 1995, pp. 5–9; Gourevitch 1998, p. 47.

[13]   Sebarenzi 2009, p. 11.

[14]   Sebarenzi 2009, p. 11. But see Prunier (1995), pp. 1–40, for more detailed analysis.

harshly over Hutu for millennia, and then being favored by European colonizers, who saw in the Tutsi more European physical features.[15] Hutu still had some opportunities under Tutsi rule, the Verticalist says, but they were never really equal. Then, when Hutu came to power, the situation flipped. Still vertical.

Whether one supports the Horizontalist or Verticalist view, everyone agrees that once Belgian colonizers instituted mandatory ethnic identity cards in 1933, ethnic categories became rigid. This rigidity made entrenched hierarchy possible. Sebarenzi echoes a common Rwandan view that with these ethnic identity cards "the seeds of discrimination and resentment were sown, and Rwanda's strong national identity began to erode."[16] When the last King of Rwanda died in 1959, power struggles between Hutu and Tutsi under Belgian colonialism culminated in a Hutu uprising, forcing 150,000 Tutsi to flee to neighboring countries. This "1959 Revolution" marks the start of the most serious rupture between Hutu and Tutsi in Rwandan history. Gourevitch reports that before 1959 "there had never been systematic political violence recorded between Hutus and Tutsis—anywhere."[17] Berry and Berry share this Horizontalist overview of Rwandan history; their analysis of Hutu extremist propaganda during the 1959 Revolution suggests that a new Verticalism was called forth as a politically useful myth.

Hutu extremists propagated a revisionist history of relations between the Hutus and the Tutsis that were not based on cohabitation and exchange but rather on segregation and violence. This myth was so successful that on the eve of independence [from Belgium, 1962], Hutu politicians rallied the people to throw out the "feudal colonists," referring not to the Belgians who had ruled Rwanda for 40 years, but to the Tutsis with whom the Hutus had lived side by side for 400 years.[18]

Colonialism may not have caused the differences between Hutu and Tutsi, but it changed their significances. The Verticalist interpretation of history

---

[15] Prunier 1995, quotes from Belgian colonial reports, which say things like this: "The Mutusi of good race has nothing of the negro, apart from his color.... His features are very fine: a high brow, thin nose and fine lips framing beautiful shining teeth... Gifted with a vivacious intelligence, the Tutsi displays a refinement of feelings which is rare among primitive people. He is a natural-born leader, capable of extreme self-control and of calculated good will." (Prunier, p.6, from *Ministère des Colonies, Rapport sur l'administration belge du Ruanda-Urundi* (1925), p.34. Quoted in Jean-Paul Harroy, *Le Rwanda, de la féodalité à la démocratie* (1955–1962) Brussels: Hayez, 1984, p. 28.) This is not an isolated comment, as Prunier shows in Chapter 1, with sources dating not only from the early colonial period, but also as late as 1970.

[16] Sebarenzi 2009, p. 13.

[17] Gourevitch 1998, p. 59.

[18] Berry and Berry 1999, p. 3.

became a springboard for the violence that would erupt across the next several decades.

Once Hutu took power after the 1959 Revolution, Tutsi had fewer educational opportunities and more limited means of employment. One genocide survivor, Françoise, born in 1962, explains her childhood as socially horizontal but institutionally vertical. She says,

> I lived in a community where Tutsi were a minority, but this situation didn't seem to influence our relationships. We had friends among Hutu as well as Tutsi, though the discrimination was more visible in our schools. Tutsi students did not have the right to perform better than Hutu students did. For example, our teachers would switch the names of Tutsi who received better marks with the names of Hutu who had not performed as well.[19]

Educational discrimination could be more extreme. Odette Nyiramilimo tells a harrowing tale of being chased from school for being Tutsi in 1973. Fleeing to relatives in Kibuye, Odette expected to be welcomed there, but instead, her Hutu brother-in-law said, "I don't give shelter to cockroaches."[20] Stories like this are not rare.

Upon gaining independence from Belgium in 1962, Rwanda elected a Hutu president, Gregoire Kayibanda. By the middle of the 1960s, almost half of the Tutsi population lived outside Rwanda. The Tutsi were (and still are) a numerical minority, approximately 10 percent of the population.[21] The children born to "the Fifty-niners" were growing up in refugee camps in Burundi, Uganda, Tanzania, and Zaire (Congo), caught between nations, neither allowed to assimilate to their 'adoptive' land nor allowed to return to their homeland. Rwanda's Hutu government perceived the potential return of these exiled Tutsi as a threat, despite its own grip on power and despite a Hutu-majority population. Significantly, many who had fled had been leaders, and would likely seek leadership again. Also, others had taken the property of the exiles, and would not

---

[19] Françoise Kayitesi, in deBrouwer and Hon Chu, p.113. See also Gourevitch 1998, pp. 63–9.

[20] Gourevitch 1998, p. 68.

[21] The Rwandan government kept close count of its citizens, with nationwide bi-annual census-taking. Des Forges reports that Tutsi were reported as 17.5 percent of the population in 1952, but declined to only 8.4 percent in 1991. Des Forges 1999, p. 40. See also Chrétien, 2003. Chrétien says that for the colonists "an equation was established between Tutsi and 'chief' (in its general meaning) to the point where the ordinary Batutsi who lived on the hills (who constituted at least 90 percent of all Batutsi) were invisible." Into the early 1950s, Belgian authorities thought the Tutsi comprised only about 5 percent of the population, when in fact, in 1956, they were "13 to 18 percent" depending on the region. Chrétien 2003, p. 285.

yield it without a fight.[22] Rwandan official resistance to accepting the 1959 returnees, decade after decade, ultimately led to the development of the Rwandan Patriotic Front (RPF), in the late 1980s, a militia trained as soldiers within the Ugandan resistance and later in the Ugandan army.[23] The RPF focused on gaining the right to return to Rwanda. One of the RPF leaders was Paul Kagame, the current president of Rwanda, now serving his second term.

In 1990 the RPF began a military campaign to force the Rwandan government to let the diaspora return. The campaign became a war, which resulted in the signing of the Arusha Accords (July 1992), winning the right to return and also power-sharing for the RPF.[24] While the RPF put pressure on the Hutu extremist government by attacking the country's borders, and moving inward, Hutu extremists within the government developed the 'Zero-Network', a death squad comprising both civilians and members of the Rwandan army.[25] They began to distribute machetes and train civilian Hutu in how to use those machetes to kill Tutsi. At the same time, they also began to invoke a mythology pre-dating colonialism to protect their own interests and to whip up anti-Tutsi fervor. This was particularly explicit in Léon Mugesera's 1992 speech, which was so virulently anti-Tutsi that the minister of justice issued an arrest warrant and Mugesera fled to Canada.[26]

This brief and selective overview of a complex period of Rwandan history might leave one thinking that neither Horizontalism nor Verticalism can possibly be true. We find a view combining aspects of each articulated by the late André Sibomana, a moderate Hutu journalist and Catholic priest, who spoke out against the genocide. Sibomana argued that, "The differences had always been there. The whites conceptualized and froze them. The extremists turned them into a political program. This was the fatal mechanism in which our country had embarked."[27] Sibomana thus suggests that horizontality lost out to verticality when Belgians instituted identity cards, rigidifying categories. At least from thence onward, verticality ruled, and extremists used ethnic divisions to promote their own power.[28]

---

[22] Sibomana 1999, p. 95.

[23] Kinzer 2008, pp. 42–69. See also Prunier 1995, pp. 67–74, 90–96.

[24] See Prunier 1995, pp. 159–212 for a detailed account of the complex negotiations that became the Arusha Accords.

[25] Malvern 2004, pp. 29–33; Prunier 1995, pp. 168–70.

[26] See Des Forges 1999, pp. 76–86 for an analysis of the Mugesera speech.

[27] Sibomana 1999, p. 92.

[28] Gourevitch reports that in early 1991, the US Ambassador pressured the Rwandan government to eliminate identity cards, to stop official recognition of ethnic divisions. The French Ambassador "quashed" this. Gourevitch 1998, pp. 89–90.

The 1994 genocide emerged within the context of a war waged from the outside by the RPF, the now-grown children of Tutsi who fled for their lives in 1959. While the RPF fought for the right to return from 1990 to 1993, the Hutu extremist government engaged in mass killings in villages known to be predominantly Tutsi. Human Rights Watch reported that, all through 1992 and 1993, small-scale massacres were launched by the Habyarimana government to test the waters, saying that these "small scale sporadic killings of Tutsi" in predominantly Hutu areas "established patterns for the genocide of 1994."[29]

Rwanda has always been a highly organized society. Under Habyirimana's presidency, going back at least to 1975, each village held mandatory weekly civic animation sessions to promote patriotism. It was only in the early 1990s, as the RPF grew stronger, that the messages of these turned to fear-mongering and ethnic division. Hyacintha Nirere, a survivor from near Butare who was 13 in 1994, reports that despite general congeniality amongst her neighbors, trust was declining after 1990. "For example, Hutu stopped their conversations whenever a Tutsi passed by."[30] These sudden silences may have been due to the topics of conversation. During this same period, the weekly animation meetings were cultivating ordinary Hutu men for the '*Interahamwe*', seasoning them to participate in civilian militia that carried out the genocide, killing neighbors and hunting down any Tutsi who fled.[31] '*Interahamwe*' literally means 'we who work together' or 'the united.'

RPF fighters called themselves the '*Inkotanyi*', which is Kinyarwanda for 'the Invincibles.' The Hutu government called them '*inyenzi*', because they were fighting a guerilla war; like cockroaches they appeared primarily at night and were hard to find during the day. This language was commonly applied to the RPF from 1990 to 1993; the big change came when the vocabulary that had previously been reserved for the militia was extended to all Tutsi. This was a major step in the broad and explicit polarization of the society.[32]

An ideological war was also being waged. Through their control of the media, President Habyirimana's inner circle, called the '*akuza*' (little house), was busy preparing the general Hutu population (beyond the *Interahamwe*) to participate in the genocide.[33] In December 1990 the

---

[29] Des Forges 1999, p. 87.

[30] Hyacintha Nirere, in deBrouwer and Hon Chu 2009, p. 118.

[31] Chrétien 2003, pp. 323–4.

[32] See Mushikiwabo and Kramer 2006, especially pp. 41–3.

[33] See Schabas 2000, 145–9; Des Forges 1999, pp. 9, 40, 176–207. For a comparison of *Kangura* to the Nazi propaganda vehicle *Der Stürmer*, see Charity Kagwi-Ndungu, in Thompson 2005, esp. pp. 332–5.

extremist newspaper *Kangura* (*Wake Them Up!*) published the notorious "Hutu Ten Commandments," which set out rules for being a proper Hutu, declaring any Hutu who disagreed with these rules to be a traitor.[34] These ten rules demanded separating from Tutsi in relationships (family, sexual, business), denying the Tutsi educational access and work opportunities, expelling Tutsi from the military, and more. Perhaps most ominous is rule number 8: "The Hutu should stop having mercy on the Tutsi."[35] In 1993 *Kangura* presented its infamous article denouncing all Tutsi, coining the phrase 'a cockroach cannot give birth to a butterfly.' *Kangura* was also noted for its vile political cartoons, which especially vilified Tutsi women, recasting their oft-touted beauty as a mark of their dangerousness. The cartoons were an important way to influence illiterate and semi-literate Rwandans, who would not need to read the text to get the message. Also, *Kangura* increased its accessibility by publishing in Kinyarwanda. *Kangura* published up until April 1994, with a circulation that maxed at about 10,000, but with a much broader readership than that, since people tended to pass each issue from friend to friend.[36]

Even broader reach was to be found through the radio. In July 1992 the *akuza* founded RTLM, *Radio-Télévision Libre des Milles Collines* (or "Free Radio and Television of the Thousand Hills") to bring the Hutu-power message to the airwaves of Rwanda. The only widely available radio station at the time was the government's Radio Rwanda, playing European classical music and reporting government-approved news.[37] As part of a propaganda strategy, RTLM "combined entertaining music, notably Zairian, with 'hot news' delivered with virulent commentary: an 'interactive' style, happy, even humorous, that conditioned the Hutu public to the most venomous kind of extremist thinking."[38] It quickly gained a wide audience. As time went on, its broadcasts became more and more explicitly racist and political, directly calling for attacks against the Tutsi. There is clearly evidence of incitement to genocide, but the International Criminal Tribunal for Rwanda (ICTR) in fact convicted Ferdinand Nahimana,

---

[34] For the content and an analysis of this issue, see ICTR 2003, pp. 45–53.

[35] Berry and Berry 1999, pp. 113–15. The back cover of this issue featured a photograph of French President Francois Mitterand, with the caption "It is in hard times that you know your real friends." Des Forges 1999, p. 92.

[36] Chrétien 2003, p. 326.

[37] Starting in 1991, the RPF broadcast Radio Muhabera from Uganda, but this propaganda station (advocating the right of return for exiled Rwandans as well as armed protest against the Hutu extremist government) never gained a wide audience. It was broadcast in English, not in Kinyarwanda, the primary language of the people, so despite its broad geographical reach, it gained little traction. http://www.article19.org/pdfs/publications/rwanda-broadcasting-genocide.pdf. See also Des Forges 1999, p. 59.

[38] Chrétien 2003, p. 327.

who founded RTLM, of *genocide, not only incitement*, for his work with RTLM. At the same trial, Hassan Ngeze was convicted of genocide for his work as the founder, owner, and Editor-in-Chief of *Kangura*. This gets us ahead of the analysis, but sets the stage for our study of specific speech acts.

Responding to the pressure brought on by the RPF offensives, the Habyarimana government began to negotiate peace talks that resulted in a temporary cease-fire agreement in August 1992. This agreement, which eventually worked out shared power between Hutu and Tutsi, came to be known as the 'Arusha Accords.' The prospect of increased Tutsi inclusion in matters of state was more than Hutu extremists could accept. While President Habyirimana publicly signed the Arusha Accords, the *akuza* were secretly executing plans for Rwanda's own 'final solution.' The context of economic distress, war, and political corruption and competition all contributed to the urgency with which the *akuza* developed their strategy to mobilize ordinary citizens to remove a minority of the population. Hutu extremists saw exterminating this minority as promising to relieve these stresses, and allow a unified Rwanda to emerge. As Andre Sibomana says, "The risk of a genocide gradually increased as the [Hutu] elite in power strengthened its domination by brandishing the ethnic threat, against a backdrop of economic crisis."[39]

Testimony from Rwandan genocide survivors raises questions about how the cultural climate changed for Tutsis from 1989 to 1994. In the US, the concept of 'chilly climate,' first introduced in sexual harassment research, brought attention to the ways that the behavior of others creates a social climate which makes personal identity factors into a liability, undermining a person's ability to function at school or work.[40] One part of creating a chilly climate is to increase the salience of identity differences, making them function in new ways. At first, the targeted person becomes aware of difference, chilling the development not only of relations but also slowing her own participation and skill development. Eventually, the chill may become more, and turn into a real threat. Applying this concept, we ask how Rwanda became, first, a chilly climate for Tutsi, and then a hot and dangerous one. Thinking of the question this way enables us to see that although the standard accounts of Rwandan colonial history may explain how the people came to be marked as 'Hutu' and 'Tutsi', this alone does not explain how these categories became toxic. In particular, how did the rigidity of the ethnic categories start to engender violent actions, in word and deed?

---

[39] Sibomana 1999, p. 92. The economic crisis began with the collapse of the coffee markets in 1989.

[40] Introduced by Bernice Sandler in 1982.

The toxic element was a widespread anti-Tutsi propaganda campaign, not only by leaders of the media but also orally transmitted, from person to person, in prefecture meetings and social gatherings. Broadcast speech acts are easy to trace, because they are part of the public record, so histories and analyses of the use of hate media to develop a climate of fear and distrust are already emerging.[41] These tend to emphasize the actions of RTLM, *Kangura*, *Umurava*, and other print media.[42] The International Criminal Tribunal for Rwanda (ICTR) trial of media leaders, Ferdinand Nahimana, Jean-Bosco Barayagwiza, and Hassan Ngeze, raised serious concerns about both the freedom and the responsibility of the press.[43] As Jacques Semelin warns, however, "it is possible to overemphasize the role of hate propaganda because there is nothing to prove that this, on its own, leads to the unleashing of massacre."[44] The causal question worried the ICTR as well, but ultimately they decided that the speech of these three men *constituted* genocidal acts, not only serving as incitements to genocide. Semelin holds that hate propaganda, "certainly contributes to the creation of a sort of *semantic matrix* that gives meaning to the increased force of a dynamic of violence that then works as a 'launching pad' for massacre."[45] A semantic matrix might seem like a stationary background graph upon which action is plotted, but I see this semantic matrix as multi-dimensional, organic, and interactive, allowing for little differentiation between background and foreground because of this organic interaction. So construed, I would argue, linguistic violence, of which hate speech and propaganda are major forms, becomes part of the broader dynamic of violence. Understanding the power of public speech acts by the media requires understanding this "semantic matrix," a dynamic arena of meaning, which should disclose what it took for such speech acts to get uptake, to be heard and acted upon, for their vision to be enacted. As Africa Rights concluded in 1995, "For the most part these journalists did not wield machetes or fire guns. Some of them did not even directly incite people to kill. But they all assisted in creating a climate of extremism and hysteria in

---

[41] Mary Kimani's analysis of RTLM programming shows that most of the invective came from the regular announcers and not from on-air guests, news, or government officials. See Kimani, in Thompson 2007.

[42] See Chrétien 1995, Chalk 1999, and Thompson 2007.

[43] See *Prosecutor v. Ferdinand Nahimana, Jean-Bosco Barayagwiza and Hassan Ngeze*, Case No. ICTR-99-52-T. All three were found guilty of genocide. All three were sentenced to life in prison, although Barayagwiza's lawyers appealed, arguing that his rights had been violated, and the court reduced his sentence to 35 years with time served further reducing it to 27 years. See also MacKinnon 2004, Temple-Raston 2005.

[44] Semelin 2007, p. 199.

[45] Semelin 2007, p. 199.

which ordinary people could be influenced to become killers."[46] Getting ordinary people to participate in practices of linguistic violence seasoned them to the structures of power that rendered collateral forms of non-linguistic violence conceivable and doable within the context.

Verticalism was gaining ground through this ideological campaign. RTLM and *Kangura* were key agencies in generating permissibility for genocidal behaviors through speech acts that further rigidified social acceptance of a sense of essential separation and justified hierarchy between Hutu and Tutsi. Power was the issue. Further, these official speech acts granted linguistic licenses to other speakers to use derogatory terms for Tutsi, making the status of being Tutsi more dangerous than most Tutsi knew.[47] The ICTR "Media Trial" emphasized the use of the radio to direct the genocide, focusing on directions given on-air to kill specific individuals, disclosing locations of hiding Tutsis, etc.[48] The radio also played a role in giving non-elite Hutu permission to kill, giving them a sense that patriotism demanded it and that Rwanda would be better when the Tutsi are gone, never to return.

The semantic matrix within which genocide can be conceived and engendered cannot arise simply from basic repetitions of hollow speech acts. Something more must generate the normative force that engenders non-linguistic action. To understand one dimension of meaning change, consider how ordinary slang tends to gain or lose its force from frequency of use. Before Bart Simpson, for example, "That sucks!" was rarely uttered on American broadcast television, but it has since become more common. The conventions governing its use changed, and the inferences one could draw from it changed. When more taboo, it was also more vulgar, making a clear but elliptical sexual reference; today many people tend to reject that inference. Meanings change as practices governing the conditions of use change. Inferences gain and lose sanction. Frequency of use and patterns of use at least partially constitute the inferential role of the expression, giving it whatever meaning and power it has. Through overuse, "That sucks" has become almost as empty has "Have a nice day"; in each we see the frequency of use draining meaning rather than building it. Hate speech seems to take a different trajectory. Initial accommodation to the linguistic

---

[46] African Rights 1995, 60. Also Carver 2000, p. 189.

[47] Francoise Mukeshimana reports that "Between 1990 and 1992, the *Interahamwe* killed Tutsi boys from Bugesera after the boys were accused of hiding suspected RPF spies. Many of the boys didn't even know that the term cockroach referred to people." DeBrouwer and Hon Chu 2009, p. 100.

[48] See MacKinnon 2004, pp. 325–30. See also Temple-Raston 2005.

violence takes it as 'just talk', ignoring the action-engendering features of such discourse. As these violent linguistic practices become more socially embedded, intertwined with discriminatory and exclusionary practices, a synergy takes hold, giving greater meaning to each. '*Inyenzi*' began as an epithet for the RPF militia raiding the borders from neighboring countries, but by 1992 and 1993 grew to include all Tutsis; this transition from a narrow to a wider scope of application was key to generating the semantic matrix within which genocide was engendered.

3. Theoretical Framework

Before turning to the main argument for the surprising action-engendering force of speech, I first present the framework in which I am working. This framework employs an inferential role theory of meaning, the notion of language games introduced by Wittgenstein, as well as sensitivity to a variety of sorts of speech acts that may occur as moves within language games. Once this framework is made clear, I present my theory of derogatory terms, which I will use in § 4 to analyze the role and social function of the use of the term '*inyenzi*' in pre-genocide Rwanda.

3.1. *Inferential Roles*

Some theorists understand language primarily in terms of the communication of intentions. When Sally says, "Peter is tall," for example, they think the best way to understand what is happening is to think of her utterance as a means to enable the hearer to figure out what Sally's (communicative) intention is. It is because of her intention to get across a certain proposition (that Peter is tall) that she says what she says. The words help the hearer get at what is important, namely, Sally's communicative intention. On this view, language use is primarily a communicative tool between speaker and hearer. What matters most is the recognition of the speaker's communicative intention.

This framework, which treats speaker's intentions as primary for understanding what a particular speech act does, is too centered on individuals, as if we each could control the meanings of what we say. Surely we do try, but often the meanings and actions associated with what we say extend far beyond our own awareness and control. In contrast, I focus on linguistic *practices*, which are non-individualistic and communal. On my view, the focus is on the (inferential) role that an utterance within a speech act plays in the linguistic practice in question. If Pio calls Albert '*inyenzi*', he may be setting in motion much more than he intends. What we do with our speech acts often outstrips our own mastery, and in cases in which the social functions of speech have been co-opted, we can see that participants might not see the full scope of the games that they are playing. Although communication of intentions is often an important part of what is happening when we use language, as we shall see, it need not be.

To understand what is done when one person hurls a racist epithet at another person, one must, of course, understand what the word means. To do that, on the inferentialist view, one must understand the term as part of a network of inferences, and one must see the hurling of the epithet as an undertaking of a commitment to justify the use of the term, which includes supplying its reference and defending its role in any assertion (or other speech act) that has been made.[49] My work also develops the idea of expressive commitments, that is, a commitment to the viability and value of a particular way of talking.[50] So if Pio hurls *"inyenzi"* at Albert, Pio becomes committed not only to explaining which inferences about Pio are licensed by that word (what can the hearer say next?), but also is committed to the viability and value of using cockroach-talk to talk about (at least some) people. Often speakers pick up practices of speech from others, without giving much thought to the inferences they are licensing or the practices they are supporting. The speaker might think only about saying something nasty about this one person, and not about the broader practices that make that speech act possible and which the speech act then further supports. An ability to play a language game does not show that a speaker has a meta-level analysis of their operations. We speak within them, and rarely speak about them.

To better understand how our linguistic behaviors work, we should begin with some basics about language games. To illustrate some of these points, I will introduce a word-game, invented and played by real children, which, on the surface, looks like a game of using a derogatory term as an epithet. We will see that there are important differences between this case and the more serious Rwandan linguistic practices, Later, we will further develop the concept of language game to more clearly elucidate the relation between speech acts and other sorts of actions.

3.2. A Children's Game

On a typical New England summer day, as I drove a carpool of children to day-camp, our daily route took us past several new homes under construction. One day, the six year olds, delighted with their own cleverness, started calling these as-yet-unsided houses "naked houses," since they did not yet wear their clapboard "clothes." Recognizing this as a basic

---

[49] The groundwork of the inferentialist approach is Brandom 1998. More recently, Kukla and Lance 2009 take inferentialism beyond asserting.
[50] See Tirrell 1999.

language-entry move, a move like setting chess pieces on a board, I still could not figure out their game. A few days later, one of the children called, "Hey, sausage-face!" out the open car window as we passed such a house. Peals of laughter followed. We passed another "naked house" a mile later; no "sausage-face." Passing another, again the call elicited many giggles. Wanting to learn what this expression meant, to identify the conditions of application, and to see what could be so funny, I kept quiet. The term seemed neither effective, nor acceptable, nor funny; I just didn't 'get it.'

After a few days of observing, I finally asked, "What does 'sausage-face' mean? Is there somebody out there with really bad skin? A lumpy nose?" My questions seemed incomprehensible to the children. Why would I think those things? They couldn't even *see* the faces they seemed to be labeling. (My questions arose from trying to apply the inferential role of 'sausage' to faces.) "Sausage-face," they explained, is (obviously) something you yell out the window at a man with no shirt on who is working on a naked house. If that epithet had been hurled at me, my interpretation would have led me to take it to be an insult about my face—it contains a direct reference to the face, after all, and sausages are not pretty. The inventors of this particular game, on the other hand, saw the compositional meaning as irrelevant, disposable. They just liked the sound of the words together. Conditions of use—their use—ruled.

Although apparently a game about insulting people through negative labeling, this game turned out to have somewhat different functions for those involved. The children were not actually *communicating* with the men, who were at such a distance from the road that they could not have heard the children's soft voices anyway. This was an in-group identification game, much like 'punch-buggy,' and the fun was getting to (legitimately) say the phrase first. Their pleasure came from their mastery of the rules of use, the sonic pleasure of the term they made up, and the competition to be the first to use that term. The camaraderie of the game was an incentive to keep the game going. It was their own invention, turning them into an 'us.' Although present in the car, I was nevertheless not in the game. I was neither a player nor a target, just an irrelevant bystander.[51]

One feature of this usage that might worry some philosophers of language is that the ordinary meanings of 'sausage' and 'face' don't seem

---

[51] Not all bystanders are irrelevant. Often communication with them is part of the function of a speech act. At a wedding, the parties being married are taking vows, but the witnesses are part of the process as well, and the rules of engagement with the parties shift once they are married.

to have any role here. In most inferentialist analyses of real speech acts that occur within real practices, the typical inferential roles would indeed have force, unless they were somehow altered by context. Here, the practice itself renders the everyday meanings (explained by inferential roles) irrelevant. The children are playing a game with language, but they are not embedding it within a host of other language games. 'Sausage-face' might almost have been any sounds at all.

As one can see, uttering a certain expression (e.g. 'sausage-face') can serve multiple functions and communication need not be one of them. This example also nicely illustrates an inferentialist view of language, without making commitments to a compositional approach to meaning. Elsewhere I have argued that the use of any term undertakes what I call an *expressive commitment* to the viability and value of the term, and the speech acts in which it gains force.[52] By saying "sausage-face," child A undertakes a commitment to the viability and value of that term, as well as undertaking commitments to identifying which item (X) in the world A is referring to as a sausage-face, and showing that the criteria of being a sausage-face are indeed met by X. (If challenged, A must prove that X is indeed a man, shirtless, working on an un-sided house.) Further, A now licenses child B to say things like, "Yes, there was a sausage-face back there," to count that instance in the daily tally, and so on. If sausage-faces get some kind of special treatment, and if B accepts A's assertion or exclamation, then A's utterance will engender subsequent verbal and non-verbal actions from B, each of which is grounded in B's legitimate reliance on A's utterance. In this way, we see that by using a term or expression, one thereby commits oneself to the various functions of that use, which include at least expressive and referential functions, plus any inferences one can draw from the imposition of the category.

Having presented and motivated some basics of this inferentialist view of language, I turn now to a brief account of derogatory terms.

3.3. *Key Features of Deeply Derogatory Terms*

My focus here is on deeply derogatory terms, rather than mere slurs or casual derogations, for deep derogations are tied to systems of oppression. "Jerk" might be a slur, and it might hurt or insult, but it does not have the power that deeply derogatory terms do. Deeply derogatory terms serve many functions. First, they express *the insider/outsider function*, which is multi-directional: the terms serve to mark members of an out-group (*as* out), and in so doing, they also mark the in-group as un-marked by the

---

[52] Tirrell 1999.

term. When speaker *A* uses a racial epithet to tell her friend *B* to stay away from a particular racial group of people, *A* sets up an insider/outsider relation, whereby *A* and *B* are not members of that group. They are insiders in their own presumed-to-be-better world, and they are outsiders to the badness of that racial group. Racist epithets of many sorts fit this pattern. 'Nigger', 'spic', 'kike', 'mick', 'Jew', '*inyenzi*', '*inzoka*', and many others seem to fit and are used accordingly.[53] Some do not fit—those that convey insider/outsider 'lifestyle' choices, without an assumption of inescapability. 'Snob' or 'jerk' might count as slurs, but they are not deeply derogatory in the sense I am developing here. Someone who is a snob can cease to be so, thus the term is a critique, not an assignment of a basic ontological status. Slurs, like 'snob' or 'jerk', might have significant social force, even if they are not deeply derogatory.[54]

Second, to be deeply derogatory, the term must meet *the essentialism condition*; deeply derogatory terms must communicate a negative message presumed to convey an essential aspect of the target to the target and the audience, and in so doing, must create and enforce hierarchy. Usually that negative message is tied to the meaning of the term, and is seen as capturing something of the object's essence. Verticalism meets essentialism here. The racial category sticks because it presumes biological differences, and these biological differences are presumed to shape inevitable social and moral differences. Derogatory terms used in propaganda usually both presuppose and convey that there is an essential difference between the groups in question. Essentialism fuels fear, generates hate, and purports to justify differential treatment. This condition does not require that essentialism be true, only that it be presumed.

---

[53] Sometimes a member of a derogated group might use the same derogatory terms that the power-group uses, even in the same way. This often reflects an internal class division, in which the speaker presumes that the term applies to the other but not to herself (except erroneously applied by ignorant members of the dominating class), but it can even be used by a speaker against herself. Such usage reflects an acceptance of the insider/outsider division. Other times, the member of the subordinated group might use the term in a *reclaimed* way, shifting the meaning. This also depends on an insider/outsider function, because typically only members of the subordinated group are allowed to use the term in the reclaimed way. For more about these sorts of cases, see Tirrell 1999.

[54] Homophobic epithets are a troublesome case, because the politics and the metaphysical assumptions are a mess. Calling someone 'fag' might not presuppose that sexual orientation is an essential trait, so that would lead my view to count it as a slur rather than a deeply derogatory term. Surely that is unacceptable. On the other hand, on my view, deeply derogatory terms are tied to systems of oppression, and homophobic practices certainly count. For designation as deeply derogatory, being tied to systems of oppression is more important than the assumption of essentialism.

Third, derogatory terms are most effective when they are connected to networks of oppression and discrimination, with the weight of history and social censure behind it. This is what most clearly marks deeply derogatory terms from other sorts of slurs. Let's call this *the social embeddedness condition.* Social context, with embedded practices and conventions, is the major source of the power of derogatory terms that are used to dominate, demean, or dehumanize people. Certainly the worst harms of derogatory terms come from those that are embedded in socially, economically, and politically oppressive practices, and not from isolated, idiosyncratic, and apparently negative expressions, like 'sausage-face.' The mere word is not the issue; at work is the derogatory term, as used in a speech act (within a hurled epithet, a report of whereabouts, an order to kill, etc.) combined with both social embeddedness and essentialism. Within a speech act, and then within a broader social context, the derogatory term takes on a force that transcends the word alone.

Fourth is *the functional variation feature.* The insider/outsider function is certainly one of the main functions that using derogatory terms can serve, but it is important to see that it can serve other functions as well. Sometimes, for example, a third-person derogation is used by a member of the dominant group to a hearer who is a member of the subordinate group as a way of labeling the third person with a label that boomerangs from the target back to the hearer. For example, Fred and Ethel see Lucy do something silly, and while Ethel laughs, Fred scornfully says, "Lucy is such a bimbo." 'Bimbo' is a gendered term, and its use here sets boundaries on acceptable and unacceptable female behavior. Whatever Lucy was doing, Ethel now knows not to do that in front of Fred. His use of the derogatory term sets gender boundaries for Ethel even though he was hurling the term at Lucy. There are many things we can see the derogatory term doing, and what it does varies with the particulars of the context of use. We can also see that communicating intentions is at best only one of the things it may do. Fred may not be intending to set behavioral boundaries (enforcing norms) on Ethel, but he does this whether or not he intends it. Used in speech acts, derogatory terms also serve many other functions: for example, they regularly enact power, incite crimes, and rationalize cruelty. The functional variation feature is a way of capturing Wittgenstein's tool box metaphor, which suggests that understanding language requires us to see the multitude of uses to which we put our words and to resist reducing these functions to one (or even a few).[55]

---

[55] Wittgenstein 1958. Especially § 7, 11,14, 23, but see also § 6, 304.

Fifth, derogatory terms used in speech acts are action-engendering within a context. To see how this works, we again return to the inferential role of such terms to see that subsequent inferences often delineate what kinds of treatments are permissible with respect to those who are so classified. Sometimes the action engendered is to assign a status-function.[56] Calling a grown woman 'girl' assigns a status-function that denies her adulthood and rationalizes male paternalistic behaviors. 'Girl' by itself is not an epithet, when applied to female children, but its inappropriate use for an adult woman serves a purpose, to rationalize paying her less for her work, treating her as incapable of making serious decisions, and similar sorts of behaviors that undercut the full expression of her autonomy. Similarly, in the long-time practice of calling African-American men 'boy' we see clearly the denial of adult status as a foundation for autonomy-undercutting behaviors. Boys don't have the same rights as men. Neither do girls. Assign the status, and the treatments follow.

Careful analysis of this set of philosophical concepts, together with an exploration of the key features of language games, will help us to understand how speech acts contribute to the preparation for and execution of a genocide, and more generally, why words are not *only* words.[57]

3.4. *Why 'Sausage-Face' is Not Derogatory*

To further illustrate these features of derogatory terms, it is worthwhile to see how the apparently derogatory expression 'sausage-face' fares with respect to the five conditions of my account. We can make explicit some basics of derogating speech acts by looking at this idiosyncratic children's language game.

First, we must ask whether the use of 'sausage-face' serves the insider/outsider function by marking an in-group and an out-group. It seems to do so in a very minimal way. The children felt free to laugh at the use and sound of the label, because they saw no weight to it, no social function beyond the game, and because it could not boomerang back to label them. Further, there are those who are players, doing the calling out, and certain people outside the car who are possible targets. No one inside the car could be a target, by virtue of the rules of the game, but improper calling might get someone who seemed to be part of the game kicked out. Usage makes each of these boundaries clear. Targets were undamaged by the label, for a variety of reasons that will become obvious. So the game was all

---

[56] Searle 1995, pp. 28, 40, and following.

[57] The phrase 'only words' has been around for a long time, but it has gained special traction since Catharine MacKinnon's book *Only Words* developed the argument that neither pornography nor the law are *only words*. See MacKinnon 1993.

about the sounds, the quickness of the call-out, and the creation of a minimal 'us,' we-who-play.

'Sausage-face' clearly fails to satisfy the second condition of derogatory terms: the essentialism condition. The conditions of application for 'sausage-face' are entirely circumstantial; the expression does not apply in virtue of some alleged essential feature. All a builder needs is a shirt, and he is targeted no more. Further, in this game, any negativity is detached from the compositional interpretation of the terms, so the potential derogation gets lost.[58]

The third condition for derogatory terms, social embeddedness, is also unmet in the 'sausage-face' example. There is no social context of oppression or discrimination connected to the use of 'sausage-face,' so any derogation that might ensue would be idiosyncratic at best. It would not have the weight of social censure behind it. Genuinely derogatory terms must be connected to other social practices. As a game develops, it may gain a force of its own, becoming embedded in practices and events that lock it into the lives of those who play. In the case of 'sausage-face,' its idiosyncratic utterances have no power, no point, except to show the quickness and cleverness of the person who attaches the label first to a newly encountered object. (It's about 'us,' not about 'them.') Disconnected from other social practices, apparently derogatory terms end up being like 'sausage-face'; their idiosyncrasy undermines their derogatory force.

So far, 'sausage-face,' which at first seemed very much like hurling a derogatory term, is failing miserably on its tests. The fourth condition, functional variability, would require 'sausage-face' to serve multiple functions. This condition should be easy to meet, because most speech act types can serve various functions, so it also is a weak delineator of derogatoriness. We saw that the children were more intent on playing with each other than on communicating with the men at whom they shout. The utterance was not about hurling an insult to be received by the target. This game could be seen as setting up insiders and outsiders, dividing into who gets called 'sausage-face' and who does the calling. It also serves to change the score between those who hurl the term, some going up in score, some going down, depending on the perceived appropriateness of the use. So it serves at least these two functions, but probably many others on particular occasions of use.

---

[58] This remains an open question for me; the children constructed it independent of any derogation, but why assume that they can control meaning this way?

Fifth and finally, the use of 'sausage-face' would be action-engendering if it were a deeply derogatory term. Again, this game is divorced from the rest of life, so there are no broader action consequences. There is no 'way that one treats a sausage-face'; the game has no extension into social reality. No one loses educational or job opportunities. No one is cast into poverty. No one's liberty and autonomy are undermined.

The apparent pointlessness of the children's game sheds light on what is missing. These five features of derogatory terms also illustrate Wittgenstein's tenet that a language is a way of life, and that a language game is "the whole consisting of the language and the actions into which it is woven." Even Wittgenstein's initial very primitive language game, introduced in § 2 of *Philosophical Investigations*, emphasizes the action-engendering aspect of the speech acts within the game.[59] If the builder were only playing a naming game, then 'Slab' might simply name an object, without engendering any action, but in the § 2 game, 'slab' very clearly engenders the assistant's action. 'Sausage-face,' said by the children, engenders no action against the target, but 'She's Tutsi' said in Rwanda in May 1994 was neither a mere label nor simply an insider/outsider designation. In that place, at that time, it was an action-engendering speech act. Of course, it was not only in the case of the extreme actions within the genocide that use of this word was action-engendering. All across Rwanda, during the early 1990s, identifying a student as Tutsi was a way to remove her from the meritocracy of the classroom; high scores would not advance her.

Derogatory terms, in use, engender actions creating and enforcing hierarchy. Thinking of real-life language uses as occurring within games emphasizes the action-engendering aspect of speech. Language games are not fully distinct from their purposes, the practices they support, and those by which they are supported. Action is built into the idea that meaning is a function of both intra- and extra-linguistic use.

In sum, we have seen that the use of derogatory terms involves an expressive commitment to the value and viability of that use. With respect to derogatory terms, in particular, we have learned that (1) the insider/outsider function is a key function of speech acts containing such terms; (2) they tend to make a negative essentialist claim about their targets; (3) they must be embedded in a social context, particularly within networks of

---

[59] Wittgenstein 1958. § 2: "Let us imagine a language ... The language is meant to serve for communication between a builder A and an assistant B. A is building with building-stones; there are blocks, pillars, slabs and beams. B has to pass the stones, and that in the order in which A needs them. For this purpose they use a language consisting of the words 'block', 'pillar', 'slab', 'beam'. A calls them out;—B brings the stone which he has learnt to bring at such-and-such a call.—Conceive this as a complete primitive language."

oppression and discrimination, to gain their derogatory force, and they gain this social embeddedness through use; (4) speech acts involving derogatory terms exhibit functional variation, particularly with respect to the different parties involved in the speech act itself; and, (5) like other speech acts, those involving derogatory terms are action-engendering. These five features work together. They are not met by the 'sausage-face' example, despite the compositional meaning of the label, with all its negative inferential consequents.

While we are clearing the ground, before turning to some deadly cases of derogatory terms, there is one more caveat. It is important not to think of derogations as mere insults, although there are some common features. Insults are about hurting the other person, inflicting a sudden (and perhaps lasting) sting. Derogations, in contrast, inflict long-lasting *harm*, which may or may not inflict immediate hurt. Derogations may be received without much notice, and still do the job of realigning the target's place in the world. Again we see that intention alone cannot carry all this weight.

The derogations with which we are concerned in Rwanda are not mere insults; they harm their targets through their functions within the speech acts in which they occur and the actions they engender. Calling someone '*inyenzi*' in Rwanda in 1994 was a reductive classification that licensed differential treatment. Its functions might include identifying a person who is a threat, stripping that person of his or her humanity, depriving the person of basic human rights, and even identifying someone to kill. Such a speech act is socially embedded in a history of using '*inyenzi*' to refer to RPF soldiers who made nightly incursions into Rwanda from Uganda and neighboring countries. From 1990 to 1994, the term was extended to all Tutsi, spreading fear across their future. We will see that such deeply derogatory terms matter, for they engender actions that others may take against the person, which in 1994 included brutal murder.

4. The Use of '*Inyenzi*' in Rwanda: Genocidal Language Games

In this section, I argue that the widespread use of the term '*inyenzi*' to refer to the Tutsi people played a crucial role in licensing the genocide that took place there. I begin by arguing that '*inyenzi*,' as used in that context, satisfied the five conditions of derogatory terms outlined above. Next, I explore the inferential role of this term in order to identify the particular actions licensed by it. Since precisely these actions took place, I conclude that there is good reason to believe that the action-engendering force of the term '*inyenzi*' played a significant role in bringing about the Rwandan genocide.

4.1. *An Actual Derogatory Use of* 'Inyenzi'

The following ten sentences, broadcast on the Hutu extremist RTLM radio on June 28, 1994, during the genocide, illustrate this use of '*inyenzi*' to damn all Tutsi, extending it beyond the initial guerilla groups, which were called the '*Inkotanyi*', the invincibles. The passage also illustrates several of the core features of derogatory speech acts. As we shall see, this passage is a complex set of speech acts with one major function: to justify all harm and destruction done to Tutsi. On RTLM, Valérie Bemeriki rapidly exclaimed:

I have always told you. All the people who joined the part controlled by the *Inyenzi Inkotanyi* are *Inyenzi* themselves. They approve the killings perpetrated by *Inyenzi*. They are criminals like the *Inyenzi Inkotanyi*. They are all *Inyenzi*. When our armed forces will get there, they will get what they deserve. They will not spare anyone since everybody turned *Inyenzi*. All those who stayed there are all *Inyenzi* since those who were against *Inyenzi* have been killed by *Inyenzi*. Those who succeeded to escape ran away to Ngara, Burundi and to the western part of our country. Those who stayed are accomplices and acolytes of the *Inyenzi*.

In ten sentences, there are ten instances of '*inyenzi*', some further emphasized through the use of '*Inkotanyi*'. The insider/outsider function that characterizes the use of derogatory terms is accomplished by the emphatic demarcation of the Tutsi as '*inyenzi*' combined with an almost incantatory repetition of 'they.' The use of 'they' exclusively for the Tutsi is so emphatic that it is a shock when the seventh sentence switches the antecedent of 'they' to 'the army'. Roger Bromley's analysis of this short speech emphasizes what we have been calling the insider/outsider function, noting its

use of polarization and dichotomization based upon pronominal distribution [I, you, our, but predominantly they], speed of delivery, and repetition of a term of abuse to produce a mesmeric, hypnotic effect. 'We' are articulated as human, the '*Inyenzi*' as sub-human, committed to 'social death,' beyond the universe of moral obligation.[60]

Polarization is an emphatic means to achieve the insider/outsider function, suggesting that you are either *inyenzi* or not, and there is no middle ground. (It may presuppose essentialism.) Bemeriki's speed of delivery stops the audience from critical distancing; there is no time to question

---

[60] Bromley, p. 5.

the implicit assumptions. The 'argument' presupposes an audience familiar with a history of Tutsi flight to neighboring countries, and government propaganda (aired frequently on this same radio station) claiming that RPF killers are 'out to get all Hutu.' The use of fear to grow anger is clear.

This insider/outsider function also constructs social power, and often combines forces with the essentialism condition. Foucault develops a distinction between juridical or negative exercises of power, on the one hand, and technical or positive exercises of power, on the other. Looking at derogatory terms from a juridical perspective brings into focus cases of hurling epithets, face to face uses designed to demean; these are hierarchical enactments of power by members of one group over members of another. Through this (limited) lens, hate speech emerges as enforcing a negative repressive power of a dominating class over those dominated, but this view obscures the fact that such uses *positively construct* both dominator and dominated. In short, we see the insider/outsider function in play here, and at the same time, we see that multiple functions are achieved. Dominating speech acts construct those dominated as lesser beings, limiting their aspirations, capabilities, potentialities, powers; such uses systematically create an underclass. Speech acts using derogatory terms also help to create the power of those who use them, those who are not targets of the terms, uniting them into a self-identifying group.[61] In Rwanda, the use of derogatory terms for Tutsi had this double effect, for at the same time that the uses of these terms were undermining the power and the humanity of the Tutsi, they were building the confidence and power of the Hutu extremists. The power of discourse, the aggregate patterns of what we may and may not say, what we do and do not say, the language games we play and the productive capacities of those games, "needs to be considered as a productive network which runs through the whole social body" (as Foucault says) because it produces the very contours of that body.

Next, missing from Bemeriki's rant, but present elsewhere, is the essentialism condition. It is absent because Bemeriki makes *inyenzi* status a *choice* for Tutsi, dependent upon their politics. Of course as soon as the passage presents the status as a political choice—a choice shown by supporting the *Inkotanyi*—it takes it away in practice, for all Tutsi left in Rwanda were deemed *ipso facto* collaborators and therefore worthy of destruction. Perhaps he smuggles essentialism back in. (This rant was

---

[61]   Of course the terms can be used by those who generally are their targets; sometimes such uses may be a way to reclaim the term, making it an in-group term of affection, for example, but sometimes the use is unreclaimed and reveals the speaker's accommodation to the injustice carried by the term as generally used. For more on reclamation, see Tirrell 1999.

delivered a year after *Kangura's* 'a cockroach cannot give birth to a butterfly' became a catch-phrase amongst Hutu.)

Elsewhere, the use of '*inyenzi*' clearly satisfies the essentialism condition. In fact, part of the point in calling non-military and non-militant Tutsi '*inyenzi*' was to imply that they shared a dangerous essence with the RPF soldiers. Derogatory terms used in propaganda generally convey that there is an essential difference between the groups in question; essentialism fuels fear, and purports to justify differential treatment. Justification of differential treatment is built into the inferential role, but essentialism closes off other actions too. There is no rehabilitation of a cockroach. A snake is a snake and must be destroyed on sight.

Third, this use of '*inyenzi*' also satisfies the social embeddedness condition. The passage quoted above relies on the social embeddedness of both '*inyenzi*' and '*Inkotanyi*' as terms of threat, posing no danger to those who are not so classified and justifying death to those who are. Calling an apolitical Tutsi '*inyenzi*' was invoking a connection to the RPF militia, and thus making the person so labeled into an object of fear. On the micro-level, when a speaker, S, hurls '*inyenzi*' as an epithet at a hearer, H, S's speech act gains force from the social and political context of exiled Tutsis trying to fight their way back into Rwanda. On the macro-level, S's epithet-hurling speech act is part of a network of similar speech acts that served the political and economic ends of Hutu extremists. As DesForges points out, "Both on the radio and through public meetings, authorities worked to make the long-decried threat of RPF infiltration concrete and immediate."[62] Authorities disseminated false information, offered tangible economic incentives for participation in fighting the RPF and eliminating all Tutsi, and gave destitute young men hope for a future with more security and prosperity. They seasoned reluctant participants by drawing them into action, "first by encouraging them to pillage, then to destroy homes, then to kill the occupants of the homes."[63] Propaganda was a key element of the implementation of the genocide, but propaganda did not act alone outside of other social forces. As Claudine Kayitesi has said, "A genocide is a poisonous bush that grows not from two or three roots, but from a whole tangle that has moldered underground without anyone noticing."[64] In Rwanda, the planners were noticing, and to achieve their own social and political goals, they were cultivating that poisonous bush with language, music, rewards, and punishments. Ordinary Rwandans noticed some changes, but did not see the big picture.

---

[62] Des Forges 1999, p. 10.
[63] Des Forges 1999, p. 11
[64] Hatzfeld 2007, p. 206.

Language did not do the whole job, but the infusion of linguistic violence into the social body engendered a breadth and depth of physical violence that went beyond war and into genocide.

Fifth and finally, as we shall see in detail in the following section, this use of '*inyenzi*' is also action-engendering. Calling someone '*inyenzi*' was signaling that they were to be killed. Calling them '*inzoka*' (snake) often brought about a dismemberment of the person's limbs, and death by exsanguination. This is tied to long-standing norms of how to treat snakes, as we shall see next.

To understand how speech acts involving deeply derogatory terms can do more than license other discursive actions and instead move into broader social and physical actions, we need a more detailed understanding of the framework we have developed so far. In the next section, I will develop a richer account of the structural components of certain sorts of language games, with an emphasis on testimony from Rwandans—survivors and perpetrators alike—about the role of speech in the preparation for and execution of the genocide.

4.2. *The Inferential Role of* 'Inyenzi'

Imagine that in January 1994, during the preparatory phase, prior to the genocide, speaker S says to hearer H: "A is an *inyenzi.*" Unlike a hurled epithet, this involves three parties, and the target need not even know about the speech act. At the very least, S has undertaken an expressive commitment to the viability and value of using insect terms to speak about A. S undertakes a commitment to showing that cockroach-talk is viable (can be extended, further inferences can be drawn) and valuable (serves the purposes of the speech act and broader language game). What are some of the inferences we can make about calling A "cockroach"? Common inferences include that cockroaches are pests, dirty, ubiquitous, multiply rapidly, are hard to kill, *ought* to be killed, show emergent tendencies when in groups, are resilient, carry diseases, can go long periods without food or water, tend to only emerge at night when they are hard to see. Each of these inferences might be justified by S's claim that A is a cockroach, although of course we can see that the use is metaphorical. If H says, "But I have seen A during the day," this would not undermine S's assertion. One can imagine S replying something like, "Yes, but it is at night that A does the work of the *Inkotanyi*", thus solidifying the reference. Further, with this utterance, S has accepted and endorsed this particular language game, which I call *reductive classification*, here applied to the Tutsi.

During the preparatory phase, what S was doing was as much about S and H as it was about A. S was cultivating a shared understanding with H that A was a kind of being that should be eliminated, and that S and H were on the same side, the side to do that job. The expressive commitment in this kind of case is a political litmus test; if H takes up the expressive commitment by using the same vocabulary, then S is reassured, at least mildly, that they are part of a united group. If H challenges S, perhaps saying, "I don't like it when you talk about my neighbor that way," then H is now marked as *ibyitso*, a traitor or "accomplice of the enemy," and soon will be at risk.[65] Expressive commitments thus play a significant role in enacting the insider/outsider function.

In addition to undertaking expressive commitments, when S asserts "A is an *inyenzi*," S also licenses H to make specific assertions about A. Think of *'inyenzi'* as having a network of possible inferential next-steps; these are inferences one is licensed to draw. H is now allowed to assert other elements of the inferential role of 'cockroach' in speaking about A, based on S's having issued those licenses in asserting the initial claim.[66] Such employment of the inferential role of *'inyenzi'*/'cockroach' would allow H to go on to say that (in some sense) A is nocturnal, a domestic pest, likely to multiply rapidly, hard to completely eliminate, spreads disease, shows emergent tendencies when in groups, and so on. These would each be asserted 'in some sense,' because the epithet is actually metaphorical, so the extensions are best interpreted with some flexibility. When *'inyenzi'* only applied to RPF soldiers, then 'nocturnal' as an inferential consequence may well have been best interpreted both literally and metaphorically, but when *'inyenzi'* was later spread to all Tutsi, 'nocturnal' was better interpreted metaphorically, indicating covert activities. Attention to the metaphors used on RTLM and in *Kangura* shows that the metaphor within this epithet was indeed extended in applying it to Tutsi. Notice also that S does not *say* that A is a Tutsi. In the context of early 1990s Rwanda, however, both S and H would know that in practice, in their local language games, this term was restricted to Tutsi. Practice rules the scope of the term. By the time of the genocide, the extension 'should be eliminated' came to be a rather immediate extension. This increased immediacy of the extermination-inference helped prepare the perpetrators for genocidal actions. This epithet, and its many uses in many kinds of speech acts, was only one way that changing discursive practices were used to change behavioral norms and expectations.

"She's a Tutsi" is an only apparently more benign case; within the perpetration phase of the genocide, it could engender diverse actions ranging from protection to murder depending upon who is speaking to

---

[65] Des Forges 1999, p. 3.
[66] Brandom 1998. *Making it Explicit*, Harvard University Press.

whom, when, and where. As André Sibomana said, "Woe betide those whose identity cards bore the word 'Tutsi': those five letters amounted to a death sentence, with immediate execution."[67] What seemed at first to be a mere classification, part of a name-game, became socially embedded in a variety of aspects of Rwandan life, and the action-engendering aspects of the mere classification became unmistakable.

In understanding the inferential roles of particular derogatory terms, we must also pay attention to the changing social and political contexts within which the terms are used, because these contexts shape the inferential roles. This is why we needed to think about Rwandan history in § 2. It is also why intentions just do not get us far enough in understanding the power of these terms and the speech acts that deliver them. As Léopord Twagirayezu, a convicted *génocidaire* from the Bugasera region, says, "It is awkward to talk about hatred between Hutus and Tutsis, because *words changed meaning after the killings.*"[68] He adds,

Before, we could fool around among ourselves and say we were going to kill them all, and the next moment we would join them to share some work or a bottle. Jokes and threats were mixed together. We no longer paid heed to what we said. We could toss around awful words without awful thoughts. The Tutsis did not even get very upset. I mean, they didn't draw apart because of those unfortunate discussions. Since then we have seen: *those words brought on grave consequences.*[69]

If Léopord is right, then even without a specific intention to harm, these initially thoughtless anti-Tutsi speech acts did cause harm. At the time, the words raised no red flags, generating little attention to the broader implications of their speech acts. Further, speakers using the terms might not have been particularly authoritative (compared to the speeches on the radio, for example), and the contexts of utterance might have diffused any sense of danger. Nevertheless, we can see that the casualness of bantering about murder and the increasing use of derogations created openings for speech acts that enacted licenses for these very actions. A radio announcer saying, "Clean the Nyamata church of its cockroaches" would have institutional authority, but as social organization fell apart, authority became diffused. Anyone could utter that sentence and get results.

These speech acts occurred within dynamic language games, which changed from the preparatory phase, through the perpetration, and yet again in the aftermath. Speech acts that, during the preparatory phase, seemed like mere words to the ordinary Rwandans later became

---

[67] Sibomana 1999, p. 87.
[68] Hatzfeld 2005, p. 218, Léopord speaking, emphasis added.
[69] Hatzfeld 2005, p. 218, emphasis added.

incitements to action, even when not in imperatives. By June 1994 the pragmatic force of both *inyenzi* (cockroach) and *ibyitso* (collaborator/ traitor) made them death sentences.

Any epithet carries with it an expressive commitment to the viability and value of that term and its use in particular sorts of context. Those who introduce derogatory terms as propaganda know what they are doing: it is no accident that such terms tend to depict the target as insects, snakes, any creature humans would be quick to kill. The value of the terms lies in this combination of vilification and its inferential and material connection to extermination. Americans were taught to view the Japanese as insects in WWII, Germans were taught to view Jews as vermin, and ordinary Rwandan Hutu were taught, through the influx of hate speech from media sources and civil authorities, to speak about, think of, and treat Tutsi as cockroaches. The viability of '*inyenzi*' may be established without speakers having a thorough grasp of the political value of the term. The value can grow on them, and in doing so, will reshape the social body, preparing it for greater violence.

In a rationalization that is typical of derogation-users across many contexts, Léopord offers Tutsi non-response as proof of the apparent innocuousness of the anti-Tutsi speech at the time.[70] Instead, we should see the apparent thoughtlessness of Hutu usage and the non-response of Tutsi as signs of practices in transition. Neither speakers nor audiences were fully in command of these speech acts, and so reactions were spotty, conclusions not drawn, actions not forthcoming. If indeed some Tutsi did see the linguistic violence for what it was, and still they did not respond, this non-response may be a measure of their own insecurity in the situation. A Tutsi aware of the threat posed by linguistic violence might feel caught in a double bind: speak up now and be punished now, or stay silent now and risk greater harm later.[71] Challenging such speech would neither feel nor be safe. Angélique Mukamanzi, a Tutsi survivor, recalls that as a schoolgirl she had both Tutsi and Hutu friends, and that the Hutu "never said bad things." She says: "I felt the first fears when people began leaving the Bugasera after the clashes in 1992. Our paths then grew loud with more and more evil words."[72]

---

[70] Surely this is not the only interpretation, but non-response from targeted groups is often cited as acceptance.

[71] Andrew Altman considers a similar situation regarding speaking out against anti-semitic speech in his, "Freedom of Expression and Human Rights Law: The Case of Holocaust Denial," this volume.

[72] Hatzfeld 2007, p. 81.

During the preparatory phase, social embeddedness is incomplete. We see this in Léopord's statement, which presents linguistic practices as dissociated from social behavior: nasty comments and friendly behavior could coexist peacefully (working together, sharing a beer). Such peaceful coexistence was perhaps made possible by not yet realizing the power of the language games they were playing and the role of these language games in the broader political struggle for power. The conventions associated with the anti-Tutsi speech acts were not yet fixed and so did not yet attach to anti-Tutsi behavior. In hindsight, however, he attributes causal power to these speech acts: *"those words brought on grave consequences."* In hindsight, he could see them as action-engendering, engendering actions that were not obvious in advance.

The testimony of both survivors and perpetrators shows marked concern for the power of discourse to shape social and material reality, giving people permission to behave in ways that previously were untenable. Some of the speech acts cited include an increased use of derogatory terms for Tutsi, increasingly frequent associations of all Tutsi as RPF 'inyenzi,' calling Hutu who were friendly with Tutsi 'ibyitso,' as well as increasing propaganda inciting fear of Tutsis and demanding specific exclusionary behaviors by Hutu.[73] Weakly construed, these linguistic behaviors were generating permission for exclusionary behaviors, thereby licensing entrenchment of a perceived or desired hierarchy. Strongly construed, these speech acts were part of a pattern that ended in genocide. We see this stronger view in the observations of Pio Mitungirehe, a *génocidaire* from Kibungo, who says,

Maybe we did not hate all the Tutsis, especially our neighbors, and maybe we did not see them as wicked enemies. But among ourselves we said we no longer wanted to live together. We even said we did not want them anywhere around us anymore, and that we had to clear them from our land. It's serious, saying that—it's already sharpening the machete.[74]

Pio's denying initial attitudes of hate suggests that the speech acts were stronger than and did not arise from speakers' intentions, suggesting instead that the speech acts conditioned attitudes over time. Even ordinary Hutu were talking about "clearing" the Tutsi from the land, a euphemism for murder that was heard repeatedly in directives issued over RTLM during the genocide. Saying such a thing is "already sharpening the

---

[73] See Kimani, in Thompson, for an analysis of many speech acts issued on RTLM. Kimani argues that the level of inflammatory content rose dramatically beginning in January 1994. pp. 110–24.

[74] Hatzfeld 2005, p. 218.

machete" because it generates licenses or permissions within the group to say similar things, which may become entrenched practices, which then sanction non-linguistic actions to back up the speech acts.[75]

Sometimes action-engendering permissions are built into an inferential role before the term is applied in a new way, so the power of specific speech acts to license material actions can sometimes be traced through the practices in which the concepts have the most play. In explaining the viciousness of the assaults on Tutsi, and why their bodies were mutilated, even posthumously, André Sibomana explains,

The extremist propaganda described Tutsi as cockroaches or snakes. For many uneducated peasants, if the official authorities state that Tutsi are snakes, it can't be wrong. If the local official of the commune orders people to kill snakes, it makes sense. When you kill a snake, you smash its head, then you cut it up in different places to make sure it's really dead. These very same forms of torture were inflicted on many Tutsi.[76]

The direct and literal application of the whole network of snake-destroying behaviors to the Tutsi is really quite remarkable. The long-standing practice of killing snakes set a model of what is to be done with snakes, and these everyday behaviors in rural Rwanda set a conceptual framework for 'snake.' The application of 'snake' to Tutsi licensed the application of a host of other terms that are part of the inferential role of 'snake.' This cultivated anti-Tutsi attitudes and licensed inferences about what should be done, granting permissions for action. When told to kill the snakes, the question 'how?' would not arise. Rwandans already knew how to kill snakes, and knew that it was mandatory. The derogatory terms used in the propaganda were well chosen, meshing everyday linguistic and non-linguistic practices, to engender genocidal actions.[77]

---

[75] We see the licenses or permissions more clearly if a speech act is repeated, rearranged, and used in a variety of contexts. The permission exists from the moment of utterance, even without follow-through. It can be undermined, though, by making it explicit, and then challenging it.

[76] Sibomana 1999. p. 71. See also Semelin p. 301 for a discussion of inscription of culture onto particular acts of violence. See also *Kangura* No. 40 (February 1993).

[77] Although '*inyenzi*' is more commonly discussed in the English-language scholarship on the genocide, '*inzoka*' was a very powerful and widespread term, reportedly even used by teachers to mock Tutsi children. The snake as a symbol of evil is basic to many cultures, including Rwanda. The extermination imperative is even stronger for snakes than for cockroaches, so of course the question arises about the relative power of the corresponding terms, speech acts, and the language games in which they appear. See Thomas Kamilindi's discussion of his young daughter's experience of being called a 'snake' during the genocide, at http://www.rwandainitiative.ca/symposium/transcript/panel2/kamilindi.html, Fergal Keene's "The Rwandan Girl who Refused to Die."

At this point, it is worth addressing a possible concern. Just how much work is being done by the social context? Do the words themselves, within the speech acts, matter much at all? If the words are just signals for action, any old word can be used (and many have been, during wars), without this elaborate apparatus of words carrying inferential roles, used in speech acts, and embedded in social and material practices. Sure, that works for codes. These derogatory terms are richer than code words, however, and their force is enacted across the population. People may use them casually, participating in a practice without being fully aware of the details of the practice. When a ten-year-old boy in the USA calls one of his classmates 'fag,' he is unlikely to fully understand the entire inferential role of that term, nor is he likely to think about, much less have mastery of, the broader social context of homophobia and hate crimes against homosexuals. Just the same, that child uses a term that brings a heavy social history and oppressive apparatus to bear on his classmate. The child probably knows that the term has negative power, and may even sense that it fulfills the insider/outsider function and may take it to meet the essentialism condition. I doubt the child has mastery of the full inferential role and its action outcomes. Although this speaker is a child, many adults speak with similar epistemic limitations, day in and day out. Few of our words lead to genocide, but we must consider our own diction and ask what apparatuses of power we invoke to control or harm others.

Asking how linguistic permissions are generated and then how those permissions grant behavioral licenses seems natural enough, but the question must not presuppose an untenable distinction between language and behavior. Speech acts *are* behavior. Using snake vocabulary to refer to humans in order to undermine their status is *doing* something—it is dehumanizing them. This expressive commitment—that using snake-talk to speak about Tutsi is viable and valuable—needs defense. In 1990s Rwanda, making this expressive commitment to the viability and value of using snake language to refer to Tutsi became one among many membership badges for the *interahamwe* and its supporters. Licensing or granting permission to derogatory speech acts is permitting action. The ultimate issue is the connection between verbal action and more macro-level physical action. To Naassan Munyandamutsa's comment that words killed his country, we can imagine the cynical advertising-soaked American saying, "*words* don't kill people, *people* kill people."[78] In light of what has

---

[78] Drawing on the NRA slogan that guns don't kill people, people kill people. Power reports that such a line was used by a Pentagon official chiding Prudence Bushnell for advocating radio jamming. Power, 2003, p. 372.

been argued here, this is too glib a response. Particular kinds of speech acts made it possible for some Rwandans to consider killing their neighbors and particular kinds of speech acts incited and sanctioned those murders. These were language games of a most serious kind.

5. Genocidal Language Games

Philosophers use Wittgenstein's concept of a language game to capture the idea that language is a human activity, with various goals—or sometimes apparently none—with various structures—ranging from minimal to complex—and with different degrees of inclusion. Some games involve a large percentage of a community; some seem to delimit community membership to "we who do this." Language games include speech acts of many kinds, and utterances that might look syntactically like the same bit of speech might constitute quite different speech acts depending upon the games in which it occurs.[79] In everyday life, we tend to think of games as non-serious, frivolous, and unimportant. Nothing could be further from the truth. Games train us in ways of being, modes of agency, patterns of effectiveness. In developing the idea of genocidal language games, I do not seek to trivialize linguistic practices that were an important part of the cultivation of the *génocidaires*, but rather to emphasize the power of language in play, in practice, in action. A language game is language in use, and it gets its power from its embeddedness in human life. One language game might be mere silliness, another might be a power play; a language game might be all seriousness in its action, and it might even be a genocidal language game that is part of a process that destroys a people.

5.1. *Major Moves*

Asking about how speech acts sanction other speech acts and make permissible non-linguistic actions leads to questions about word/world relations, particularly the territory marked out as pragmatics in the late twentieth century. Over half a century ago, in "Some Reflections on Language Games," Wilfrid Sellars posited that a language game would have three general categories of moves.[80] *Language entry transitions* take a speaker from a physical and social context *into* a language game. This would seem to fit initial naming of things and persons. Internal transitions within the language game, *language-language moves*, enable participants to make inferences based upon other moves that have already been made in

---

[79] The hierarchy of the model is this: linguistic practices are constituted by language games, and language games are constituted by speech acts.

[80] Sellars 1954, pp. 204–28.

the game. A can talk about B's dog, based only on what B has said about the dog, even if A never encountered B's dog. *Language exit transitions* take the player from inside the game to a position outside the game.[81] These moves carry the action-engendering force of the game into the world.

§ 5.1.a. Language Entry Moves

Language *entry* transitions are the ways that "one comes to occupy a position in the game"; the movement is from world to word.[82] Observation sentences, such as "This is red," were what Sellars had in mind. These utterances take a speaker from a perception to a position in a language game; notice that, pragmatically speaking, these are pretty basic speech acts. (They do not seem, on the surface, to engender any action.) Sellars calls these 'transitions' instead of 'moves,' perhaps to respect Wittgenstein's denial that naming something is actually even a move in a language game. Wittgenstein says,

> For naming and describing do not stand on the same level: naming is a preparation for description. Naming is so far not a move in the language-game—any more than putting a piece in its place on the board is a move in chess. We may say: nothing has so far been done, when a thing has been named. It has not even got a name except in the language-game. (*Philosophical Investigations* § 49)

Wittgenstein is right about setting up the chess board, with its two players each equally outfitted from the start. Looking at other games, though, we can see that not all entry transitions are equal. If you enter soccer as the goalie, that is quite a different thing than entering as a wing. Each entrance carries with it different powers and responsibilities from the outset. Any game that has positions will work the same way. So we can see that each entry will shape a range of permissible internal moves, and probably also shape the permissible exit transitions. How much this is settled from the very start will vary with the game.

It is possible that the Belgians who instituted Rwandan identity cards may have thought that they were simply labeling observable properties that mark different kinds of persons, "This one is Tutsi. That one is Hutu." Even so, many Rwandans today deny that such direct observation would ever have been possible.[83] It would be a mistake to think of the

---

[81] Sellars distinguishes between *moves*, which are transitions internal to the game, and *transitions*, which involve "a situation which is not a position in the game and a situation which is a position in the game" (Sellars 1954, p. 210).

[82] Sellars 1954, p. 210.

[83] See Sibomana 1999, pp. 82–7. Prior to the 1931 institution of identity cards, Sibomana says, ethnic identity was somewhat fluid: "a cattle-owning Hutu could enter the Tutsi group, while an impoverished Tutsi could become a Hutu" (87). See also Chretain's history, and Lyons and Straus, p. 81.

world-to-word relation as emerging because the world prompts the word, even in the case of something as simple as "This is red," given the variety of words that something red in the world can prompt: 'rouge,' 'rojo,' 'rosso,' 'rot,' 'rood,' to name a few. Further, increased Hutu use of 'inyenzi' and 'inzoka' was not a response to a brute fact of nature about the Tutsi. To believe so would be to blame the victim, and to overlook the ontological slip from word to world. It would be to miss the power play that produces the discourse that shapes the social body. Rwandan journalist Thomas Kamilindi recalls that his young daughter was disturbed by 'inzoka':

One day somebody said, "That one is a snake. They have to kill her." She still wasn't even three years of age at the time. She said to me, "Daddy, am I a snake? Am I really a snake?..."[84]

Even a child can tell when the application of a name or label is an entrance into a hostile game.

The world-to-word relationship centers on people attaching words to the world. The metaphysics of this is quite subtle, although most of the time we would simply say that a person sees the thing and names it. But what makes it possible for a person to see a thing? Speaking several years after the genocide, innocent Rwililiza says, "Here in Rwanda, it's a big deal to be Hutu or Tutsi. In a marketplace, a Hutu can spot a Tutsi at fifty yards, and vice-versa, but admitting that there is a difference is taboo, even among ourselves."[85] Take typical Americans to that marketplace and we will not observe this difference that is so basic to Rwandan social ontology, because we do not have the language games ready to hand to enable us to perform this task. The micro-level issues involved in carving the world up into nameable units are complex and well discussed by Sellars and many others since.

Name games are various but share some basic structures. There is a first use. That first use, say of a newborn child's name, puts the child's name into use, into the game, as it were, and forges a connection between the child and what is said about her. The use of a name, by a non-baptizing speaker for the first time, may work to get a speaker into a game as well. In classes, it is much easier for students who did not previously know each other to cross-refer during discussion ("I'd like to return to Mary's point") if everyone in the group has already *used* each other's name. In doing so, they have entered the name-game, and then the use of any one particular name is not an awkward announcement of undue attention. Of course, these students already had names long before entering the class, but unless

[84] http://www.rwandainitiative.ca/symposium/transcript/panel2/kamilindi.html
[85] Hatzfeld 2007, p. 108.

they are all named within the context of this classroom, we see the all-too-familiar phenomenon of just a few people in the class having names familiar to and used by all. This example captures the specificity of what can be permissible or impermissible within a given language game, and also illustrates the nesting and overlapping of language games. Most of the time, we join ongoing games. If speaker A calls person B a racist name while speaking with person C, A signals that he is participating in an ongoing racist practice. If C then uses the term, C gets into the game. If C challenges A's use of the term, then not only does C not get into that game, but C attacks the game. Silence leaves the game intact, and leaves open the question whether C will play.[86]

§ 5.1.b. Language-Language Moves

Once one is within the language game, other moves become permissible from that position. These internal moves within the language game, *language-language moves*, are transitions from one speech act to another; the anchors of these transitions (positions) are often inferences based on approved patterns. S says that A is a member of the RPF, so then H is permitted to apply the epithet '*inyenzi*' to A because the practice of calling RPF soldiers '*inyenzi*' was already established as a simple inference within Hutu circles in the early '90s. When I say, "JJ is a dog," you may ask what breed JJ is, whether he needs a lot of exercise, whether he is friendly or scares the neighbors. There are, of course, limits to automatic inferential licenses in any language game; mastery of the game requires mastery of these limits. If you already knew, for example, that JJ is human, and so inferred that I was using 'dog' metaphorically, then the language-language moves would change accordingly. In Rwanda, Hutu extremists had a lot at stake in making unjustified inferences (from 'Tutsi' to '*inyenzi*') stick. Without them, ordinary Hutu would have feared Tutsi less, and would have been unlikely to participate in the genocide. To keep and expand political power and to gain control of more land and resources, Hutu extremists needed ordinary Hutu to believe that ordinary Tutsi were a threat to their own lives and well-being. Sliding from the *Inkotanyi* being *inyenzi* to all Tutsi being *inyenzi* is a strong start.

§ 5.1.c. Language Exit Moves

As we have seen from the social embeddedness condition as applied to deeply derogatory terms, real-life language games are integrated into ways of life, and so actions within the game result in changed permissions governing behaviors beyond the game. For example, when a patient sees

---

[86] Simple silence lets things be, but of course there are game-stopping silences, and silences that can change the course of a game.

a doctor, she typically explains her symptoms, and the doctor makes a diagnosis and offers a prescription. So far we are still talking about speech. When the doctor says, "Take two of these pills and stay home from work," the patient is now authorized to move beyond the give-and-take of discourse by actually ingesting the pills and taking the time to rest. The doctor's prescribing speech act is a *language exit transition*, moving from a location within the language game to a behavior that is not a position in the game. It is an exit-move.

Imperatives are obvious language exit moves, which is to say that they are action-engendering discourse. J.L. Austin's categories of verdictives, exercitives, and commissives would generally count as language departures. Trying to explain why he participated in the massacre of Tutsis, Pancrace Hakizamungili says:

When you receive a new order, you hesitate but you obey, or else you're taking a risk. When you have been prepared in the right way by the radios and the official advice, you obey more easily, even if the order is to kill your neighbors. The mission of a good organizer is to stifle your hesitations when he gives you instructions. For example, when he shows you that the act will be total and have no grave consequences for anyone left alive, you obey more easily, you don't worry about anything. You forget your misgivings and fears of punishment. You obey freely.[87]

Hesitation is stifled through the cultivation of perceptions of inevitability and impunity. Organizers create a climate of acceptance through specific kinds of speech acts: (a) preparatory speech acts—such as using epithets— that train potential participants to dehumanize their targets, (b) clear and official commands, (c) clear targets, (d) threats against those who resist, and (e) promises of rewards to those who participate. Authority is key here, the authority of the speaker who issues the threats and promises makes a difference to how easily misgivings can be set aside. In early stages in Rwanda, authority set the everyday derogations into motion, but once the genocide was underway, nearly any identification of Tutsi had sufficient authority. Here we see Foucault's point about the productivity of power; authority, once concentrated, became spread throughout the Hutu social body.

The use of an epithet—a naming game—can involve all three types of moves. A transition from world-to-word can be seen in the application of 'inyenzi' to the RPF *inkotanyi* (invincibles/warriors), who struck at night, seemed to come out of nowhere, and could not be stopped. Analogical observation underlies initial uses of that particular term to that particular

---

[87] Hatzfeld 2005, p. 71. See also Prunier 1995, pp. 141–2.

group. The application of '*inyenzi*' spread beyond the invading militia by an extension of the term to all who share their ethnicity. This is a simple, but common, logical error: "All *inyenzi inkotanyi* are Tutsi, therefore all Tutsi are *inyenzi*." This language-language move has significant implications for those to whom the term is newly applied. A speaker who then uses the term in this new way, in referring to a particular person, would be making a language exit move. While still in the game, the speaker has now also done something beyond the game; he/she is bringing the weight of anti-Tutsi social and political policy to bear upon this individual. *Language exit moves are the site of action-engenderment.*

5.2. *Exit Moves and Status-Functions*

We began by rejecting the conception of deeply derogatory terms as being best understood primarily as insulting slurs designed to communicate one person's dislike, displeasure, or disapproval of another. We rejected the view that the use of a derogatory term is best understood as the communication of the speaker's intention (mental state) to the hearer. As we have seen, words can be used, and have power, without the speaker having the intention that such a theory implies. Pio might not be in command of '*inyenzi*' when he uses it, just as the American schoolboy might not really understand 'fag,' but each does damage with these terms just the same. Without denying the potential utility of intentions for some explanations, we instead understand deeply derogatory terms as operating within social practices that sanction certain inferences to go with each term, giving it a role in our patterns of sanctioned speech acts. These terms, used in speech, enact the power of one group over another.

Understanding certain aspects of the exit moves present in racist speech—understood as a social practice—is clarified by the concept of status-functions. John Searle originally introduced status-functions to explain institutional realities such as how certain pieces of paper can be money. Searle argues that we move from brute facts and merely physical objects (atoms, wood, paper) to social or institutional objects by way of collective consciousness and through collective assigning of status-functions to objects. These pieces of paper are money because *we say* they count as money; this *saying* involves both the speech act and its supporting behaviors. We *treat* that paper and those metal bits as money by trading with them, and so they come to *be* money. Status-functions, of the form 'X counts as Y in C,' where X is an object, an event, or even a human being, and Y is something more complex, crucially depend on collective acceptance of treating X as a Y within C by members of that community. Citizenship is a Y function, but so is slavery. Neither is a brute fact, and each is possible only within contexts that can make sense of the heightened or diminished powers of these statuses. Searle highlights the positive powers often associated with the imposition of a new status: "in general, the creation of a status-function is a matter of conferring some new power."[88]

In most language games that use racist derogations, the derogation is a *function* attached to a person, whose status changes because of the imposition of the function.[89] Racist derogations are status-functions, for they tell the target, "You count as a so-and-so here." With exponential growth from 1990 to 1994, '*inyenzi*' became a social-kind word, delimiting a group of people who are slated for certain sorts of treatment by others.[90] Today, the government of Rwanda wants all use of 'Tutsi' and 'Hutu' stopped, so that Rwandans can unite *as* Rwandans instead of living out divisive ethnicities.[91] The imposition of racist status-functions diminishes the power of the target and increases the power of others who are not members of that socially constituted kind. The language exit moves are built right into the inferential roles of the terms, because these terms are what they are because of the subsequent treatment they purport to justify. Status-functions are action-engendering exit moves.

The action-engendering power of speech acts containing derogatory terms arises from an interaction between the status-function and the inferential role of the derogatory term applied. Status functions carry with them inferential roles that have treatment-consequents. If X counts as money in C, then A is rational to work for it, save it, spend it, etc. In general, A is not rational to burn it, waste it, or simply throw it away. Couching these action-consequents in terms of rationality makes sense because rationality is largely about making justified inferences. This raises the question: which treatments are purportedly justified by a particular status-function? This question cannot be answered in the abstract, because the answer will always be anchored by a particular social and historical context. In the case of Rwandan Tutsi, we saw that the status-function

---

[88] Searle 2007, p. 95.

[89] Although Searle does not apply his theory directly to racist and ethnic and sexist derogatory terms, he does express concern about shifting institutional identifications around the world, citing Bosnia, for example, and asserting that although it may seem like brute force prevails over institutional facts, the opposite is the case. "The guns are ineffectual except to those prepared to use them in cooperation with others and in structures, however informal, with recognized lines of authority and command. And all of that requires collective intentionality and institutional facts." (117).

[90] One *génocidaire* says that before 1990, there was no 'Hutu' or 'Tutsi,' and blames the RPF for the reemergence of emphasis on these categories. See Lyons and Straus, *Intimate Enemy*, p. 81. This apparently self-serving claim nevertheless reveals the need for further empirical study of the history of these terms and their correlates.

[91] See Republic of Rwanda 2001, and Lacey 2004.

'*inyenzi*' led to vilification and then genocide. As the Bikindi case (below) will show, the *inyenzi* status-function became so entrenched that, during the genocide, the action-engendering force of the derogatory term came to be applied *even without explicit use of the derogatory term*.

Action-engendering speech acts come in many grammatical guises. In Wittgenstein's iconic complete—albeit primitive—language game, which we discussed earlier, a builder calls out a word, "Slab!," "Block!," etc., and an assistant brings a particular object in each case. In everyday speech, imperatives wear their status as action-engendering on their sleeves, but many other grammatical forms and many kinds of speech acts engender action in more subtle ways. A simple question or a straightforward indicative declaration can, within a particular context, prompt immediate action from others. "Why was this room not cleaned?" asks the hotel manager, or perhaps she says, "That floor is still dirty." Each of these would be action-engendering if said to someone whose responsibility included cleaning that room or that floor.

The story of Simon Bikindi's visit to Gisenyi prison unfolds like a horrible parody of the "Slab!" language game. One of the most famous songwriters and performers in Rwanda, Simon Bikindi became a leading propagandist for the Hutu power movement. On the occasion described below, he visited the prison with Hassan Ngeze, the editor of *Kangura*. These visitors were not only media celebrities, but also people of very high rank in the Hutu-Power structure. Notice the patterns of speech and action revealed in the following summary of real events, taken from the transcript of Bikindi's trial before the ICTR.

25. In June 1994, SIMON BIKINDI went to Gisenyi prison in the company of Hassan Ngeze, Major Kabera, the prison Director Gasirabo and more than ten body guards. The prison guard Rukara called out the names of 12 prisoners who came out of their cells and were told to stand beside the prison latrine pit. Simon BIKINDI then asked the prison director Gasirabo why the 12 prisoners were still alive whilst in Kigali all Tutsis had been killed. The prison director Gasirabo responded that he had been given these prisoners to keep them and he did not know if they were to be killed. Ngeze then asked all the Tutsis prisoners to raise their hands in the air, and 10 of the prisoners who were Tutsi did. Reading from a list of twelve prisoners, Simon BIKINDI then called out the names of Tutsi prisoners, starting with Matabaro and Kayibanda. Matabaro came forward to stand near to where Simon BIKINDI stood, and he was hit in the back of the head with the back of an axe by one of the bodyguards. Simon BIKINDI then called out the name of Kayibanda who was also hit on the back of the head with the back of an axe by BIKINDI's body guard. Matabaro and Kayibanda both died as a result of the blows. Eight of the other persons whose names were on the list, all Tutsis, were killed by BIKINDI's bodyguards, using bayonets. *By reading out from a*

list of Tutsi prisoners, by asking why they had not yet been killed, Simon BIKINDI instigated, and aided and abetted the immediate killings of two of the prisoners, namely Matabaro and Kayibanda. In respect of the other eight Tutsi prisoners who were killed immediately afterwards by Simon BIKINDI's bodyguards, by his initial question as to why all the Tutsi prisoners had been not been killed before his arrival at the prison, he instigated, and aided and abetted their subsequent killings by his bodyguards. (Italics added.)[92]

The court's judgment, marked here by italics, indicates that they see the action-engendering work of Bikindi's speech acts. Bikindi simply calls out the name of a prisoner, the prisoner comes forward, and a guard deals him a fatal blow on the head. Clearly André Sibomana was not exaggerating when he said, as quoted earlier, "Woe betide those whose identity cards bore the word 'Tutsi': those five letters amounted to a death sentence, with immediate execution."[93] Calling out the prisoners' names, directing them to the side of the latrine pit (often a prelude to death), and telling the Tutsi to raise their hands—these are all language-exit moves, engendering actions from either the Tutsis or the guards.

When is a question not a question? When it is an indirect speech act. Simon Bikindi's question about "why the 12 prisoners were still alive whilst in Kigali all Tutsis had been killed," is an indirect speech act, directly parallel to the hotel manager saying, "Why is this room not clean?" to the housekeeper. Bikindi does not *assert* that they should already be dead, nor does he utter the imperative "Kill them!" Just the same, Bikindi's question—in the context of the identify-and-destroy practices of the genocide—made the requisite action clear enough to all the parties involved.[94]

Indirect speech acts are socially embedded in many practices. They communicate more than they literally say because the speaker relies on a mutually shared set of background beliefs, goals, assumptions, and mutually shared rational strategies for interpreting linguistic and non-linguistic behavior.[95] With an indirect speech act, there is room for interpretation, but context usually limits the possibilities. Searle comments, "For a sentence like 'Can you reach the salt?' or 'I would appreciate it if you would get off my foot', it takes some ingenuity to imagine a situation in which their utterances would not be requests."[96] When Bikindi asks why the

---

[92] ICTR 2005. The Prosecutor v. Simon Bikindi, Case No. ICTR-01-72-T, paragraph 25, p. 8, as transcribed: http://www.unictr.org/Portals/0/Case/English/Bikindi/indictment/bikindi05.pdf

[93] Sibomana 1999, p. 87.

[94] Tutsi lack of resistance does not prove indeterminacy of the speech act; testimony from perpetrators and survivors indicates that Tutsi rarely begged for their lives when confronted by their killers.

[95] Searle 1979, pp. 31–2.

[96] Searle 1979, p. 31.

Tutsi prisoners are not dead, and then calls them forward by name, the actions of the warden and the guards make the contextually required interpretation of Bikindi's speech acts clear. Everyone understood what to do; the actions engendered and the exit positions indicate the internal inferential moves that were made. The ICTR conclusion that Bikindi's speech acts prove that "he instigated, and aided and abetted their subsequent killings by his bodyguards" further underscores the way in which these simple utterances, used in a complex context, played multiple roles in this deadly language game.

The Rwandan linguistic practices that developed in the early 1990s involve a variety of kinds of speech acts, many of them indirect, so we must note the entry moves of getting into the anti-Tutsi rhetoric game or practices, the moves within the practices, and the exit to non-linguistic behaviors, including rape, murder, and ultimately genocide. We must be sensitive to the role of extra-linguistic context in settling the question of what was done through an utterance. These very broad categories of moves within language games help to track the linguistic practices that generated a sense of permissibility amongst many Hutu for the genocide.

6. Conclusion

At the outset of this analysis, we considered Foucault's remark that power "needs to be considered as a productive network which runs through the whole social body, much more than as a negative instance whose function is repression."[97] Particular kinds of linguistic practices conveyed through language games produce a social body capable of enacting genocide. We have been working with a simplified model of genocide, as the complete extermination of a people. Now it is time to note that genocide encompasses more than physical death, it includes the destruction of a culture, extreme psychological damage that allows people to live but feel as if they died, and more. The constant, deep, and widespread derogation of a group should be seen as part and parcel of genocide, not only as an antecedent to it.

The practice of derogation is made up of many kinds of language games, which comprise many kinds of speech acts. These derogatory acts, games, and practices are repressive *prima facie* but even more, they produce a positive set of licenses and permissions which foster behaviors that both construct the positive identities of all parties to the games, and permit destructive actions which undermine the very logic of the game and

---

[97] Foucault 1980, p. 119.

practice. What's the harm if we give someone a new label, like 'sausage-face'? Perhaps none, if the term stays isolated, a mere child's identification game, unembedded in social practices and systems of power. In real life, derogatory terms act as status-functions, which shape a person's life prospects in significant ways. It is through the language-exit dimension of these status functions that we can see their action-engendering power.

The philosophical analysis of genocidal language games presented here argues that the derogatory terms used against Tutsi during the Rwandan genocide were action-engendering. I argued that the widespread use of such terms played a significant role in bringing about the Rwandan genocide. The first step was the entrance of the derogatory terms to the linguistic practices—the language games—of the people. Naming the Tutsi *as* 'inyenzi' was the start of the game. Next, the inferential roles of the terms and the full character of their status-functions developed through use. As these language-language moves developed, the kinds of inferences people became licensed to make expanded and became more entrenched. Finally, and most emphatically, we saw that the power of the terms was brought beyond discourse into material action through the exit moves that were licensed. At first these exit moves were forms of discrimination at school and at work, perhaps extending to the social world of the neighborhood soccer match, but often limited to institutional settings where individuals could beg off their own responsibility. Ultimately, because of the action-engendering force of derogatory terms like 'inyenzi' and 'inzoka,' morally prohibited actions like murder, rape, mayhem, and mutilation came to be regarded as socially appropriate and even required.

To understand the full force of these deeply derogatory terms, we must remember how they exemplify the five features set out in this analysis. Functional variability is important, but evidence suggests that the development of the insider/outsider function is key to dividing a society and keeping it divided. If the inferential roles of the derogations map onto divisions that are perceived as essential kinds, the division becomes further entrenched. In Rwanda we saw that the road to genocide included taking Hutu and Tutsi to be essential traits, and 'inyenzi' to mark the evil of the Tutsi, even when she or he might seem just fine on the surface. Genocidal language games require the essentialism condition, because if a cockroach can give birth to a butterfly, death is not the only solution.

This suggests that the harms of speech acts using derogatory terms are significantly weakened to the degree that the essentialism condition is weakened. If true, this could help explain why in some contexts, some individuals escape the harms of speech acts involving derogatory terms that deeply plague others. The escapees deny the essentialism, seeing the term used as a political action on the part of the user, and so escape the naturalizing force of that speech act. Understanding the saying to be an action, they take it to represent someone else's view of the world and of them. By resisting taking what is said to depict reality, the escapees demystify it. Alertness to the normative import is key.

The social embeddedness of some derogatory terms gives them their breath and their depth. If derogatory terms are idiosyncratic, like 'sausage-face,' they might reveal something about the speaker or the few people who play the game. Deeply derogatory terms are not idiosyncratic, but become embedded in their own inferential networks, as well as in social practices that include how people are treated. Deeply derogatory terms are nested within practices of injustice. They empower some people, and weaken others. The social embeddedness condition was key to the entrenchment of '*inyenzi*' and its spread in frequency of use. Genocidal language games need broad engagement to do their work.

"She's an *inyenzi*," while grammatically akin to "She's a child," is a speech act of a very different order when appropriately embedded in a climate of fear and a culture of distrust. Social embeddedness and essentialism work together to create a coherent order of social practices, norms, and related concepts. Their partnership is crucial: essentialism naturalizes and reifies the categories, while social embeddedness obscures the political context that these categories construct and maintain. This stops questions before they start. Switching from calling the RPF guerilla fighters '*Inkotanyi*' (invincible), to calling them '*inyenzi*' (cockroach) as a descriptive derogation, is a fairly straightforward speech act typical of wartime propaganda. Spreading this epithet across the entire Tutsi population fostered essentialism, opening the door to genocide.

Once we are aware of the different kinds of moves within language games, we can be more sensitive to entries, internal language-language moves, and language-departure or exit moves. In genocide, the exit moves are so dramatic, the consequences of these actions so overwhelming, that we see the power of the conceptual framework in stark relief. In relatively peaceful political systems, our naming practices, our patterns of deep derogation (tied to systems of oppression), and the inferences that these terms sanction, also do damage to the individuals upon whom they most obviously work. Less obvious, but also important, is the damage this set of practices does to the society as a whole and to the individuals who live and work within these practices.

Gandhi is said to have held that "a language is an exact reflection of the character and growth of its speakers." If so, then perhaps an analysis of the derogatory terms and other forms of linguistic violence prevalent in a society is an important diagnostic of the level of material violence already present or potentially developing. We must understand linguistic violence, and find ways to fix the problems it reveals. Saying is a kind of doing, generalizing out to other kinds of action through the inferential content of what we say and through the permissions and licenses we thereby grant. Linguistic violence is the canary in the mine. We ignore it at our peril.

References

African Rights 1995: 60. *Rwanda: Death, Despair and Defiance*. London: African Rights. (Revised edition).

Article 19. http://www.article19.org/pdfs/publications/rwanda-broadcasting-genocide.pdf

Berry, John A. and Carol Pott Berry 1999. *Genocide in Rwanda*: A Collective Memory. Washington, DC: Howard University Press.

Brandom, Robert 1998. *Making It Explicit*. Cambridge, MA: Harvard University Press.

Bromley, Roger 2007. *Beast, Vermin, Insect: 'Hate' Media and the Construction of the Enemy—the Case of Rwanda, 1990–1994*. http://www.inter-disciplinary.net/ptb/hhv/vcce/vcce1/Bromley%20paper.pdf

Carver, Richard 2000. "Broadcasting and Political Transition: Rwanda and Beyond," *African Broadcast Cultures: Radio in Transition*. Richard Fardon and Graham Furniss, eds. Oxford: James Currey.

Chalk, Frank 1999. "Radio Propaganda and Genocide," MIGS Occasional Paper, November 1999, presented in an earlier form to the Conference on "Synergy in Early Warning," Centre for Refugee Studies York University, Toronto, Ontario, 16 March 1997.

Chrétien, Jean-Pierre, J. F. Dupaquier, M. Kabanda, and J. Ngarambe 1995. *Rwanda: Les Médias du Génocide*. Paris, France: Karthala (with Reporters Sans Frontières).

Chrétien, Jean-Pierre 2003. *The Great Lakes of Africa: Two Thousand Years of History*, translated by Scott Straus. NY: Zone Books.

De Brouwer, Anne-Marie and Sandra Ka Hon Chu, eds. 2009. *The Men Who Killed Me: Rwandan Survivors of Sexual Violence*. Vancouver: Douglas and MacIntyre.

Des Forges, Alison 1999. *Leave None to Tell the Story: Genocide in Rwanda*. NY: Human Rights Watch.

Foucault, Michel 1980. *Power/Knowledge: Selected Interviews and Other Writings 1972–1977*, "Truth and Power," edited by Colin Gordon, trans. Colin Gordon et al. NY: Vintage.

Gourevitch, Philip 1998. *We Wish to Inform You that Tomorrow We Will be Killed With Our Families: Stories From Rwanda*. NY: Picador (Farrar, Strauss, Giroux).

Hatzfeld, Jean 2005. *Machete Season: The Killers in Rwanda Speak*. Preface by Susan Sontag. Translation: Linda Coverdale (2005). NY: Farrar, Straus and Giroux.

Hatzfeld, Jean 2005 Machete Season: *The Killers in Rwanda Speak,* Preface by Susan Sontag. Translation: Linda Coverdale (2005). NY. Farrar, Status and Giroux.

Hatzfeld, Jean 2007. *Life Laid Bare: The Survivors in Rwanda Speak,* translated by Linda Coverdale (2005). NY: Farrar, Straus and Giroux.

ICTR (International Criminal Tribunal for Rwanda) 2003. *Prosecutor v. Ferdinand Nahimana, Jean-Bosco Barayagwiza and Hassan Ngeze,* Case No. ICTR-99-52-T. http://www.unictr.org/Portals/0/Case/English/Ngeze/judgement/Judg&sent.pdf

ICTR 2005. *Prosecutor v. Simon Bikindi,* Case No. ICTR-01-72-T http://www .unictr.org/Portals/0/Case/English/Bikindi/indictment/bikindi05.pdf

Kagwi-Ndungu, Charity 2007. "The Challenges in Prosecuting Print Media for Incitement to Genocide," in Thompson, 2007, pp. 330–42.

Kamilindi, Thomas 2006. http://www.rwandainitiative.ca/symposium/transcript/panel2/kamilindi.html

Keene, Fergal 1997. "The Rwandan Girl Who Refused to Die," reprinted from *The Sunday Times* (London), at http://www.pbs.org/wgbh/pages/frontline/shows/rwanda/reports/refuse.html

Kimani, Mary 2007. "RTLM: The Medium that Became a Tool for Mass Murder," in Thompson, Allan, 2007, pp. 110–24.

Kinzer, Stephen 2008. *A Thousand Hills: Rwanda's Rebirth and the Man Who Dreamed It.* Hoboken, NJ: John Wiley & Sons.

Kukla, Rebecca, and Mark Lance 2009. *Yo! and Lo!: The Pragmatic Topography of the Space of Reasons.* Cambridge, MA: Harvard University Press.

Lacey, Marc 2004. "A Decade After Massacres, Rwanda Outlaws Ethnicity," *The New York Times,* April 9, 2004.

MacKinnon, Catherine A. 2004. *Prosector v. Nahiman, Barayagwiza, & Ngeze.* Case No. ICTR 99-52-T, in *The American Journal of International Law,* Vol. 98, No. 2 (April 2004), pp. 325–30.

MacKinnon, Catharine A. 1993. *Only Words.* Cambridge, MA: Harvard University Press.

Malvern, Linda 2004. *Conspiracy to Murder: The Rwandan Genocide.* London: Verso.

Mamdani, Mahamood 2004. *When Victims Become Killers: Colonialism, Nativism, and the Genocide in Rwanda.* Princeton, NJ: Princeton University Press.

Mills, Charles 1998. "But What Are You Really? The Metaphysics of Race," in his *Blackness Visible: Essays on Philosophy and Race.* Ithaca, NY: Cornell University Press. pp. 41–67.

Munyandamutsa, Naasson 2007. Speaking at "The Language of Genocide" symposium, Harvard University, 27 March.

Mushikiwabo, Louise, and Jack Kramer 2006. *Rwanda Means the Universe: A Native's Memoir of Blood and Bloodlines.* NY: St. Martin's Press.

OAU (Organization for African Unity) 2000. "Rwanda: The Preventable Genocide" (OAU Doc. IPEP/Panel (May 29, 2000) at 12.33).

Power, Samantha 2003. *A Problem from Hell: America in the Age of Genocide*. NY: Harper.

Prunier, Gérard 1995. *The Rwanda Crisis: History of a Genocide*. NY: Columbia University Press.

Republic of Rwanda 2001. *Law 47/2001 of 18/12/2001, On Prevention, Suppression, and Punishment of the Crime of Discrimination and Sectarianism*. See: http://www.grandslacs.net/doc/4040.pdf, also: http://www.grandslacs.net/doc/4040.pdf, also: http://www.unhcr.org/refworld/pdfid/4ac5c4302.pdf

Rusesagabina, Paul 2006. (with Tom Zoellner) *An Ordinary Man: The True Story Behind "Hotel Rwanda."* London: Bloomsbury.

Schabas, William 2000. "Hate Speech in Rwanda: The Road to Genocide." 46 *McGill L.J.*: 141–71.

Searle, John 1979. "Indirect Speech Acts," in his *Expression and Meaning: Studies in the Theory of Speech Acts*. Cambridge: Cambridge University Press, pp. 30–57.

Searle, John 1995. *The Construction of Social Reality*. NY: The Free Press.

Sebarenzi, Joseph 2009. *God Sleeps in Rwanda: A Journey of Transformation*. NY: Atria Books.

Sellars, Wilfrid 1954. "Some Reflections on Language Games," *Philosophy of Science*, 21(3), pp. 204–28.

Semelin, Jacques 2003. "Toward a Vocabulary of Massacre and Genocide," *Journal of Genocide Research*, 5(2): 193–210, especially 201.

Semelin, Jacques 2007. *Purify and Destroy: The Political Uses of Massacre and Genocide*. NY: Columbia University Press, p. 199.

Sibomana, André 1999. *Hope for Rwanda: Conversations with Laure Guilbert and Hervé Deguine*. London: Pluto Press.

Straus, Scott, and Richard Lyons 2006. *Intimate Enemy: Images and Voices of the Rwandan Genocide*. Cambridge, MA: Zone Books.

Temple-Raston, Dina 2005. *Justice on the Grass: Three Rwandan Journalists, Their Trial for War Crimes, and a Nation's Quest for Redemption*. NY: The Free Press.

Thompson, Allan (ed.) 2007. *The Media and the Rwanda Genocide*. London/Ann Arbor: Pluto Press.

Tirrell, Lynne 1999. "Derogatory Terms: Racism, Sexism, and the Inferential Role Theory of Meaning," in *Language and Liberation: Feminism, Philosophy and Language*, Kelly Oliver and Christina Hendricks, eds. Albany NY: SUNY Press, pp. 41–79.

Wittgenstein, Ludwig 1958. *Philosophical Investigations*, translated by G. E. M. Anscombe. NY: MacMillan.

Words That Silence? Freedom of Expression and Racist Hate Speech[1]

Caroline West

1. Introduction

Debates over the regulation of racist hate speech are often set up as posing a choice between free speech and other values (e.g. equality). It may well be that other values would be best promoted by restricting racist hate speech. But I will have little directly to say about that here. My aim instead is to examine the prevailing assumption that the value of *freedom of speech* itself is necessarily only or best served by permitting racist hate speech. Racist hate speech could function to undermine freedom of speech, rather than to exemplify or enhance it. If so, there might be a free speech argument against permitting racist hate speech.

How (if at all) racist hate speech could undermine free speech turns partly on what it takes for speech to be free. A variety of different accounts of freedom of speech have been proposed, and these may have quite different implications for what kinds of interference with communication can legitimately be taken to limit free speech. For instance, there is a view according to which speech is free just so long as the government does not interfere by imposing coercive restrictions on what people can (or cannot) say. From that vantage point, it is hard to see how racist hate speech could even in principle interfere with anyone's freedom of speech, for racist hate speakers and their audiences are typically private actors. But this conception seems too narrow an account of free speech. It implies, for instance, that a society in which a small coterie of media barons exert absolute

---

[1] Thanks to David Braddon-Mitchell, Robert Bezimienny, Ishani Maitra, and Mary Kate McGowan for helpful comments and suggestions.

control over what opinions can (and cannot) be published or televised counts as one in which everyone is perfectly free to speak, providing that the media barons are private entrepreneurs; and that seems implausible.

On the other hand, there is a possible conception of free speech as requiring a guarantee of a sympathetic and receptive audience disposed to hear the speaker just as they intend to be heard.[2] On that picture, it is relatively easy to see how private actors preaching racial hatred and intolerance could interfere with free speech; but, as critics are quick to point out, it is equally easy to see that there is likely to be nothing very special about racist hate speech in this regard. If free speech requires a guarantee of an audience that listens carefully to every word we utter and grasps perfectly exactly what we mean to say, then very few of us are ever really free to speak.

The correct conception of free speech plausibly lies somewhere in between these two extremes. I will not attempt to determine exactly where the correct account lies. Rather, I will outline three relatively minimal conditions that I will argue any conception of something worthy of the label 'freedom of speech' must satisfy. These conditions are not, or not simply, motivated by commonsense intuitions about what kinds of interference with communication are (or are not) aptly described as making speech unfree, but rather by the sorts of justifications commonly advanced by moral and political theorists in favour of something called 'free speech'. I will argue that these justifications imply that free speech requires (at least) minimal distribution, minimal comprehension, and minimal consideration. (I say more about what these amount to in part 1). It may be that a plausible case can be made for thinking that free speech requires more than simply the satisfaction of the minimal conditions I will describe—in which case, there may be more ways in which racist hate speech could interfere with free speech than I will discuss here. But my aim is to show what it would take for racist hate speech to undermine free speech under a conception of free speech that ought to be acceptable to all who wish to claim for free speech the kind of value traditionally attached to it. This will provide what may be a somewhat novel—but, I hope, useful—framework within which we can consider the question of whether or how racist hate speech could function to interfere with free speech. That will be my task in part 2.

I should stress that my focus here will be on whether the kinds of moral and political considerations commonly advanced in favour of something called 'free speech' necessarily tell in favour of permitting racist hate speech.

---

[2] Leslie Green attributes this conception to some feminist theorists: in particular, Rae Langton and Jennifer Hornsby. (Green 1998: 285–312. The quotation appears at p. 303.) Langton rejects this interpretation of her view in her contribution to the same volume (Langton 1998: 261–84, see esp. 276–7).

This should be distinguished from the legislative or jurisprudential question of what kinds of communicative expression are (or are not) protected by, say, the First Amendment of the United States Constitution.[3] The First Amendment offers one influential view about the nature of freedom of expression.[4] But it is by no means the only account available, nor necessarily the correct one. Of course, the two issues may be related. One might think that if constitutional principles turned out to conflict with principles of political morality that would be a reason for revising the constitutional principles (but not, I hope, for revising political morality).

I should also emphasize that my aim is to clarify what it would take for racist hate speech to undermine freedom of speech. Whether racist hate speech *does* in fact function so as to undermine freedom of speech is obviously an important question, but it depends on further empirical matters that fall largely outside the scope of this paper. My aim then is to show how racist hate speech *could* undermine free speech, *if* it functioned in certain ways.

Silencing and the Scope of a Free Speech Principle

The idea that the value of freedom of speech could on occasion best be promoted by regulating speech of a certain type will not come as a surprise to readers familiar with recent feminist work on pornography. '[T]he free speech of men silences the free speech of women', claims Catharine MacKinnon, who argues that regulation of pornography is justified—indeed, required—in order to protect women's (First Amendment) right to freedom of speech.[5]

The silencing argument has not found favour with traditional liberal defenders of a right to pornography. The objection has not been to the empirical claims that the production and consumption of pornography may in fact silence women in a variety of ways (by, for example, making it difficult for women to voice their opinions, or preventing their views from receiving a fair hearing, or causing what they say to be misunderstood), but

---

[3] For instance, it is no part of my argument here that members of minority racial groups targeted by racist hate speech could have a First Amendment claim against racist hate speakers. This claim seems problematic, not least because the First Amendment has generally been understood by the courts to protect the speech of individuals only against state, not private, action; and racist hate speakers are generally not state actors. Rather, I claim that considerations of free speech might not justify permitting racist hate speech as speech, *if* racist hate speech were to silence its targets in the ways that I discuss in part 2.

[4] Given the debates in First Amendment jurisprudence about exactly what 'speech' is and isn't protected by the First Amendment, it might be more accurate to say that the First Amendment offers not one view of free speech, but rather one family of views.

[5] MacKinnon 1987: 156. MacKinnon favours regulation of pornography by civil, rather than criminal, means.

rather to the conceptual claim that freedom of speech includes such 'positive' liberties as these. The argument that pornography silences women, says Ronald Dworkin, is 'premised on an unacceptable proposition: that the right to free speech includes a right to circumstances that encourage one to speak, and a right that others grasp and respect what one means to say'.[6] He continues,

These are obviously not rights that any society can recognize or enforce... Many political and constitutional theorists, it is true, insist that if freedom of speech is to have any value, it must include some right to the opportunity to speak: they say that a society in which only the rich enjoy access to newspapers, television, or other public media does not accord a genuine right to free speech. But it goes far beyond that to insist that freedom of speech includes not only opportunity to speak to the public but a guarantee of a sympathetic or even competent understanding of what one says.[7]

I think Dworkin and others are mistaken to suppose that the silencing argument against pornography need rest on the very strong claim that the right to free speech includes a *guarantee* that what a speaker says will be considered or correctly understood by the audience.[8] But let us set this aside, and consider instead a milder and more general question: Is it plausible in principle to suppose that freedom of speech includes nothing more than the opportunity to distribute meaningful sounds and scrawls to a reasonably wide public audience, as Dworkin, in good liberal company, seems to imply?

In thinking about how we should understand the nature of freedom of speech, a useful approach is to begin from the explanations of why it is that the opportunity to produce meaningful sounds and scrawls is valuable; that is, to consider the justifications that are typically offered for protecting something called 'speech'. 'Freedom of speech' is supposed to name a normatively significant kind in moral and political theorizing, so our conception of *speech* in the context of discussions of free speech should presumably be determined by what the best justification of something called 'free speech' justifies us in protecting.

Of course, a number of different justifications of free speech have been offered and there is some disagreement among liberals about which of these justifications is to be preferred.[9] But for now we can set aside these

---

[6] Dworkin, 'Women and Pornography', p. 38. Dworkin is here discussing the coherence of a silencing argument against pornography, but his remarks would apply *mutatis mutandis* to a silencing argument against racist hate speech.

[7] *loc. cit.* For a similar line of objection see Green 1995: 64–79.

[8] West 2003: 391–422.

[9] For an excellent discussion and overview of the various justifications for free speech see Schauer 1982.

in-house debates. For although there are differences as to exactly why something called 'free speech' is valuable, there is general agreement that freedom of speech involves at base the liberty to *communicate*—that is to say, the freedom to distribute words and their expressive equivalents is taken to be important because, and insofar as, words (and pictures and the like) are the vehicle by which people communicate their thoughts and views to others. It is not the sounds or scrawls *per se* that are valuable and worthy of protection. Words in themselves are merely instruments or tools.[10] It is the *ideas* and *opinions* that words are used to express that are the (either intrinsically or instrumentally) valuable things. If we were creatures that lacked a voice box and communicated with each other wholly telepathically, then presumably the freedom to distribute various grunts and incidental noises would not be the important value liberals take free speech to be. It would be the process by which the thoughts move silently from one head to another that would then warrant protection on free speech grounds. The opportunity to distribute words and the like to a public audience matters because, being the non-telepathic creatures that we are, having the opportunity to distribute words to others is a necessary condition for being able to communicate our thoughts and ideas to them.

Free Speech and Comprehension Failure

But it is easy enough to see that it might not be sufficient. The communication of ideas is typically a two-sided process, involving a speaker and an audience. To communicate an idea to another person, a speaker must not simply be able to produce words that can be heard or seen by an audience; the audience must also be in a position to grasp what the speaker means to say by producing those words. Otherwise, no communication in the sense that matters—that is, no communication of the speaker's thoughts and ideas—can take place.

Elsewhere, I imagined a dictator who implants a device—a 'Meaning Obliterator'—in the heads of audiences.[11] The Meaning Obliterator allows speakers to distribute words, but intervenes so as to prevent would-be audiences from grasping the meaning of the speakers' words. 'Overthrow the dictator', dissidents chant; 'Numfuttal', 'Numfuttal', 'Numfuttal' is all the audience are able to grasp as they hear the dissidents chant. The device allows speakers to distribute meaningful noises, but it makes those sounds seem like meaningless gibberish to the audience.

---

[10] Langton 1993.
[11] Braddon-Mitchell and West 2004: 437–60.

If having the opportunity to distribute meaningful words to a reasonably wide public audience were all it took for speech to be free, then dissidents in the situation just described would be free to speak. But it seems clear that they are not free to speak in any meaningful sense. By implanting the Meaning Obliterator in the heads of audiences the dictator renders the speakers' words useless: they cannot use them to communicate their thoughts and ideas to others who may wish to hear them. By so interfering, the dictator silences would-be speakers just as surely as had he deprived them of the opportunity to distribute words at all—for instance, by locking them away in a soundproof room. Preventing someone from producing or distributing words is one way to prevent them communicating their views to others; preventing the audience from grasping the intended meaning of the words that are produced is another.

If the opportunity to communicate our opinions and ideas to one another is the usual grounds for valuing free speech (or is entailed by the grounds for valuing free speech) then free speech requires that, in addition to being able to hear or see speakers' words, audiences are not entirely prevented from grasping the intended meaning of those words. So it would be a mistake to suppose that free speech, if it is to be the value liberals take it to be, requires nothing in the way of an audience being able to grasp what a speaker means to say. Liberals should accept that freedom of speech requires at least something in the way of the opportunity to have one's words comprehended, as well as heard; otherwise, by their own lights, what is protected is not 'speech' in any meaningful or normatively significant sense.

Of course, there are important further questions about precisely how to spell out a comprehension requirement so as to avoid imposing what may seem to be unreasonably cumbersome duties and disabilities on the audience. In cases where an audience does not speak the speaker's language, for example, comprehension will not be able to occur. But presumably few of us would want to say that it is a requirement of free speech that audiences learn every human language; or even every language whose speakers they are likely to encounter, which would be burdensome enough in contemporary multilingual societies. Similarly, if speakers express themselves unclearly (if they use convoluted language or have a thick accent, for example), comprehension may fail to occur through no fault of the audience. We presumably do not want to say that the speaker is rendered unfree to speak by her own lack of clarity.

But we can agree that free speech does not require comprehension on this scale without insisting (implausibly) that it requires absolutely nothing in the way of the possibility of comprehension. We are not forced to choose between the view that free speech requires a guarantee of perfect comprehension of what a speaker says, at one extreme, and the view that it requires nothing in the way of comprehension, at the other. Both these positions seem unacceptable; and there are many other possibilities in between. For instance, without committing ourselves to any of the consequences just described, we can say that at the very least freedom of speech requires that comprehension of a speaker's words is not systematically prevented by the actions of another agent. The following *minimal comprehension requirement* captures this basic idea, without imposing the kinds of cumbersome duties and disabilities on audiences just described: free speech requires that were a speaker to produce the appropriate words, and were an audience to want to hear what the speaker has to say, there is no agent (individual, group, or institutional) whose actions systematically prevent the audience from comprehending the intended meaning of the speaker's words.[12]

So understood, freedom of speech remains a negative liberty. It requires not a *guarantee* of uptake comprehension, to which Dworkin and others rightly object; but rather that comprehension is not prevented by the actions of another agent. Individuals are not entitled to all means necessary to ensure that they will be correctly understood, but others are not permitted to act in ways that prevent comprehension from occurring. It allows, with Dworkin, that a speaker is not silenced in the relevant sense when she is discouraged from speaking by an unsympathetic speech environment in which what she has to say is likely to be ridiculed. It is in fact silent on the question of what free speech requires in the way of the possibility or opportunity to produce and distribute words. And it does not imply that free speech has been infringed when an audience chooses to ignore or dismiss what a speaker has to say. So understood, the requirement seems liberally acceptable. Something like it seems to be required if a free speech principle is supposed to protect the communication of ideas, as

---

[12] This is narrower than Langton and Hornsby's 'minimal receptiveness', which requires 'that a hearer has the capacity to grasp what communicative act a speaker might be intending to perform' ('Free Speech and Illocution', 1998: 21–37, 25). Notice that, as stated, there is no requirement that the interference be that of a government agent. Of course, a comprehension requirement could be restricted in that way; but it does not strike me as very plausible to include this restriction as part of an account of what it takes *in principle* for speech to be free. The Meaning Obliterator would prevent communication regardless of whether it was implanted by a private agent or by a government one; and it is not clear why government intervention with speech is distinctively *intrinsically* bad. If the issue of *who* instigates interference with comprehension matters, it matters only indirectly and contingently, insofar as agents of the government happen generally to be better able or more likely than private actors to interfere with speech in this way in virtue of having the special powers of the state at their disposal. I take the same point to apply to interference with comprehension and consideration of words.

opposed merely to the opportunity to make meaningful noises and scrawls.

Free Speech and Minimal Consideration

Arguably, however, freedom of speech includes more than minimal distribution and comprehension of words. For it seems to take more than the opportunity to distribute words whose comprehension is not interfered with in the ways just described for speech to be useful in many of the ways that liberals claim it to be.

To see why, we can imagine another science-fiction case. The 'Input Buffer' is a device that can be implanted in the heads of audiences.[13] The device allows the speaker's words to be distributed and comprehended, but it prevents the information that is heard and understood from entering as input into the deliberations of receivers, and so from posing any threat to receivers' existing beliefs and desires. The device allows the receivers' beliefs and desires to evolve naturally, except that they are completely insensitive to what they have heard. Of course, implanting such a device would infringe the liberties of receivers. But there is an important sense in which it would also interfere with the interests of speakers. To be sure, the device does not actually prevent communication from occurring: it permits the speaker's words to be both heard and understood by anyone who cares to listen. But it makes communication pointless. When we attempt to communicate with others—when we seek to inform or persuade them, for instance—we typically do so in the reasonable expectation that what we say stands some, non-negligible chance of having some impact on them. If we are free to say what we like, but whatever we say stands little or no chance of influencing those around us, regardless of its merits, then while we can speak, our speech will be futile.

The Input Buffer is, of course, an extreme case. It makes it the case that speakers have *no* chance whatsoever of informing or persuading others through speech, however rationally compelling the case they put to others may be. I use it only to illustrate that there are at least some ways in which consideration might be interfered with that everyone is likely to agree constitute unacceptable interference with expressive freedom. The question is then not *whether* free speech requires the possibility of having one's speech considered, but rather *how much* it requires and exactly what kinds of interference with it we should take to diminish free speech. It is, of course, open to someone to deny this, and to insist that a device such as the

---

[13] This and other kinds of cases are discussed in more detail in Braddon-Mitchell and West 2004.

Input Buffer poses no obstacle whatsoever to free speech. But then it would be difficult to claim for free speech the sort of value that many liberals think attaches to it, a significant portion of which is widely taken to derive from its benefits in informing the public and private deliberations of audiences.[14]

The point was well appreciated by Mill, who is quite explicit that the benefits of free speech can only obtain where opinions are not simply voiced, but also attended to: '[T]ruth has no chance', writes Mill, 'but in proportion as every side of it, every opinion which embodies even a fraction of the truth, not only finds advocates, but is so advocated as to be listened to'.[15] It is clear that by 'listened to' Mill meant more than merely that words can be heard by an audience. The expression must also be able to be considered, so that such merits as the ideas may have can emerge to inform the deliberations and actions of receivers. Mill thinks free speech is valuable as a precondition for knowledge and the fulfilment of the progressive interests of humankind; and knowledge requires allowing one's existing beliefs to be tested against competing ones, which in turn requires attending to competing ideas expressed by others and critically assessing those ideas according to their intrinsic merits. In other words, a Millian justification of free speech as a necessary precondition for knowledge implies that, in addition to a distribution requirement, there is also what we might call a *consideration requirement* on speech. For speech to play a role in facilitating knowledge, audiences must reasonably often be in a position not simply to hear what speakers say, but also to attend to it, to give it some consideration, and to update their beliefs and desires in light of the perceived merits of the information received. This, needless to say, threatens to impose duties on audiences that go well beyond those that many contemporary liberals are prepared to accept.[16]

---

[14] This may be a case in which the commonsense meaning of 'free speech' may come apart from the quasi-technical sense. A society in which a dictator implants Input Buffers is perhaps a society in which there is 'free speech' in the ordinary sense, but not, I suggest, in the technical sense relevant to moral and political discussions of free speech.

[15] Mill 1975: 65.

[16] It would be a synoptic task well beyond the scope of this paper to attempt to explore what each of the justifications that have been offered for free speech imply about the need for audience attention and consideration. But it is worth noting that a Millian justification does not seem to be alone in supposing the value of speech to lie partly in its capacity to influence the deliberations and decisions of others. Dworkin's own view, for instance—which holds that equal concern and respect demands that every citizen be permitted a chance to influence the moral and political environment around them through speech, no matter how misguided or disagreeable what they say may seem to others—also seems to require that there are no significant barriers to consideration. For speech that is systematically and dogmatically

Of course, like comprehension, attention and consideration can come in degrees; and a consideration requirement might be formulated to require correspondingly more or less of audiences in the way of attention and consideration. A very strong view would hold that each person has a duty (albeit perhaps an imperfect one) to go forth, ears pricked, in search of every possible idea that a speaker somewhere might be expressing, to give careful and fair-minded consideration to every single one of them (no matter how apparently trivial or absurd) and scrupulously to update their existing beliefs and desires in light of their deliberations. A consideration requirement of this kind would demand a superhuman level of single-minded dedication to the cause of knowledge, would crowd out other important values and interests in our lives, and would probably, in any case, be counter-productive (insofar as, over a certain threshold, more information and consideration tends to impede, rather than enhance, successful deliberation). The attainment of knowledge or informed decision-making plausibly neither justifies nor requires consideration on this scale.

But, once again, considerations of these kinds need not lead us to reject wholesale the idea that free speech requires something in the way of consideration. Even skeptics may want to agree that the implantation of Input Buffers in members of the populace would interfere with communication in ways that undermine the point and value of speech. So while heavy-handed duties of consideration may not be in order, *some* degree of audience attention and consideration may seem to be necessary for speech to be valuable in the way that Mill, among others, supposes it to be.

A more moderate consideration requirement might have it that audiences have a *prima facie* duty at least not to systematically and dogmatically block their ears to certain types of ideas with which they are presented, even if they may legitimately ignore some token ideas; and that they make at least *some* effort to evaluate information fair-mindedly and to update their own beliefs and desires accordingly, so that if overwhelming and obvious reasons are given for modifying their beliefs or desires they may. A still more *minimal consideration requirement* would recognize no positive duties of attention or consideration at all, holding instead only that agents refrain from acting in ways that systematically prevent the speech of another from being attended to or considered.

Whatever exactly is required for free speech in the way of audience attention and consideration, we can nevertheless agree that in general

ignored, or that would not enter anyone's deliberations even if it were listened to, can influence no one—except perhaps the speaker.

things go *better* for speech when there are not obstacles that systematically prevent various ideas from receiving attention and consideration (so that such merits as they may have may emerge to improve the quality of public and private decisions); and, conversely, that in general things go *worse* for speech when there exist barriers to attention and consideration that mean that certain ideas stand little or no chance of gaining currency, regardless of their merits. Barriers to consideration may represent a genuine cost to free speech values that needs to be factored into an overall determination of whether, on balance, a given policy enhances or diminishes free speech— even if this cost may be outweighed by greater benefits for speech elsewhere (say, in the form of increased distribution or comprehension).

In this section, I have suggested that closer attention to some of the considerations commonly advanced in favour of free speech suggest that we should think of free speech as having not one, but three, dimensions: 1) production and distribution; 2) comprehension; and 3) consideration. If so, when evaluating whether a particular policy is likely to enhance or else to diminish free speech we must take into account not only its implications for what words can be produced and distributed, but also the likely effects on comprehension and consideration. Permitting racist hate speech may allow for more words to be produced and distributed than would regulating it—although, as I discuss in the following section, even this might be disputed. But if the benefits of permitting greater production and distribution of words come at the cost of significant losses to comprehension and/ or consideration elsewhere, then the net effect of permitting racist hate speech may in fact be to diminish freedom of speech. I turn now to exploring how racist hate speech could interfere with communication along each of these dimensions.

2. Racist Hate Speech and Silencing

Racist hate speech expresses derogatory feelings about, or attitudes towards, people on the basis of their race in order 1) directly to inflict psychological injury on them (in the case of face-to-face encounters) or 2) to incite in third parties hostility towards or hatred for them, or both. So defined, racist hate speech differs from merely racially discriminatory speech (speech that advocates a negative view of a particular racial group) in that its primary function or purpose is to cause psychological injury to its targets and/or to arouse hostility or hatred for the group targeted.[17]

---

[17] See Sumner 2004: 14–15.

This way of defining racist hate speech is in one respect broader than some alternative definitions, and in another way narrower. It is narrower in that it does not include in the category of racist hate speech expressions whose primary function is merely to *insult* targets on the basis of their race. Being insulted is unpleasant, but it does not in itself justify regulation of speech; and it misconstrues the distinctive nature of the harm that a visceral expression of racial hostility causes to those it targets to characterize it merely as insult.

The definition is broader than some alternative definitions in that it does not restrict racist hate speech to that which employs racist epithets (e.g. 'nigger', 'kike', 'coon', 'spic') in order to wound or stigmatize.[18] Restricting racist hate speech to speech that contains racist epithets has the obvious pragmatic virtue of singling out a relatively narrow class of speech, clearly distinguishable by its content from racially discriminatory speech that may be a legitimate part of scientific, historical, or political debate. But it is unlikely that this narrow definition serves to pick out a natural social kind. Using derogatory or hateful epithets is one way to incite in an audience hatred or contempt for those so labelled. But it is not the only way. For example, if members of a racial group are repeatedly pilloried as 'animals'—whether verbally, or in visual caricatures that depict them with exaggerated ape-like features, living in caves or jungles, or the like—this plausibly functions to incite in audiences hatred or contempt for those so depicted, regardless of whether an epithet such as 'nigger' additionally appears. While the presence of epithets is a marker of racist hate speech in my view (insofar as it is a generally reliable indicator that the speech is designed to inflict psychological harm or to incite racial hatred), I do not take it to be either necessary or sufficient for it.

Racist Hate Speech and Production Interference

As we noted in part 1, one way in which communication may be interfered with is when there are barriers or blockages to the production and/or distribution of words and their expressive equivalents. In the most extreme kind of case, would-be speakers are literally prevented from producing or distributing words: they are gagged or locked away in a soundproof room, for instance. Uncontroversially, interference of this kind constitutes a limitation on free speech. Close to this extreme are cases where would-be speakers are intimidated into simple silence through threats of violence or significant retribution of other kinds. Many political dissidents in Burma or Zimbabwe at present are silenced in this sense. They are not literally

---

[18] See, for instance, that offered by Brink 2001: 119–57.

prevented from producing or distributing words of dissent; in some sense of 'could', they could speak. But they know that, if they do, there is a very real chance that they will end up beaten, incarcerated, or dead. In a situation where speaking out would be very costly, only the exceptionally courageous (or foolhardy) are likely to speak. Most people, quite reasonably, will remain silent.

Could racist hate speech silence by threatening its targets into simple silence? Charles Lawrence thinks that it might. He writes,

> When the Klan burns a cross on the lawn of a Black person...the effect of this speech does not result from the persuasive power of an idea operating freely in the market. It is a threat; a threat made in the context of a history of lynching, beatings, and economic reprisals that made good on earlier threats...The threat does not need to be explicit because racially motivated violence is a well-known historical and contemporary reality...The Black student who is subjected to racial epithets, like the Black person on whose lawn the Klan has burned a cross, is threatened and silenced by a credible connection between racist hate speech and racist violence.[19]

Lawrence is surely right that an important part of what distinguishes racist hate speech from merely offensive speech and garden-variety name-calling is its place in a broader network of practices of racial discrimination that includes, among other things, a contingent but very real association with racist violence. Racist hate crimes are typically preceded and accompanied by racist hate speech; and both victims and perpetrators generally know this. Racist hate speech is the clearest expression of the kind of hostility that fuels racial discrimination and violence, short of the acts themselves; and it indicates to its targets the presence of these attitudes and behavioural dispositions in the speaker. For this reason, it is very plausible to think that racially hostile speech could sometimes quite reasonably be interpreted by its targets as constituting a threat. For example, the message 'Death nigger' that appeared on the door of a counsellor at Purdue University might reasonably be interpreted by its target as a threat. So too may the message, 'The Knights of the Klu Klux Klan are watching you', that appeared on flyers distributed to students by White Supremacists at Northwest Missouri State University.[20] It is true that even speech of this most overtly threatening kind does not typically explicitly threaten its targets for speaking out. But it does not need to. If it is public knowledge that speaking out in a certain situation carries with it a credible risk of serious retribution, then this is usually enough to keep most (prudent) would-be speakers silent.

[19] Lawrence 1993: 53–88, 79.
[20] These and other examples are discussed in Lawrence 1993.

While there are particular instances of racist hate speech where it seems clear that the speech constitutes a threat, it may seem less clear that racist epithets or invective *in general* have this function. Whether a particular instance of speech is reasonably interpreted by its target as a threat seems sensitive not simply to the general social environment in which it occurs, but also to the particular context in which it occurs. Even speech with explicitly threatening content may perhaps not count as a threat if it is uttered in a context where the nature of the speaker or the circumstances make it highly unlikely that the threat could ever be carried though. Compare: 1) a frail, old, wheelchair-bound white man says, 'Nigger, I'm going to give you what you deserve', to a physically imposing, successful black lawyer passing by in a shopping mall; and 2) the same utterance produced by a white male employer to a junior black employee. The latter could reasonably be interpreted by its target as a threat; but the former probably could not. Perhaps one could argue that even in the former case the utterance counts as a threat in virtue of being a token of a type of speech whose *typical* instances are associated with racial discrimination and violence.[21] If so, then even narrow or minimal conceptions of free speech will imply that racist hate speech is a proper object for regulation. The right to free speech does not extend to the right to use speech to threaten or intimidate others.

But racially hostile speech may not need to count as a threat in order to have the effect of deterring its targets from producing words. Describing some of the immediate effects of such speech on its targets, Lawrence writes:

[T]he visceral emotional response to personal attack precludes speech. Attack produces an instinctive, defensive psychological reaction. Fear, rage, shock, and flight all interfere with any reasoned response. Words like 'nigger', 'kike', and 'faggot' produce physical symptoms that temporarily disable the victim, and the perpetrators often use these words with the intention of producing this effect. Many victims do not find words of protest until well after the assault, when the cowardly assaulter has departed.[22]

Racist hate speech does not function as an invitation to conversation. It does not offer reasons or arguments with which its audience can engage; and the visceral hostility it expresses effectively forecloses, rather than opens, the opportunity for further discussion. In the immediate aftermath of a verbal attack, it is rare that victims are able to produce words at all, let alone to gather themselves together to offer a clear-headed and balanced

---

[21] This deserves fuller consideration than I have space to give it here.
[22] Lawrence 1993: 68.

response of the kind likely to be conducive to a rational discussion of the issues (even supposing, as seems unlikely, that a hate speaker were of a mind to engage in rational discussion).[23] This explains why it may be somewhat psychologically unrealistic to suppose that here the corrective to bad speech is more speech—at least, if 'more speech' is supposed to come from those directly targeted by hate speakers.[24] And there are particular instances where it would clearly be ridiculous to expect those targeted to attempt to counter hostile expression with more speech to the contrary. When confronted by a hate-filled speaker in a lonely location, or in a bar surrounded by other people who clearly share the speaker's attitude, it would be plain foolhardy for targets to attempt to use the occasion as an opportunity to persuade the speaker of the error of his ways.

In addition to its immediate disabling effects, racist hate speech may have indirect and longer-lived silencing effects. There is considerable evidence that being subjected to racist verbal abuse reduces the self-esteem of targets, especially when individuals are targeted repeatedly. It is not hard to see how this could work. If others repeatedly tell you that you are worthless or contemptible—if they say that you are dumb, dirty, or lazy, simply in virtue of your race which you are powerless to change or conceal—then it is likely that eventually you will come yourself to believe that this is so, especially if the message of inferiority is reinforced in subtle and not so subtle ways by the culture at large.[25] (One needs only to think of the well-known effects on children of parental verbal abuse to get a sense of the way in which racist hate speech may impact psychologically on its targets; and indeed there is evidence that some of the effects of racist abuse on its targets are not dissimilar to the short-term effects of sexual abuse on children.)[26] Low self-esteem has numerous adverse outcomes. One less commonly emphasized effect concerns its impact on speech. Individuals who suffer low self-esteem tend to believe they have nothing worth saying, and so are generally less likely to voice their opinions. Even when they do speak, they are less likely to persist in arguing their case in the face of disagreement or opposition. They tend to seek affirmation from others and typically desire to avoid confrontation. Insofar as being subjected

---

[23] Commenting on these effects, David Brink notes that 'Insofar as hate speech, like fighting words, expresses visceral attitudes and elicits inarticulate reactions, it doesn't engage deliberative values central to Millian and constitutional principles that normally protect speech', 140. Racist hate speech, he argues, may for this reason constitute a 'well-motivated exception to the usual prohibition on content-specific censorship', 141, n. 47.

[24] For a sustained and empirically grounded criticism of the 'more speech' response, see Nielsen, this volume.

[25] For further discussion of this point see Delgado 1993: 89–110, esp. pp. 94–5.

[26] Summer (2004), p. 160.

to racist abuse contributes to a process whereby targets come to internalize feelings of worthlessness, it makes it less likely in general that they will speak at all; and less likely still that, when they do speak, the opinions that they voice will be ones that contest established opinions.[27]

In these and other ways, racist hate speech may cause those it targets to withdraw from participation in public life and discourse. This is unfortunate for society as a whole, insofar as it adversely affects the quality of the deliberations that take place without the benefit of their input. But it is especially unfortunate for those who are silenced, not least because deliberations that take place without their input may issue in decisions that fail to take account of their interests. While everyone may lose if some people are deterred from participating in collective decision-making, especially if those silenced have worthwhile things to say, those who are silenced are likely to bear a disproportionate share of the loss.

This is to focus on the effects that racist hate speech may have on its targets' propensity to produce words and to participate in public discussions. But it might be claimed that these costs are offset by greater production and distribution elsewhere. When publicized, incidents of racist hate speech can and do prompt further discussion—typically by others at a later time—about the importance of values of tolerance and mutual respect, and even about the permissibility of racist hate speech itself. Taking these downstream effects into account it could be that, even if racist hate speech deters members of minority racial groups it targets from speaking out, its net effect is to enhance the production and distribution of words in the community.

In the end, it is an empirical matter whether the net effect of permitting racist hate speech is to enhance or to diminish the number and variety of words that enter the public arena for consideration. But suppose that it were true that permitting racist hate speech resulted in more words being produced and distributed than would be the case if it were regulated. There are still at least two reasons why it might be too hasty to conclude that free speech is thereby enhanced. First, permitting or enhancing the production and distribution of words of a certain type will only enhance free speech if it does not bring with it significant losses to communication

---

[27] In research summarized by Taylor and Obiechina, about one in three Blacks endorse racist stereotypes about Blacks as mentally defective (intellectually, morally, emotionally) and physically gifted (athletically, sexually). One hypothesis is that these expectations are linked via the latent belief that 'Blacks are animals', which is used to 'explain' why Blacks are mentally defective and physically gifted (Taylor and Kouyate: 327–56). Since much racist hate speech quite explicitly labels or likens its targets to animals, it would not be surprising if it contributed to producing or reinforcing that latent belief.

along the dimensions of comprehension or consideration. If more words are produced and distributed, but the cost of this extra production and distribution is that other ideas can be less well comprehended or considered, then the net effect may be to diminish free speech, not to enhance it. (How racist hate speech could affect comprehension and consideration is the focus of the next two sections.)

Second, one might think it matters for free speech not merely how many words can be produced and distributed in a community, but also how the opportunity to produce words (and to have those words comprehended and considered) is distributed among the different members of the community. Suppose that the policy that results in the greatest total production and distribution of words in a community also has the result of making it considerably less likely that some members of the community will speak. More words are produced and distributed overall, but at the cost that some people have less opportunity to speak. Does this policy enhance or diminish free speech?

The answer may turn partly on whether one accepts a consequentialist or a non-consequentialist approach to free speech. If one thinks of the value of free speech as grounded in some agent-neutral value (e.g. truth), then how the opportunity to speak is distributed among the different members of the population will matter only indirectly, insofar as it bears on the prospects for the emergence of truth. If, on the other hand, one thinks of free speech as an agent-relative value that each individual member of society has an interest in, then it will be a matter of direct concern if a policy has the effect of differentially deterring some people from expressing their views—even if this leads to more speech overall, and even if you think that what those silenced would have said can be perfectly well or better said by someone else. While a consequentialist approach to free speech may be willing to allow the disabling of some speakers if it leads to a better outcome overall, non-consequentialists are likely to regard it as a matter of direct concern if racist hate speech has the effect of differentially rendering some (e.g. members of racial minorities targeted by it) significantly less able or likely to speak.

In this section, I have considered a number of ways in which racist hate speech could interfere with the production and distribution of words. If Lawrence is right that the use of racist epithets threatens or intimidates its targets into simple silence, then racist epithets will deserve no protection on free speech grounds, even on a narrow conception of free speech. Whether silencing of the other kinds discussed could count as limiting free speech will depend on whether it is plausible to think that free speech requires anything more than minimal production and distribution. The distinction between interference that limits free speech and that which does not is often thought to be marked by a distinction between 'coercive' and 'non-coercive' forms of interference. The distinction is supposed to be between situations in which we are 'forced' in a way that seems especially bad to say (or not to say) something and those in which we are not. But the distinction between 'coercive' and 'non-coercive' kinds of interference is really not very clear, partly because coercion seems to come in degrees as well as kinds. While it would be trivial to say that *anything* that exerts some external causal influence over what we do (or do not) say counts as 'coercive', it is not trivial to single out some particular set of circumstances (e.g. social persecution) that makes it considerably more difficult for members of some groups in society to speak than it is for others. Even if we think it would be a mistake to view interference of this kind as falling in the category of objectionable coercion, we may nonetheless wish to recognize that at least sometimes it may constitute a *prima facie* cost to freedom of speech; a cost that we may wish to factor into an overall determination of whether, on balance, permitting racist hate speech enhances or retards free speech.

Racist Hate Speech and Comprehension Failure

In part 1, I described an extreme case of comprehension failure involving a device (the Meaning Obliterator) which functions to prevent audiences from comprehending speakers' words entirely. Even skeptics are likely to agree that interference of this kind undermines free speech (otherwise, the commitment to free speech threatens to appear a peculiar fetish for the production and distribution of meaningful noises and scribbles). The Meaning Obliterator is, of course, the stuff of science fiction. But once it is apparent how communication could be prevented by the operation of such fictional devices, it is easier to see how it could—at least in principle—be prevented by less far-fetched means.

Consider one type of case, much discussed in the literature on pornography and silencing.[28] A woman says, 'No', intending to refuse sex. But her audience fails to recognize her intention to refuse, perhaps because he believes that women are coy and wish not to appear sexually forward. Let us set aside the empirical question of whether there in fact are men like this, i.e. men who literally believe that a woman who says 'No' does not intend to refuse sex by so speaking. There is certainly a nearby possible world in which there are such men. In that world, a woman who says 'No' will be unable to use the word 'No' to communicate her opinion—

---

[28] See Langton, 'Speech Acts and Unspeakable Acts' and Jennifer Hornsby, 'Speech Acts and Pornography', in Dwyer 1995: 220–32.

namely, refusal—to her audience. Although she can utter the appropriate words, something prevents the audience from understanding what she means to say by producing them in that context. What prevents the audience from grasping the intended meaning of the speaker's words in this case is not a science fiction device, but background beliefs held by the audience (perhaps tacitly) about women's nature and behaviour in sexual situations. Some theorists have argued that women are in fact differentially silenced in this way; and that pornography bears significant responsibility for it by producing in consumers beliefs that render them unable to recognize women's communicative intentions.[29]

Taking our cue from this example, one way in which racist hate speech could interfere with comprehension would be by producing in its audience beliefs that prevent them from recognizing the communicative intentions of speakers from the minority racial groups that it targets. However, racist hate speech could undermine comprehension in a slightly different and considerably more radical way than the 'no-means-yes' case just described. Pornography prevents comprehension, if it does, by producing in its (mostly male) audience beliefs that prevent them from grasping the nature of women's communicative intentions in certain contexts. Racist hate speech could in principle prevent comprehension in a yet more extreme way: by producing in its audience beliefs that prevent them from recognizing that the speaker has any communicative intentions *at all*. While pornography may *change* audience perceptions of the meaning of women's utterances in sexual contexts, racist hate speech could, in the extreme case, *remove* it altogether.

A couple of more general examples will help to illustrate both the kind of silencing that I have in mind and how it might occur. Suppose a professional philosopher were to utter the sentence, 'Descartes was a very fine philosopher'. This is a meaningful sentence in English. Competent English speakers who know a little about philosophy or the history of thought will be able to grasp its meaning and will take it that, by producing this sentence, the speaker means to communicate to them his or her commitment to the proposition it expresses. Suppose, by contrast, that this sentence were to be produced by a parrot. Nothing about the content of the sentence has changed. It remains a meaningful sentence in English, and appropriately acculturated English-speaking audiences can grasp that meaning. But no one would take a *parrot* that produces this sentence to mean *anything* by it. Notwithstanding what we now know about the

---

[29] For a nice discussion of how the production and distribution of pornography could be responsible for silencing, see Maitra 2004: 189–208.

cognitive and linguistic abilities of many species of parrot, no one would expect even an exceptionally smart parrot to be sufficiently well cognitively equipped and versed in human intellectual traditions as to be able to grasp the content of what it has said. The parrot is merely parroting or mimicking a grammatical string of meaningful words, presumably one it has overheard or has been trained to say, in much the same way as young children sometimes repeat a string of words that they have heard uttered by their parents whose content they cannot yet understand ('High interest rates are bad for the economy', for example).

These cases provide a general illustration of how a speaker's ability to communicate an opinion to others is conditional, among other things, on audience beliefs (tacit or otherwise) about the cognitive abilities of the speaker. If an audience believes that a speaker lacks the cognitive wherewithal to understand what they say then, even though the speaker can produce the appropriate words, she will be unable thereby to communicate her opinion to others.

In the examples just described, the audience's beliefs about the speaker's cognitive abilities are correct. Plausibly, a parrot or a very young child really is incapable of understanding the proposition expressed by the sentence 'Descartes was a very fine philosopher' or 'High interest rates are bad for the economy'. So whatever a parrot or a young child may be intending to do by producing those words, it is not to communicate that opinion to others. Since the speaker is incapable of having the opinion, the fact that others believe they cannot does not prevent them from communicating it. But suppose that a speaker *is* in fact capable of grasping the meaning of the words they produce, while the audience falsely believes that they are not. In that case, the speaker would be prevented from communicating their opinion by the audience's (false) belief.

This is, of course, an extreme case. It may seem far-fetched to suggest that anyone could seriously take the cognitive capacities of adult human beings to be akin to those of a parrot or a child, whatever the colour of their skin. Perhaps. But absurd though such ideas may seem to many educated people now, it is worth bearing in mind that they were widely held, indeed mainstream.[30] People said that people of colour were sub-

---

[30] Jared Diamond claims that the belief that non-whites are innately biologically inferior to whites persists among 'many (perhaps most) Westerners', although few feel comfortable acknowledging it. In the absence of an obviously better explanation for differences in technological and other achievements between white and non-white societies, Diamond says, 'most people will continue to suspect that the racist biological explanation is correct after all' (1998: 19). Diamond cites laying this suspicion to rest as the most important reason for seeking to develop a better, alternative explanation.

human, more closely related to monkeys than to human beings. It was said that they were like children: unable to use reason to moderate their desires, to make rational decisions, or to entertain complex ideas or plans. Admittedly, it is hard to know how many people genuinely believed these things, and how many merely professed to believe them as a convenient *post facto* justification for slavery and other racial oppression. But considerable effort was certainly put into showing that they were true. In 1906, for instance, a series of widely publicized papers by Robert Bennett Bean appeared in reputable scientific journals of the time purporting to offer scientific 'proof' of the inferiority of the Negro based in 'peculiarities of the Negro brain'. Bean's findings of differences in the shape and size of the brains of African-Americans compared with those of whites led him to conclude that 'the Negro evidently stands in an intermediate position [between] ... man and the orang-outang'.[31] In April 1907 an editorial in *American Medicine* sought to make clear the broader social significance of Bean's findings. Bean had identified 'the anatomical basis for the complete failure of the negro schools to impart the higher studies—the brain cannot comprehend them any more than a horse can understand the rule of three'. The editorial continues, '[L]eaders in all political parties now acknowledge the error of human equality ... It may be practicable to rectify the error and remove a menace to our prosperity—a large electorate without brains'.[32] The author of these comments was no marginalized racial extremist, but a respected member of the medical establishment.

Although subsequently thoroughly discredited, work such as Bean's forms part of the historical and cultural backdrop to present-day racist hate speech. Much racist hate speech implicitly or explicitly recalls and endorses these historically prevalent views about the natural inferiority and limited intellectual capacities of non-whites, by labeling them 'animals' or 'monkeys', attributing to them traits associated with monkeys, or depicting them in visual caricatures with exaggerated ape-like characteristics, living in trees or in jungles, or the like. ('Nigger, do you want some bananas? Go back to the jungle' is one fairly typical example.) Since racist hate speech expresses ideas such as these, it could produce or reinforce in its audience beliefs of this kind. (The very familiarity of these ideas may make them appear considerably less incredible to contemporary audiences than they otherwise might.) Messages of this kind may reproduce or reinforce in audiences the belief that Blacks are by nature intellectually simple,

---

[31] Bean 1906: 353–432, 380. Readers may recall Himmler's chilling speech to the SS group leaders at Potsdam which made similar claims about Jews. Although extreme, these are by no means historically isolated examples.

[32] *American Medicine*, April 1907, p. 36.

incapable of complex or fully rational thought. If so, then among the effects of racist hate speech will be to prevent Blacks from communicating their opinions to others in a quite radical way: by preventing them from communicating all but the most simple opinions entirely.

To what extent, if at all, racist hate speech causes anyone to believe that Blacks and other people of colour are literally incapable of entertaining complex ideas or of rational, independent thought is an empirical issue that cannot be settled from a philosopher's armchair. So far as I am aware, no studies to date have investigated the effects of racist hate speech on comprehension, so we have as yet no firm evidence either way. But racist hate speech certainly *could* interfere with comprehension in this way, and we should not let our own liberal sensibilities blind us to this possibility. If racist hate speech did cause comprehension failure of this kind, then even skeptics should agree that there is a clear sense in which considerations of free speech would not protect racist hate speech. Like threats and intimidation, words that cause comprehension failure of this kind are not 'speech' in the relevant sense.

One might suspect (and hope) from the armchair that cases of such extreme comprehension failure are in fact comparatively rare. The question would then be whether there are actual cases of comprehension failure that are sufficiently close to this extreme to which racist hate speech contributes.

Racist Hate Speech and Consideration Failure

We should distinguish comprehension failure from another kind of silencing that might occur when, for instance, an audience is caused to think that speakers are intellectually limited or otherwise inferior. In this case, the audience grasps what the speaker means to say perfectly well, but ignores it or dismisses it out of hand because they believe the speaker is not the kind of person worth listening to. This constitutes consideration failure. There is considerable evidence that racist hate speech—especially when directed by a member of a dominant group against a member of a historically marginalized group—functions to undermine the attention and consideration that is paid to the speech of those it targets.[33]

This is not surprising. If certain groups are sufficiently pilloried this may have a purely causal impact on the audience, such that they are less likely to attend to what members of the targeted group have to say or to give it much consideration. Here is Lawrence again:

---

[33] See Greenburg and Pyszczynski 1985, and Greenberg, Kirkland, and Pyszczynski 1988.

Racist speech...distorts the marketplace of ideas by muting or devaluing the speech of Blacks and other despised minorities. Regardless of intrinsic value, their words and ideas become less saleable in the marketplace of ideas. An idea that would be embraced by large numbers of individuals if it were offered by a white individual will be rejected or given less credence if its author belongs to a group demeaned and stigmatized by racist beliefs.[34]

The point here is an important, if familiar, one. How much attention and consideration is paid to what a speaker has to say varies in accordance with the esteem in which the speaker is held in a community. Esteem matters less for a speaker's ability to communicate ideas that conform to established opinion. Accepted opinions bring with them credence of their own; and the credence attached to established ideas may in fact sometimes spill over to confer additional credibility on the speaker in the eyes of the audience. Esteem is absolutely critical, however, when it comes to a speaker's ability to communicate new or unfamiliar ideas, especially ideas that challenge prevailing orthodoxies. When a member of a respected group in society expresses an unorthodox or unpopular opinion they may not succeed in persuading others to their point of view, but their opinion tends at least to be listened to and given some consideration. This occurs simply in virtue of the fact that, however implausible the idea may at first sight seem, it is the opinion of someone esteemed, someone generally taken to be worth listening to. But when members of a group generally held in low regard express an unorthodox or unpopular view, that opinion is considerably less likely to be attended to or considered—at least, absent a conspicuous counter-veiling reason for thinking that the speaker in question has some special domain-specific expertise regarding the particular subject matter at hand.[35]

This, I take it, is part of what Catharine Mackinnon has in mind when she notes that powerful and respected members of society get to do more, say more, *have their words count for more*, than do the powerless.[36] The ability

---

[34] Lawrence, pp. 78–9.

[35] Esteem may function in complex ways. Some speakers may be members of a social group generally held in comparatively low regard, yet be judged to have special competence in a particular, limited domain. For instance, it could be that women's speech in general is paid less attention than the like speech of men, except in domains where women are assumed to have a special expertise—such as on the merits of washing powder, where women in general may be judged as more credible than men (except perhaps when compared with a man in a white laboratory coat). Not so, however, when a woman expresses an unorthodox opinion about political or economic policy. In these domains, critical to effecting social and political change, women as a group may be judged less competent than men and their views correspondingly judged less likely to be correct.

[36] MacKinnon 1987.

to have one's speech attended to and considered by others is both a consequence of occupying a position of social power and part of what constitutes and maintains that position of power, for it is a significant part of what enables individuals to use speech to influence others and so to shape the social and political environment around them. Conversely, the inability to have one's speech attended to and considered is both a mark of powerlessness and part of what constitutes one as powerless. Those whose speech is widely ignored or unreflectively dismissed cannot use speech, as the powerful can, to influence the beliefs and attitudes of others and, through this, impact on the community around them.

It should be clear why consideration failure is of special concern when those affected are members of historically marginalized groups. It is not that oppressed minorities are more virtuous or more likely to be right, although this may sometimes be true. It is rather that consideration failure can here form part of a self-reinforcing cycle of marginalization. Many of the groups most commonly targeted by hate speech have quite literally been denied a voice in public affairs. Only comparatively recently have many of them been granted the right to vote, for instance. As a result, they live in a society whose dominant culture and institutions have arisen substantially without their input and often without much if any concern for their interests. Effecting social reform by means of rational persuasion requires that members of these groups are in a position to use speech to challenge established patterns of thought and practice. This in turn requires that their views—which are likely frequently to be unfamiliar and sometimes confrontational—stand a reasonable chance of being given some consideration by others. Only then can minority views genuinely compete with established opinion. But the attitudes of intolerance and disrespect that underpin and sustain existing discrimination may themselves prevent the views of those disadvantaged from receiving the fair hearing required to challenge these attitudes. Insofar as racist hate speech functions to reproduce and reinforce in its audience attitudes of hostility and contempt for minority groups it targets, it may operate as a kind of protective buffer to the ideology of racism, shielding it from challenge by sapping the power of minority speech to contest it. This cycle must somehow be interrupted if members of historically marginalized groups are to have a reasonable chance of reshaping the moral and political environment through speech.

Conclusion

In part 1, I suggested that free speech has not one, but three dimensions: production and distribution; comprehension; and attention and consideration. In part 2, I sketched a number of ways in which racist hate speech could interfere with communication along each of these dimensions. In determining whether free speech considerations tell for or against permitting racist hate speech we need to balance the benefits of allowing the production and distribution of words of racial hate against its costs, to take into account its likely effects of comprehension and consideration, as well as production and distribution. If permitting the production and distribution of words of a certain kind has the result that other words cannot be comprehended or considered (as in the extreme cases), then restricting those words may enhance, not diminish, free speech.

Notice that these trade-offs are not between free speech and other values, but between various dimensions of free speech itself. Some liberals have argued that regulation of hate speech should be resisted as a matter of principle because our commitment to free speech must be absolute.[37] The objection here is to the proposal that free speech can be traded off in the service of other values (e.g. equality). That is not my suggestion here. My point is rather that, even if the commitment to free speech is taken as absolute, we may be faced with difficult questions about how to balance the interest in being able to produce and distribute words of a certain kind against the interest in being able to have words comprehended and considered. Where permitting words of a certain kind to be produced and distributed brings with it the costs that other words can be less well comprehended and considered, we must decide how these costs and benefits should be balanced against each other in order to determine what it is that is deserving of absolute protection. The prospect of such balancing could only be avoided if we insisted that free speech demands that the production and distribution of words must be permitted *no matter what* the resulting costs to comprehension or consideration—even where the result is that other people's words stand zero chance of being understood or considered at all. And that, I argued, is implausible—at least, if free speech is to be the value it is presently taken to be. If the dissemination of words of racial hatred functioned to preclude comprehension or consideration of words produced by its targets entirely—if, that is, it functioned like the Meaning Obliterator or the Input Buffer—then a commitment to free speech, however absolute, might seem to require that it be prevented, not permitted. Permitting people to voice their hatred for other people on the basis of their race may allow more words to be produced and distributed, but if the costs of this extra production and distribution is that other speech cannot be comprehended or considered at all (as in the extreme cases), then permitting those words to be produced

[37] See, for instance, Jacobson 2007.

and distributed arguably precludes, rather than promotes, freedom of speech.

Suppose it turned out that permitting the dissemination of words of racist hate were to have the effect of reducing production, comprehension, or consideration of the words of the targets of such speech considerably, but not to zero. In that case, it will be much less clear whether permitting the dissemination of words of racist hate diminishes free speech. It will be a matter of deciding what policy strikes the best balance between the various aspects of free speech. This may depend not simply on the degree to which production and distribution of words of racist hate interferes with the chances of comprehension and consideration, but also on the relative importance of the speech interests at stake. We may need to balance how important it is for people to be able to express their hatred for racial minorities against how important it is for racial minorities to have their views on a much wider range of subjects better heard, better understood, and better considered. Perhaps the best balance for free speech requires permitting racist hate speech, or perhaps it does not. Perhaps there are policies other than regulating racist hate speech that would be preferable. These are difficult questions. But it would be a mistake simply to assume that considerations of free speech tell in favour of permitting racist hate speech. That assumption could well turn out to be false.

References

Unsigned editorial, *American Medicine* (April, 1907): 197.

Bean, R. B. 1906. 'Some Racial Peculiarities of the Negro Brain', *Am J. Anat* 5: 353–432, 380.

Braddon-Mitchell, David and Caroline West 2004. 'What is Free Speech?' *Journal of Political Philosophy* 12, no. 4: 437–60.

Brink, David 2001. 'Millian Principles, Freedom of Expression, and Hate Speech', *Legal Theory* 7: 119–57.

Delgado, Richard 1993. 'Words That Wound: A Tort Action for Racial Insults, Epithets, and Name Calling', in Mari J. Matsuda et al. (eds.), *Words That Wound: Critical Race Theory, Assaultive Speech and the First Amendment*. Boulder, Colorado: Westview: 89–110, esp. pp. 94–5.

Diamond, Jared 1998. *Guns, Germs and Steel*. London: Vintage, p. 19.

Dworkin, Ronald 1993. 'Women and Pornography', The New York Review of Books, 21 October 1993, p. 38.

Green, Leslie 1998. 'Pornographizing, Subordination and Silencing', in Robert C. Post (ed.), *Censorship and Silencing: Practices of Cultural Regulation*. L.A., CA: The Getty Research Institute, pp. 285–312.

Greenburg, Jeff and Tom Pyszczynski 1985. 'The Effect of an Overheard Slur on Evaluation of Target: How to Spread a Social Disease', *J. Experimental Soc. Psychology* 21: 61–72.

Greenberg, Jeff, S. L. Kirkland, and Tom Pyszczynski 1988. 'Some Theoretical Notions and Preliminary Research Concerning Derogatory Ethnic Labels', in G. Smitherman-Donaldson and T. van Dijk (eds.), *Discourse and Discrimination*. Detroit, MI: Wayne State University Press.

Hornsby, Jennifer 1995. 'Speech Acts and Pornography', in Susan Dwyer (ed.), *The Problem of Pornography*. Belmont, CA: Wadsworth: 220–32.

Jacobson, Daniel 1995. 'Freedom of Speech Acts? A Response to Langton', *Philosophy & Public Affairs* 24, no. 1: 64–79.

Jacobson, Daniel 2007. 'Freedom of Speech: Why Freedom of Speech Includes Hate Speech', in Jesper Ryberg, Thomas S. Petersen, and Clark Wolf (eds.), *New Waves in Applied Ethics*. Basingstoke, Hampshire: Palgrave Macmillan.

Langton, Rae 1993. 'Speech Acts and Unspeakable Acts', *Philosophy & Public Affairs* 22, no. 4.

Langton, Rae 1998. 'Subordination, Silence and Pornography's Authority', in Robert C. Post (ed.), *Censorship and Silencing: Practices of Cultural Regulation*. L.A., CA: The Getty Research Institute, pp. 261–84, see esp. 276–7.

Langton, Rae and Jennifer Hornsby 1998. 'Free Speech and Illocution', *Legal Theory* 4: 21–37, 25.

Lawrence, Charles R. 1993. 'If He Hollers Let Him Go: Regulating Racist Speech on Campus', in Mari J. Matsuda et al. (eds.), *Words That Wound: Critical Race Theory, Assaultive Speech and the First Amendment*. Boulder, CO: Westview: 53–88, 79.

MacKinnon, Catharine 1987. *Feminism Unmodified*. Cambridge, MA: Harvard University Press, p. 156.

Maitra, Ishani 2004. 'Silence and Responsibility', *Philosophical Perspectives* 18: 189–208.

Mill, 1975. *On Liberty*, reprinted in *Three Essays*. Oxford: Oxford University Press; originally published 1859, p. 65.

Nielsen, Laura Beth, this volume. 'Power in Public: Reactions, Responses, and Resistance to Offensive Public Speech'.

Schauer, Frederick 1982. *Free Speech: A Philosophical Inquiry*. Cambridge: Cambridge University Press.

Sumner, L. W. 2004. *The Hateful and the Obscene: Studies in the Limits of Free Expression*. Toronto: University of Toronto Press, pp. 14–15.

Taylor, Jerome and Malick Kouyate 2003. 'Achievement Gap Between Black and White Students: Theoretical Analysis with Recommendations For Remedy', in G. Bernal (ed.), *Handbook of Racial & Ethnic Minority Psychology*. London: Sage Publications, pp. 327–56.

West, Caroline 2003. 'The Free Speech Argument Against Pornography', *Canadian Journal of Philosophy* 33, no. 3: 391–422.

Index

Printed in the United Kingdom by the MPG Books Group Ltd